Adobe®
Premiere® Pro

Classroom in a Book®

Adobe

www.adobepress.com

Contents

Lesson 1

The Workspace

Lesson 2

Sequencing and Basic Real-Time Editing

Lesson 8   ## Fundamentals of Multipoint Editing

Lesson 9   ## Advanced Editing One: Single-Frame Techniques

Getting Started

Adobe® Premiere® Pro software is a revolutionary nonlinear video editing application. Powerful real-time video and audio editing tools give you precise control over virtually every aspect of your production. Built for the exceptional performance of Microsoft® Windows® XP systems, Adobe Premiere Pro takes video production to an entirely new level.

Whether you want to edit digital video on your laptop or work with multiple layers of uncompressed analog footage on a professional, hardware-based real-time editing system, Adobe Premiere Pro allows you to work with ease and efficiency. Take advantage of a new, real-time editing experience that provides immediate feedback and enables you to edit with amazing speed. Produce richer, more vibrant audio using sample-level editing, VST filters, track-based effects, and 5.1 surround sound. Easily create sophisticated titles for all of your productions with the new Adobe Title Designer.

Premiere Pro's scalable editing platform allows you to work closely with your other video software and hardware tools and supports the latest industry standards, including OHCI, ASIO, AAF, and VST.

Native DV support provides plug-and-play capabilities with a wide variety of camcorders and other new devices. If your computer doesn't offer a DV input option or you're looking to import analog, Premiere Pro provides support for the widest variety of capture cards. Running on Windows XP allows you to take advantage of the latest operating system enhancements.

Seamless integration has been engineered between Adobe Premiere Pro and other Adobe programs, including Adobe Photoshop®, After Effects®, Illustrator®, Encore® DVD, Audition®, and GoLive® software. Use the Edit Original command to modify native Photoshop, After Effects, and other files. Import logos, vector artwork, and technical drawings as native Illustrator files. And export streaming media with chapters and URL triggers that can be imported directly into GoLive or to make Encore® DVD files. Once your production is complete, Adobe Premiere Pro provides you with a number of export options. Export to the Web, videotape, DV, DVD, CD, Video CD (VCD), and more.

Whether you are a video professional or an aspiring producer, you'll enjoy the versatility, ease of use, and power of Adobe Premiere Pro software.

About *Classroom in a Book*

Adobe Premiere Pro Classroom in a Book is part of the official training series for Adobe graphics and publishing software developed with the support of experts at Adobe Systems. The lessons are designed to let you learn at your own pace. If you're new to Adobe Premiere Pro, you'll learn the fundamental concepts and features you'll need to master the program. If you've been using Adobe Premiere for awhile, you'll find that *Adobe Premiere Pro Classroom in a Book* teaches many advanced features, including tips and techniques for using the latest version of Adobe Premiere Pro.

Although each lesson provides step-by-step instructions for creating a specific project, there's room for exploration and experimentation. You can follow the book from start to finish or do only the lessons that correspond to your interests and needs.

While a beginner or intermediate user might be best served by going through all the lessons in order, each lesson is built to stand alone to give a primer on its subject. For this *Classroom in a Book*, a six-and-one-half minute short film, entitled *Books & Beans*, was developed to convey a sense of building an entire movie as you course through each exercise. By the last lessons on Audio and Output, you will have reconstructed the entire motion picture.

Prerequisites

Before beginning to use *Adobe Premiere Pro Classroom in a Book*, you should have a working knowledge of your computer and its operating system. Make sure that you know how to use the mouse and standard menus and commands and that you know how to open, save, and close files. If you need to review these techniques, see the printed or online documentation included with your Windows operating system. It is also helpful, but not necessary, to have experience with Adobe Premiere, Adobe Illustrator, Adobe Photoshop, Adobe After Effects, Adobe Encore DVD, and Adobe Audition.

Installing the Adobe Premiere Pro program

Before you begin using *Adobe Premiere Pro Classroom in a Book*, make sure that your system is set up correctly and that you've installed the required software and hardware. You must purchase the Adobe Premiere Pro software separately. For system requirements and complete instructions on installing the software, see the *InstallReadMe* file on the application CD.

You must install the application from the Adobe Premiere Pro CD onto your hard disk; you cannot run the program directly from the CD. Follow the on-screen instructions. Make sure your serial number is accessible before installing the application; you can find the serial number on the registration card, on the CD sleeve, or on the back of the CD case.

Because this version contains a large database of digital video media, it is mastered to DVD-ROM. Thus a DVD drive is required for copying user files to your hard drive.

Media tools in the XP environment

The Windows XP operating system comes with the onboard media tools you'll need to reproduce the images and sounds in your projects. Investigate on the Web to familiarize yourself with available enhancements and advanced media tools that are on the market to make your producing and editing experience as precise and pleasurable as it can be.

To play sound, a sound card and speakers must be installed. For best quality when previewing audio, you may want to connect external speakers to your system.

With the launch of Adobe Premiere Pro comes the ability to make layered, nested sequences, use whole timeline assemblies like simple stand-alone clips, and design and output 5.1 sound to a room full of speakers.

See the *Adobe Premiere Pro User Guide* for installation instructions.

Starting Adobe Premiere Pro

You start Premiere Pro just as you would any software application.

1 Launch the program as follows:

• Choose Start > Programs > Adobe > Premiere Pro > Adobe Premiere Pro.

In the lessons that follow, you will learn about this and the other editing workspaces available in Adobe Premiere Pro.

2 In the Load Project Settings dialog box, choose DV - NTSC Real-time Preview > Standard 48kHz, and click OK.

This will allow you to smoothly play older clips saved in earlier versions of the program.

Note: For the lessons in this book, you will work with this preset. For your own work, you will typically use the preset included with your capture card software or the appropriate preset included with Premiere Pro.

 Adobe Premiere Pro is very easy to customize. When working on your own projects, if you don't see a preset that matches your video, select the preset that most closely matches your editing environment. Click Custom, specify your project settings, and then click Save. In the Save Project Settings dialog box, type a name and description (if desired), and click OK. The new settings are saved as a preset file that appears in the list of available presets in the Load Project Settings dialog box. For more information, see "Specifying project settings", in the Adobe Premiere Pro User Guide.

3 After you click OK, the Adobe Premiere Pro application window appears. You will see the Editing workspace and its three main windows (the Project window, the Monitor window, and the Timeline window) and the default palettes. If necessary, you can rearrange windows and palettes so they don't overlap, by choosing Window > Workspace > Editing. The workspace components automatically adjust.

Copying the *Classroom in a Book* files

The *Adobe Premiere Pro Classroom in a Book* DVD includes folders containing all the electronic files for the lessons. Each lesson has its own folder, and you must copy the folders to your hard drive to do the lessons.

Digital Video is a verbose technology. Given that the sample footage is stored at full-frame size in true colors, a great deal of hard disc space is required to run it. You'll need at least 5 GB (gigabytes) on your C:\ Drive to fit all of the files needed to take the lessons of the book.

To install the *Classroom in a Book* files on your C:\ drive:

1 Insert the *Adobe Premiere Pro Classroom in a Book* DVD into your DVD-ROM drive.

2 On the **C:** drive of your computer, create a folder named PrPro_CIB.

3 Copy both of the directories located on the DVD-ROM—**Lessons** and **Movies**—to the hard drive. Drag the two directories from the DVD into the C:\PrPro_CIB folder.

4 For the large database of files to stay linked to each other, leave the directory exactly like described. Your path to the lesson files will therefore be:

• **C:\PrPro_CIB**, your main directory.

• **Lessons** directory and **Movies** directory, inside the PrPro_CIB directory.

Note: As you work through each lesson, you will overwrite the Start files. To restore the original files, recopy the corresponding Lesson folder from the Classroom in a Book *DVD-ROM to the PrPro_CIB folder on your hard drive.*

Copying the lesson files to alternate drives

If it is necessary for you to use a disc drive other than drive C:\, then you might encounter the Where is the File '[*file_name*]' box in Lessons 10-through-12, and Lesson 14. This means Premiere Pro is searching for files specifically linked to project files in those four lessons.

The following chart will guide you through the Where is the File box, if it appears on your display, when you are taking the exercises in Lessons 10-through-12 and Lesson 14.

FILE NAME	Navigate to linked file in
Opening.avi	04Lesson
Cup.avi	10Lesson
Greet1.avi	09Lesson
Admire1.avi	07Lesson
Order1.avi	08Lesson
Gaze1.avi	03Lesson
Doorslam.wav	09Lesson
Sigh.avi	03Lesson
Black frame.psd	11Lesson
Presents.prtl	11Lesson
Dooropen.avi	08Lesson
Dooropen.wav	08Lesson
Clip01.avi	14Lesson\Premiere Source
Trailer.wmv	PrPro_CIB\Movies

Using default preferences

Adobe Premiere Pro provides *default*, or factory preset, settings. Like many software programs, Premiere Pro also maintains a *preferences file* that stores the settings you most recently used in the program. You may find instances in your own projects when restoring the default preferences will be useful or necessary.

Note: *Deleting the preferences file also resets the window and palette positions.*

To quickly locate and delete the Premiere Pro preferences file:

1 On your system, choose Start > Find > Files or Folders and search for **Premiere Pro Prefs**. Choose Options > Save Results and then File > Save Search.

2 Create a shortcut for the Preferences folder. Locate and select the Preferences folder, found within the System folder. From the title bar, choose File > Create Shortcut. A file called Preferences alias will appear within the System folder. This file lands on your desktop. Double-clicking the shortcut will open the Preferences folder to give you quick access to the Adobe Premiere Pro Preferences file.

3 Double-click the saved search file any time you want to open the Preferences folder.

To restore default preferences for Premiere Pro:

1 If Premiere is running, exit Premiere.

2 Delete the Premiere Pro Prefs file found in <windows install drive>: \Documents and Settings\<username>\Application Data\Adobe\Premiere. The <windows install drive> is usually C: and the <username> pertains to the currently logged on user.

Note: The AppData folder is usually hidden. You can access it by choosing Folder Options > View in Windows Explorer and selecting Show hidden files and folders.

To save your current Premiere Pro preferences:

1 Exit Adobe Premiere Pro.

2 Select the Premiere Pro Prefs file from <windows install drive>: \Documents and Settings\<username>\Application Data\Adobe\Premiere.

Note: Use your operating system's Search command to locate this file.

3 Drag the Preferences file shortcut to your desktop or to another folder that you can locate quickly while you are working.

To restore your saved settings after completing the lessons:

1 Exit Premiere Pro.

2 Drag the Preferences file from the desktop back into the folder holding the Adobe Premiere Pro Preferences file.

3 In the Warning box that appears, confirm that you want to replace the existing version of the file indicated.

Additional resources

Adobe Premiere Pro Classroom in a Book is not intended to replace documentation that comes with the Premiere Pro program. Only the commands and options used in the lessons are explained in this book. For comprehensive information about program features, refer to these resources:

• The *Adobe Premiere Pro User Guide*, which is included with Adobe Premiere Pro software, contains a complete description of all the features found in Premiere Pro.

• Online Help, an online version of the *User Guide*, is accessible by choosing Help > Contents from the Premiere Pro title bar.

• The Adobe Web site (www.adobe.com), can be viewed by choosing Help > Adobe Online if you have a connection to the World Wide Web.

Adobe certification

The Adobe Training and Certification Programs are designed to help Adobe customers improve and promote their product proficiency skills. The Adobe Certified Expert (ACE) program is designed to recognize the high-level skills of expert users. Adobe Certified Training Providers (ACTP) use only Adobe Certified Experts to teach Adobe software classes. Available in either ACTP classrooms or on-site, the ACE program is the best way to master the use of Adobe products. For Adobe Certified Training Programs information, visit the Partnering with Adobe Web site at http://partners.adobe.com.

The World of Digital Video

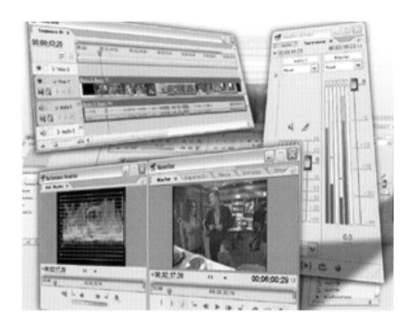

When you edit video, you arrange source clips so that they tell a story. That story can be anything from a fictional television program to a news event and more. Understanding the issues that affect your editing decisions can help you prepare for successful editing and save you valuable time and resources.

This lesson describes the role of Adobe Premiere Pro in video production and introduces a variety of key concepts:

- Measuring video time.
- Measuring frame size and resolution.
- Compressing video data.
- Capturing video.
- Superimposing and opacity.
- Using audio in a video.
- Creating final video.

How Adobe Premiere fits into video production

Making video involves working through three general phases:

Preproduction Involves writing the script, visualizing scenes by sketching them on a storyboard, and creating a production schedule for shooting the scenes.

Production Involves shooting the scenes.

Post-production Involves editing the best scenes into the final video program and correcting and enhancing video and audio where necessary. Editing includes a first draft, or *rough cut (or offline edit),* where you can get a general idea of the possibilities you have with the clips available to you. As you continue editing, you refine the video program through successive iterations until you decide that it's finished. At that point, you have built the *final cut or online edit.* Premiere Pro is designed for efficient editing, correcting, and enhancing of clips, making it a valuable tool for post-production.

The rest of this chapter describes fundamental concepts that affect video editing and other post-production tasks in Premiere Pro. All of the concepts in this section and the specific Premiere Pro features that support them are described in more detail in the *Adobe Premiere Pro User Guide.*

If any stage of your project involves outside vendors, such as video post-production facilities, consult with them before starting the project. They can help you determine what settings to use at various stages of a project and can potentially help you avoid costly, time-consuming mistakes. For example, if you're creating video for broadcast, you should know whether you are creating video for the NTSC (National Television Standards Committee) standard used primarily in North America and Japan; the PAL (Phase Alternate Line) standard used primarily in Europe, Asia, and southern Africa; or the SECAM (Sequential Couleur Avec Memoire) standard used primarily in France, the Middle East, and North Africa.

Measuring video time

In the natural world, we experience time as a continuous flow of events. However, working with video requires precise synchronization, so it's necessary to measure time using precise numbers. Familiar time increments—hours, minutes, and seconds—are not precise enough for video editing, because a single second might contain several events. This section describes how Premiere Pro and video professionals measure time, using standard methods that count fractions of a second in terms of frames.

How the timebase and frame rates affect each other

You determine how time is measured in your project by specifying the project *timebase*. For example, a timebase of 30 means that each second is divided into 30 units. The exact time at which an edit occurs depends on the timebase you specify, because an edit can only occur at a time division; using a different timebase causes the time divisions to fall in different places.

The time increments in a source clip are determined by the *source frame rate*. For example, when you shoot source clips using a video camera with a frame rate of 30 frames per second, the camera documents the action by recording one frame every 1/30th of a second. Note that whatever was happening between those 1/30th of a second intervals is not recorded. Thus, a lower frame rate (such as 15 fps) records less information about continuous action, while a high frame rate (such as 30 fps) records more.

You determine how often Premiere Pro generates frames from your project by specifying the *project frame rate*. A project frame rate of 30 frames per second means that Premiere Pro will create 30 frames from each second of your project.

For smooth and consistent playback, the timebase, the source frame rate, and the project frame rate should be identical.

Editing Video Type	Frames per second
Motion-picture film	24 fps
PAL and SECAM video	25 fps
NTSC video	29.97 fps
Web or CD-ROM	15 fps
Other video types, e.g., non-drop-frame editing, 3D animation	30 fps

Note: NTSC was originally designed for a black-and-white picture at 30 fps, but signal modifications made in the mid-20th century to accommodate color pictures altered the standard NTSC frame rate to 29.97 fps.

Sometimes the time systems don't match. For example, you might be asked to create a video intended for CD-ROM distribution that must combine motion-picture source clips captured at 24 fps with video source clips captured at 30 fps, using a timebase of 30 for a final CD-ROM frame rate of 15 fps. When any of these values don't match, it is mathematically necessary for some frames to be repeated or omitted; the effect may be distracting or imperceptible depending on the differences between the timebase and frame rates you used in your project.

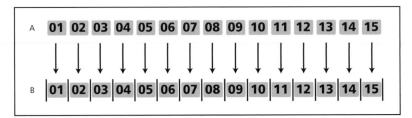

A. 30 fps video clip (one-half second shown) **B.** *Timebase of 30, for a video production When the source frame rate matches the timebase, all frames display as expected.*

ADOBE PREMIERE PRO | **13**
Classroom in a Book

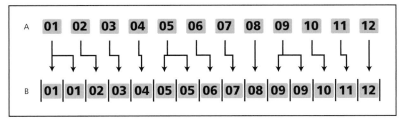

A. 24 fps motion-picture source clip (one-half second shown) **B.** *Timebase of 30, for a video production. To play one-half second of 24 fps frames at a timebase of 30, source frames 1, 5, and 9 are repeated.*

💡 *It is preferable to capture your clips at the same frame rate at which you plan to export your project. For example, if you know your source clips will be exported at 30 fps, capture the clips at 30 fps instead of 24 fps. If this is not possible (for example, DV can only be captured at 29.97 fps), you'll want to output at a frame rate that evenly divides your timebase. So, if your capture frame rate and your timebase are set at 30 fps (actually 29.97), you should output at 30, 15, or 10 fps to avoid "jerky" playback.*

When time systems don't match, the most important value to set is the timebase, which you should choose appropriately for the most critical final medium. If you are preparing a motion picture trailer that you also want to show on television, you might decide that film is the most important medium for the project, and specify a timebase of 24.

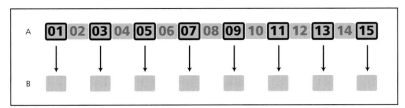

A. Timebase of 30 (one-half second shown) **B.** *Final frame rate of 15, for a Web movie. If the timebase is evenly divisible by the frame rate, timebase frames are included evenly.*

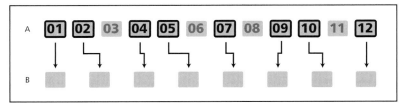

A. Timebase of 24 for a motion-picture film (one-half second shown) **B.** *Final frame rate of 15, for a Web movie. The time is not evenly divisible by the frame rate, so frames are included unevenly. A final frame rate of 12 fps would generate frames more evenly.*

The important thing to remember is this: You'll get the most predictable results if your timebase and frame rate are even multiples of one another; you'll get the best results if they are identical.

[?] *For more information, see the Adobe Web site* (www.adobe.com) *and do a search for available resources.*

Counting time with timecode

Timecode defines how frames are counted and affects the way you view and specify time throughout a project. Timecode never changes the timebase or frame rate of a clip or project—it only changes how frames are numbered.

You specify a timecode style based on the media most relevant to your project. When you are editing video for television, you count frames differently from counting frames when editing video for motion-picture film. By default, Premiere Pro displays time using the SMPTE (Society of Motion Picture and Television Engineers) video timecode, where a duration of 00:06:51:15 indicates that a clip plays for 6 minutes, 51 seconds, and 15 frames. At any time, you can change to another system of time display, such as feet and frames of 16mm or 35mm film. Professional videotape decks and camcorders can read and write timecode directly onto the videotape, which lets you synchronize audio, video, and edits, or edit off line (see Capturing DV on page 29).

When you use the NTSC-standard timebase of 29.97, the fractional difference between this timebase and 30 fps timecode causes a discrepancy between the displayed duration of the program and its actual duration. While tiny at first, this discrepancy grows as program duration increases, preventing you from accurately creating a program of a specific length. *Drop-frame timecode* is an SMPTE standard for 29.97 fps video that eliminates this error, preserving NTSC time accuracy. Premiere Pro indicates drop-frame timecode by displaying semicolons between the numbers in time displays throughout the software, and displays non-drop-frame timecode by displaying colons between numbers in timecode displays.

Drop-frame timecode uses semicolons (left)
and non-drop-frame timecode uses colons (right).

When you use drop-frame timecode, Premiere Pro renumbers the first two frames of every minute except for every tenth minute. The frame after 59:29 is labeled 1:00:02. No frames are lost because drop-frame timecode doesn't actually drop frames, only frame numbers.

A picture on a television or computer monitor consists of horizontal lines. There is more than one way to display those lines. Most personal computers display using *progressive scan* (or non-interlaced) display, in which all lines in a frame are displayed in one pass from top to bottom before the next frame appears. Television standards such as NTSC, PAL, and SECAM standards are *interlaced*, where each frame is divided into two *fields*. Each field contains every other horizontal line in the frame. A TV displays the first field of alternating lines over the entire screen, and then displays the second field to fill in the alternating gaps left by the first field. One NTSC video frame, displayed approximately every 1/30th of a second, contains two interlaced fields, displayed approximately every 1/60th of a second each. PAL and SECAM video frames display at 1/25 of a second and contain two interlaced fields displayed every 1/50th of a second each. The field that contains the topmost scan line in the frame is called the *upper field*, and the other field is called the *lower field*. When playing back or exporting to interlaced video, make sure the *field order* you specify matches the receiving video system, otherwise motion may appear stuttered, and edges of objects in the frame may break up with a comb-like appearance.

Note: *For analog video, the field order needs to match the field order of the capture card (which should be specified in the preset). For DV, the field order is always lower field first. Be sure to select the correct preset first; doing so will correctly specify the field order.*

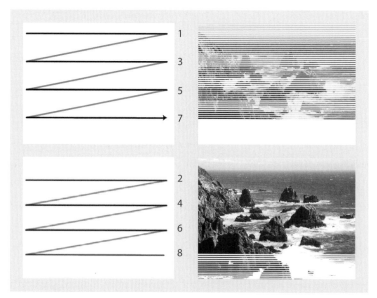

Interlaced video describes a frame with two passes of alternating scan lines.

Progressive-scan video describes a frame with one pass of sequential scan lines.

If you plan to slow down or hold a frame in an interlaced video clip, you may want to prevent flickering or visual stuttering by *de-interlacing* its frames, which converts the interlaced fields into complete frames. If you're using progressive-scan source clips (such as motion-picture film or computer-generated animation) in a video intended for an interlaced display such as television, you can separate frames into fields using a process known as *field rendering* so that motion and effects are properly interlaced.

For more information, see "Processing interlaced video fields" in the Adobe Premiere Pro User Guide *and the Adobe Web site* (www.adobe.com).

Measuring frame size and resolution

Several attributes of *frame size* are important when editing video digitally: pixel and frame aspect ratio, clip resolution, project frame size, and bit depth. A *pixel* (picture element) is the smallest unit that can be used to create a picture; you can't accurately display anything smaller than a pixel.

Aspect ratio

The *aspect ratio* of a frame describes the ratio of its width to its height in the dimensions of a frame. For example, the frame aspect ratio of NTSC video is 4:3, whereas DVD, HDTV, and motion-picture frame sizes use the more elongated aspect ratio of 16:9.

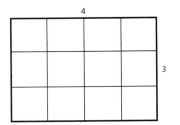
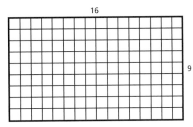

A frame using a 4:3 aspect ratio (left), and a frame using the 16:9 aspect ratio (right)

Some video formats use a different aspect ratio for the pixels that make up the frame. When a video using *nonsquare pixels* (that is, pixels that are taller than they are wide, or wider than they are tall) is displayed on a square-pixel system, or vice versa, shapes and motion appear stretched. For example, circles are distorted into ellipses.

Frame with square pixels (left), frame with tall horizontal pixels (center), and center frame again displayed using square pixels (right)

Nonsquare pixels

Premiere Pro provides support for a variety of non-square pixel aspect ratios, including DV's Widescreen (Cinema) pixel aspect ratio of 16:9 and the Anamorphic pixel aspect ratio of 2:1.

When you preview video with non-square pixel aspect ratios on your computer screen, Premiere Pro displays a corrected aspect ratio on the computer monitor so that the image is not distorted. Motion and opacity settings, as well as geometric effects, also use the proper aspect ratio, so distortions don't appear after editing or rendering your video.

Frame size

In Premiere Pro, you specify a *frame size* for playing back video from the Timeline and, if necessary, for exporting video to a file. Frame size is expressed in pixels by the horizontal and vertical dimensions of a frame; for example, 640 by 480 pixels. In digital video editing, frame size is also referred to as *resolution.*

In general, higher resolution preserves more image detail and requires more memory (RAM) and hard disk space to edit. As you increase frame dimensions, you increase the number of pixels Premiere Pro must process and store for each frame, so it's important to know how much resolution your final video format requires. For example, a 720 x 480 pixel (standard DV) NTSC frame contains 345,600 pixels, while a 720 x 576 PAL image contains 414,720 pixels. If you specify a resolution that is too low, the picture will look coarse and pixelated; specify too high a resolution and you'll use more memory than necessary. When changing the frame size, keep the dimensions proportional to the original video clip.

If you plan to work with higher resolutions or you are concerned about your CPU's processing capabilities, you can specify one or more scratch disks *for additional RAM and hard disk space. For more information, see "Using scratch disks" in the* Adobe Premiere Pro User Guide.

Overscan and safe zones

Frame size can be misleading if you're preparing video for television. Most NTSC consumer television sets enlarge the picture; however, this pushes the outer edges of the picture off the screen. This process is called *overscan*. Because the amount of overscan is not consistent across all televisions, you should keep action and titles inside two safe areas—the action-safe and title-safe zones.

The action-safe zone is an area approximately 10% less than the actual frame size; the title-safe zone is approximately 20% less than the actual frame size. By keeping all significant action inside the action-safe zone and making sure that all text and important graphic elements are within the title-safe zone, you can be sure that the critical elements of your video are completely displayed. You'll also avoid the distortion of text and graphics that can occur toward the edges of many television monitors. Always anticipate overscan by using safe zones, keeping important action and text within them, and testing the video on an actual television monitor.

You can view safe zones in the Monitor window's Source view, Program view, or both by clicking on the safe zones icon below the monitor.

Safe zones in the Program view: ***A.*** *Title-safe zone* ***B.*** *Action-safe zone*

Safe zones are indicated by white rectangles in Premiere's Title Designer window.

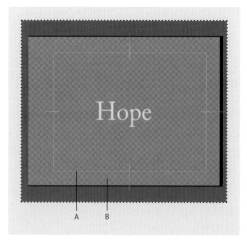

A. *Title-safe zone* **B.** *Action-safe zone*

For more information on customizing safe zones in the Monitor and Title windows, see Lesson 11, "Titles and Credits" in this book.

Bit depth

A *bit* is the most basic unit of information storage in a computer. The more bits used to describe something, the more detailed the description can be. *Bit depth* indicates the number of bits set aside for describing the color of one pixel. The higher the bit depth, the more colors the image can contain, which allows more precise color reproduction and higher picture quality. For example, an image storing 8 bits per pixel (8-bit color) can display 256 colors, and a 24-bit color image can display approximately 16 million colors.

Adobe Premiere Pro can work with video captured and stored at any bit depth, but internally it converts clips to the YUV color format used in broadcasting. The YUV format stores high-quality video using only 16 bits per pixel. (The RGB color format requires 24 bits per pixel.) This allows for higher quality with faster processing.

The YUV color space was invented in the early fifties as a way to add color to broadcast television while maintaining backward compatibility with black and white sets and simultaneously limiting the amount of bandwidth required for the signal. In the YUV system, the three color components of RGB are mathematically converted to a luminance signal (i.e., the black and white) plus two color signals. Because of the way the conversion is done, the amount of data for the total signal is greatly reduced without a loss of quality.

To get the best picture quality possible:

• Save RGB source clips and still images with 24 bits of color (although you can use clips with lower bit depths).

• If the clip contains an alpha channel mask, save it from the source application using 32 bits per pixel (also referred to as 24 bits with an 8-bit alpha channel, or *millions of colors*). For example, QuickTime® movies can contain up to 24 bits of color with an 8-bit alpha channel, depending on the exact format used.

Internally, Premiere Pro always processes clips using 24 bits per pixel regardless of each clip's original bit depth (16 bits for YUV, plus an 8-bit alpha channel). This helps preserve image quality when you apply effects or superimpose clips.

If you're preparing video for NTSC, you should keep in mind that although both 16-bit YUV and 24-bit RGB provide a full range of color, the color range of NTSC is limited by comparison. NTSC cannot accurately reproduce saturated colors and subtle color gradients. The best way to anticipate problems with NTSC color is to preview your video on a properly calibrated NTSC monitor during editing.

For more information, see the Adobe Web site (www.adobe.com) *and do a search for available resources.*

Understanding video data compression

Editing digital video involves storing, moving, and calculating extremely large volumes of data compared to other kinds of computer files. Many personal computers, particularly older models, are not equipped to handle the high *data rates* (amount of video information processed each second) and large *file sizes* of uncompressed digital video. Use *compression* to lower the data rate of digital video to a range that your computer system can handle.

Compression settings are most relevant when capturing source video, previewing edits, playing back the Timeline, and exporting the Timeline. In many cases, the settings you specify won't be the same for all situations:

• It's a good idea to compress video coming into your computer. Your goal is to retain as much picture quality as you can for editing, while keeping the data rate well within your computer's limits.

• You should also compress video going out of your computer. Try to achieve the best picture quality for playback. If you're creating a videotape, keep the data rate within the limits of the computer that will play back the video to videotape. If you're creating video to be played back on another computer, keep the data rate within the limits of the computer models you plan to support. It you're creating a video clip to be streamed from a Web server, keep an appropriate data rate for Internet distribution.

Applying the best compression settings can be tricky, and the best settings can vary with each project. If you apply too little compression, the data rate may be too high for the system, causing errors such as dropped frames. If you apply too much compression, lowering the data rate too far, you won't be taking advantage of the full capacity of the system and the picture quality may suffer unnecessarily.

Note: DV has a fixed data rate of 3.5 megabytes per second, nominally 25 megabits per second; the DV standard compression ratio is 5:1.

Analyzing clip properties and data rate

Premiere Pro includes clip analysis tools you can use to evaluate a file, in any supported format, stored inside or outside a project.

1   Locate and select the Opening.avi clip from Lesson 1 and click Open.

2 From Premiere, choose File > Get Properties For > File.

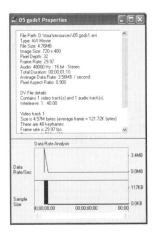

The *Properties window* provides detailed information about any clip. For video files, the analyzed properties can include file size, number of video and audio tracks, duration, average frame, audio and data rates, and compression settings. You can also use the Properties window to alert you to the presence of any dropped frames in a clip you just captured.

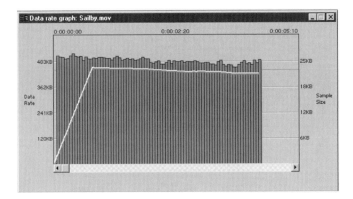

At the bottom of the Properties window, you'll notice a data graph. You can use this to evaluate how well the output data rate matches the requirements of your delivery medium. It charts each frame of a video file to show you the render keyframe rate, the difference between compression keyframes and differenced frames (frames that exist between keyframes), and data rate levels at each frame.

The data rate graph includes:

- Data rate: the white line represents the average data rate.
- Sample size: the red bars represent the sample size of each keyframed frame.

If there are differenced frames, they appear as blue bars, representing the sample size of the differenced frames between compression keyframes. In this case, there are not any.

3 When you are finished, close the Data Rate Graph window and the Properties window.

? *For more information, see the Adobe Web site* (www.adobe.com) *and do a search for available resources.*

Choosing a video compression method

The goal of data compression is to represent the same content using less data. You can specify a compressor/decompressor, or *codec*, that manages compression. A codec may use one or more strategies for compression because no single method is best for all situations. The most common compression strategies used by codecs and the kinds of video they are intended to compress are described in this section.

Spatial compression Spatial (space) compression looks for ways to compact a single frame by looking for pattern and repetition among pixels. For example, instead of describing each of several thousand pixels in a picture of a blue sky, spatial compression can record a much shorter description, such as "All the pixels in this area are light blue." *Run-length encoding* is a version of this technique that is used by many codecs. Codecs that use spatial compression, such as QuickTime Animation or Microsoft RLE, work well with video containing large solid areas of color, such as cartoon animation.

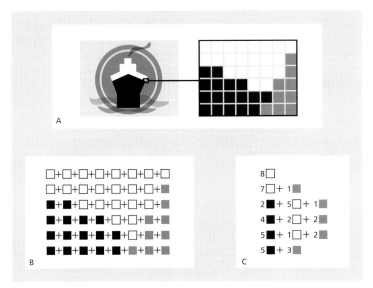

*Digital images are composed of pixels (**A**), which consume a lot of disk space when stored without compression (**B**). Applying run-length encoding stores the same frame data in much less space (**C**).*

In general, as you increase spatial compression, the data rate and file size decrease, and the picture loses sharpness and definition. However, some forms of run-length encoding preserve picture quality completely, but require more processing power.

Temporal compression Temporal (time) compression compacts the changes during a sequence of frames by looking for patterns and repetition over time. In some video clips, such as a clip of a television announcer, temporal compression will notice that the only pixels that change from frame to frame are those forming the face of the speaker. All the other pixels don't change (when the camera is motionless). Instead of describing every pixel in every frame, temporal compression describes all the pixels in the first frame, and then for each frame that follows, describes only the pixels that are different from the previous frame. This technique is called *frame differencing*. When most of the pixels in a frame are different from the previous frame, it's preferable to describe the entire frame again. Each whole frame is called a *keyframe*, which sets a new starting point for frame differencing. You can use Premiere Pro to control how keyframes are created (see the *Adobe Premiere Pro User Guide*). Many codecs use temporal compression, including Cinepak.

If you can't set keyframes for a codec, chances are it doesn't use temporal compression. Temporal compression works best when large areas in the video don't change, and is less effective when the image constantly changes, such as in a music video.

In this animation clip, the only change is the circle moving around the ship.

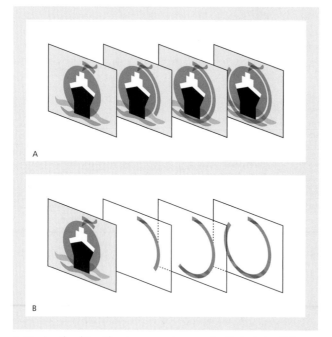

A. Storing the clip without compression records all pixels in all frames.
B. Applying temporal compression creates a keyframe from the first frame, and subsequent frames record only the changes.

Lossless compression Some codecs use *lossless* compression, which ensures that all of the information—and thus all of the quality—in the original clip is preserved after compression. However, preserving the original level of quality limits the degree to which you can lower the data rate and file size, and the resulting data rate may be too high for smooth playback. Lossless codecs, such as Animation (at the Best quality setting), are used to preserve maximum quality during editing or for still images where data rate is not an issue.

Note: To ensure smooth playback, full-frame, full-size video using lossless compression requires a very large defragmented hard disk and very fast computer system built for high data rate throughput.

Lossy compression Most codecs use *lossy* compression, which discards some of the original data during compression. For example, if the pixels making up a sky actually contain 78 shades of blue, a lossy codec set for less-than-best quality may record 60 shades of blue. While lossy compression means some quality compromises, it results in much lower data rates and file sizes than lossless compression, so lossy codecs such as Cinepak or Sorenson Video are commonly used for final production of video delivered using CD-ROM or the Internet.

Asymmetrical and symmetrical compression The codec you choose affects your production workflow, not just in file size or playback speed, but in the time required for a codec to compress a given number of frames. Fast compression speeds up video production, and fast decompression makes viewing easier; but many codecs take far more time to compress frames than to decompress them during playback. This is why a 30-second clip may take a few minutes to process before playback. A codec is considered *symmetrical* when it requires the same amount of time to compress as to decompress a clip. A codec is *asymmetrical* when the times required to compress and decompress a clip are significantly different.

Compressing video is like packing a suitcase—you can pack as fast as you unpack by simply throwing clothes into the suitcase, but if you spend more time to fold and organize the clothes in the suitcase, you can fit more clothes in the same space.

DV compression DV is the format used by many digital video camcorders. DV also connotes the type of compression used by these camcorders, which compress video right inside the camera. The most common form of DV compression uses a fixed data rate of 25 megabits per second (3.5 megabytes per second) and a compression ratio of 5:1. This compression is called "DV25." Adobe Premiere Pro includes native support for DV25 and other DV codecs, and can read digital source video without further conversion.

No single codec is the best for all situations. The codec you use for exporting your final program must be available to your entire audience. So, while a specialized codec that comes with a specific capture card might be the best choice for capturing source clips, it would not be a good choice for exporting clips, since it is unlikely that everyone in your audience would have that specific capture card and its specialized codec. This is a significant concern when exporting streaming media, since the three most popular streaming architectures (RealMedia, Windows Media, and QuickTime) use proprietary codecs in their players; a RealMedia stream, for example, cannot be played back through a Windows Media player, and vice versa. So, for the convenience of audiences with diverse players set as the default in their browsers, streaming media is usually encoded in multiple formats.

🛈 *For more information, see the Adobe Web site* (www.adobe.com) *and do a search for available resources.*

Capturing video

Before you can edit your video program, all source clips must be instantly accessible from a hard disk, not from videotape. You import the source clips from the source videotapes to your computer through a post-production step called *video capture*. Consequently, you must have enough room on your hard disk to store all the clips you want to edit. To save space, capture only the clips you know you want to use.

Source clips exist in two main forms:

Digital media Is already in a *digital* file format that a computer can read and process directly. Many newer camcorders digitize and save video in a digital format, right inside the camera. Such camcorders use one of several *DV formats*, which apply a standard amount of compression to the source material. Audio can also be recorded digitally; sound tracks are often provided digitally as well—on CD-ROM, for example. Digital source files stored on DV tape or other digital media must be *captured* (transferred) to an accessible hard disk before they can be used in a computer for a Premiere Pro project. The simplest way to capture DV is to connect a DV device, such as a camcorder or deck, to a computer with an Institute of Electrical and Electronic Engineers (IEEE) 1394 port (also known as FireWire or i.Link). For more sophisticated capture tasks, a specialized DV *capture card* might be used. Premiere Pro supports a wide range of DV devices and capture cards, making it easy to capture DV source files.

Analog media   Must be *digitized*. That means it must be converted to digital form and saved in a digital file format before a computer can store and process it. Clips from *analog* videotape (such as Hi-8), motion-picture film, conventional audio tape, and continuous-tone still images (such as slides) are all examples of analog media. By connecting an analog video device (such as an analog video camera or tape deck) and an appropriate *capture card* to your computer, Adobe Premiere Pro can digitize, compress, and transfer analog source material to disk as clips that can then be added to your digital video project.

Note: Video-digitizing hardware is built into some personal computers, but often must be added to a system by installing a compatible hardware capture card. Adobe Premiere Pro supports a wide variety of video capture cards.

If your system has an appropriate capture card, Adobe Premiere Pro also lets you perform manual and time-lapse *single-frame video captures* from a connected camera or from a videotape in a deck or camcorder, using *stop-motion animation*. For example, you can point a camera at an unfinished building and use the time-lapse feature to capture frames periodically as the building is completed. You can use the stop-motion feature with a camera to create clay animations or to capture a single frame and save it as a still image. You can capture stop-motion animation from analog or DV sources.

Note: Premiere Pro supports device control. This enables you to capture stop motion, or perform batch capture of multiple clips, by controlling the videotape from within the Capture window in Premiere. However, stop motion does not require device control within Premiere. If you don't have a controllable playback device, you can manually operate the controls on your camcorder or deck and in the Capture window.

For more information on capturing video, see "Capturing and Importing Source Clips" in the *Adobe Premiere Pro User Guide.*

Capturing DV

When you shoot DV, the images are converted directly into digital (DV) format, right inside the DV camcorder, where your footage is saved on a DV tape cassette. The images are already digitized and compressed, so they are ready for digital video editing. The DV footage can be transferred directly to a hard disk.

To transfer DV to your hard disk, you need a computer with an OHCI-compliant interface and an IEEE 1394 (FireWire or i.Link) port (standard on newer Windows PCs and newer-model Macintosh computers). Alternatively, you can install an appropriate DV capture card to provide the IEEE 1394 port. Be sure to install the accompanying OHCI-compliant driver and special Adobe Premiere Pro plug-in software that may be required. Adobe Premiere Pro comes with presets for a wide variety of DV capture cards but, for some, you may need to consult the instructions provided with your capture card to set up a special preset.

Adobe Premiere Pro provides settings files for most supported capture cards. These *presets* include settings for compressor, frame size, pixel aspect ratio, frame rate, color depth, audio, and fields. You select the appropriate preset from the Available Presets list in the Load Project Settings dialog box when you begin your project.

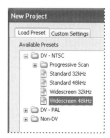

 To enhance DV capture, Adobe Premiere Pro provides device control for an extensive range of DV devices. See the Adobe Web site for a list of supported devices (www.adobe.com).

If you have an appropriate digital video device attached to or installed in your computer, you can do the following:

1 To specify the DV device in your computer, choose Edit > Preferences > Device Control.

2 Click the Option button in the Preferences window to see the DV Device Control Options dialog box and select your DV device. Click OK.

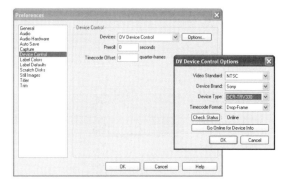

Capturing analog video

When capturing analog video, you need to first connect the camcorder or deck to the capture card installed in your system. Depending on your equipment, you may have more than one format available for transferring source footage—including component video, composite video, and S-video. Refer to the instructions included with your camcorder and capture card.

For convenience, most video-capture card software is written so that its controls appear within the Premiere Pro interface, even though much of the actual video processing happens on the card, outside of Premiere. Most supported capture cards provide a settings file—a preset—that automatically sets up Premiere Pro for optimal support for that card. Most of the settings that control how a clip is captured from a camera or a deck are found in the Capture Settings section of the Project Settings dialog box. Available capture formats vary, depending on the type of video-capture card installed.

For more information, or if you need help resolving technical issues that you may encounter using your capture card with Premiere Pro, see the Adobe Premiere Web site (www.adobe.com/premiere) for links to troubleshooting resources.

Using the Movie Capture window

You use the Movie Capture window to capture DV and analog video and audio. To open and familiarize yourself with the Movie Capture window, from the title bar at the top of your screen choose File > Capture. This window includes:

- Preview window that displays your currently recording video.

- Controls for recording media with and without device control.

- Movie Capture window menu button.

- Settings panel for viewing and editing your current capture setting.

- Logging panel for entering batch capture settings (you can only log clips for batch capture when using device control).

Movie Capture window: **A.** *Preview area* **B.** *Controllers*
C. *Movie Capture menu button* **D.** *Settings panel* **E.** *Logging panel*

Note: *When doing anything other than capturing in Premiere Pro, close the Movie Capture window. Because the Movie Capture window has primary status when open, leaving it open while editing or previewing video will disable output to your DV device and may diminish the performance.*

Capturing clips with device control When capturing clips, *device control* refers to controlling the operation of a connected video deck or camera using the Premiere Interface, rather than using the controls on the connected device. You can use device control to capture video from frame-accurate analog or digital video decks or cameras that support external device control. It's more convenient to simply use device control within Premiere Pro rather than alternating between the video editing software on your computer and the controls on your device. The Movie Capture or Batch Capture windows can be used to create a list of *In points* (starting timecode) and *Out points* (ending timecode) for your clips. Premiere then automates capture—recording all clips as specified on your list. Additionally, Premiere captures the timecode from the source tape, so the information can be used during editing.

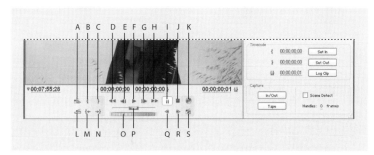

Movie Capture window with device control enabled: **A.** *Next screen*
B. *Set In Point* **C.** *Set Out Point* **D.** *Rewind* **E.** *Step back* **F.** *Play* **G.** *Step forward*
H. *Fast forward* **I.** *Pause* **J.** *Stop* **K.** *Record* **L.** *Previous scene* **M.** *Go To In Point*
N. *Go To Out Point* **O.** *Jog* **P.** *Shuttle* **Q.** *Slow Reverse* **R.** *Slow play* **S.** *Scene detect*

Capturing clips without device control If you don't have a controllable playback device, you can capture video from analog or DV camcorders or decks using the Adobe Premiere Pro Capture window. While watching the picture in the Movie Capture window, manually operate the deck and the Premiere controls to record the frames you want. You can use this method to facilitate capture from an inexpensive consumer VCR or camcorder.

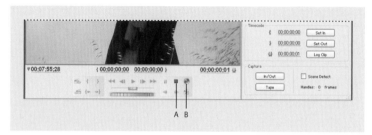

Using the Movie Capture window without device control: **A.** *Stop* **B.** *Record*

Batch-capturing video

If you have a frame-accurate deck or camcorder that supports external device control and a videotape recorded with timecode, you can set up Premiere for automatic, unattended capture of multiple clips from the same tape. This is called *batch capturing*. You can *log* (create a list of) the segments you want to capture from your tape, using the Batch Capture window. The list (called a *batch list* or *timecode log*) can be created either by logging clips visually using device control or by typing In and Out points manually.

To create a new entry in the Batch List window, click the Add icon (▣). When your batch list is ready, click one button—the Capture button in either the Batch Capture or Movie Capture window—to capture all the specified clips on your list. To open and familiarize yourself with the Batch Capture window, from the title bar at the top of your screen, choose File > Batch Capture.

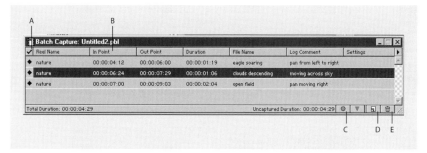

Batch Capture window: **A.** *Check-mark column* **B.** *Sort by In point button*
C. *Capture button* **D.** *Add New Item button* **E.** *Delete selected button*

Note: *Batch Capture is not recommended for the first and last 30 seconds of your tape because of possible timecode and seeking issues; you will need to capture these sections manually.*

Components that affect video capture quality

Video capture requires a higher and more consistent level of computer performance—far more than you need to run general office software, and even more than you need to work with image-editing software. Getting professional results depends on the performance and capacity of all of the components of your system working together to move frames from the video-capture card to the processor and hard disk. The ability of your computer to capture video depends on the combined performance of the following components:

Video-capture card You need to have a video-capture card installed or the equivalent capability built into your computer to transfer video from a video camcorder, tape deck, or other video source to your computer's hard drive. A *video-capture card* is not the same as the *video card* that drives your computer monitor. Adobe Premiere Pro software is bundled with many video-capture cards.

Note: *Only supported video-capture cards should be used with Adobe Premiere Pro. Not all capture cards certified for use with Adobe Premiere 5.x are certified for use with 6.x and higher. Please refer to the list of certified capture cards found on the Adobe Web site (www.adobe.com).*

Your video-capture card must be fast enough to capture video at the level of quality that your final medium requires. For full-screen, full-motion NTSC video, the card must be capable of capturing 30 frames (60 fields) per second at 640 x 480 pixels without dropping frames; for PAL and SECAM, 25 frames (50 fields) per second at 720 x 576 pixels. Even for Web video that will be output at a smaller frame size and a lower frame rate, you'll want to capture your source material at the highest quality settings available. You'll be using a lot of hard-disk space, but it's better to start with high quality (more data) so you'll have more choices about what information to discard when you reach the encoding stage. If you start with low quality (less data), you might regret having fewer options down the road.

Hard disk   The hard disk stores the video clips you capture. The hard disk must be fast enough to store captured video frames as quickly as they arrive from the video card; otherwise, frames will be dropped as the disk falls behind. For capturing at the NTSC video standard of just under 30 frames per second, your hard disk should have an average (not minimum) access time of 10 milliseconds (ms) or less, and a sustained (not peak) data transfer rate of at least 3 MB per second—preferably around 6 MB per second. The *access time* is how fast a hard disk can reach specific data.

The key to optimal performance is to have as much contiguous defragmented free space as possible on your hard disk. Fragmented disks greatly inhibit access for Real-Time Preview, capture, or playback.

The *data transfer rate* is how fast the hard disk can move data to and from the rest of the computer. Due to factors such as system overhead, the actual data transfer rate for video capture is about half the data transfer rate of the drive. For best results, capture to a separate high-performance hard disk intended for use with video capture and editing. The state of high-end video hardware changes rapidly; consult the manufacturer of your video-capture card for suggestions about appropriate video storage hardware.

Central processing unit (CPU)   Your computer's processor—such as a Pentium® 4 chip—handles general processing tasks in your computer. The CPU must be fast enough to process captured frames at the capture frame rate. A faster CPU—or using multiple CPUs in one computer (multiprocessing)—is better. However, other system components must be fast enough to handle the CPU speed. Using a fast CPU with slow components is like driving a sports car in a traffic jam.

Codec (compressor/decompressor)   Most video-capture cards come with a compression chip that keeps the data rate within a level your computer can handle. If your video-capture hardware doesn't have a compression chip, you should perform capture using a fast, high-quality codec such as Motion JPEG. If you capture using a slow-compressing or lossy codec such as Cinepak, you'll drop frames or lose quality.

Processing time required by other software If you capture video while several other programs are running (such as network connections, nonessential system enhancers, and screen savers), the other programs will probably interrupt the video capture with requests for processing time, causing dropped frames. Capture video while running as few drivers, extensions, and other programs as possible.

Data bus Every computer has a data bus that connects system components and handles data transfer between them. Its speed determines how fast the computer can move video frames between the video-capture card, the processor, and the hard disk. If you purchased a high-end computer or a computer designed for video editing, the data bus speed is likely to be well matched to the other components. However, if you've upgraded an older computer with a video-capture card, a faster processor, or a hard disk, an older data bus may limit the speed benefits of the new components. Before upgrading components, review the documentation provided by the manufacturer of your computer to determine whether your data bus can take advantage of the speed of a component you want to add.

For more information, go to the Adobe Web site (www.adobe.com) *and search for available resources.*

Capturing to support online or off-line editing

Depending on the level of quality you want and the capabilities of your equipment, you may be able to use Premiere Pro for either online or off-line editing. The settings you specify for video capture are different for online or off-line editing.

Online editing The practice of doing all editing (including the rough cut) using the same source clips that will be used to produce the final cut. As high-end personal computers have become more powerful, online editing has become practical for a wider range of productions such as broadcast television or motion-picture film productions. For online editing, you'll capture clips once, at the highest level of quality your computer and peripherals can handle.

Off-line editing The practice of preparing a rough cut from lower-quality clips, then producing the final version with higher-quality clips, sometimes on a high-end system. Off-line editing techniques can be useful even if your computer can handle editing at the quality of your final cut. By batch-capturing video using low-quality settings, you can edit faster, using smaller files. When you digitize video for off-line editing, you specify settings that emphasize editing speed over picture quality. In most cases, you need only enough quality to identify the correct beginning and ending frames for each scene. When you're ready to create the final cut, you can redigitize the video at the final-quality settings.

Note: *Typically, off-line editing is not employed when working with DV, because Premiere Pro handles DV at its original quality level.*

For more information on all the topics covered in this section on capturing video, see "Capturing and Importing Source Clips" in the *Adobe Premiere Pro User Guide*.

Batch-capturing video

If you have a frame-accurate deck or camcorder that supports external device control and a videotape recorded with timecode, you can set up Premiere Pro for automatic, unattended capture of multiple clips from the same tape. This is called batch capturing. You can log (create a list of) the segments you want to capture from your tape, using the Capture window. The list (called a batch list or timecode log) can be created either by logging clips visually using device control or by typing In and Out points manually.

To create a new entry in the batch list, click the Log Clip button in the lower-right section of the capture window. The Log Clip window comes up where you can give the file a name and add meta-information about the clip. Logged clips appear as off-line clips in the Project window. When your batch list is ready, select the clips in the project window and choose File > Batch Capture.

Note: *Batch Capture is not recommended for the first and last 30 seconds of your tape because of possible timecode and seeking issues; you will need to capture these sections manually.*

Automatic Scene Selection

To save yourself the trouble of manually logging and capturing scenes, you can also use the automatic scene detection feature of Premiere Pro. When Scene Detect is on, Premiere Pro looks for discontinuities in the timecode on the tape and captures a separate file for each scene that it finds.

Using the DV Device Control Options

Adobe Premiere Pro makes it easy to choose an appropriate setting for your DV device control. You simply choose a preset from a default list of tested devices.

To choose a DV device option preset:

1 Choose Edit > Preferences > Device Control.

2 In the Device Control section, choose DV Device Control from the Devices menu.

3 Click the Options button below the Device menu.

4 In the DV Device Control Options dialog box, set any of the following options and click OK:

Video Standard Specifies the video format.

Device Brand Specifies the device manufacturer.

Device Type Specifies the device model number.

Timecode Format Specifies the device timecode format.

Check Status Tells you if the device is connected.

Go Online for Device Info Opens the Web page that lists the latest compatible devices.

Understanding opacity and superimposing

Opacity allows a clip (or any portion of a clip) to reveal a second, underlying clip, so that you can create composites, transitions, or other effects. A variety of opacity types are available in Premiere Pro. The opacity types are described in this section.

Matte or mask An image that specifies transparent or semitransparent areas for another image. For example, if you want to superimpose an object in one clip over the background of another clip, you can use a mask to remove the background of the first clip. You can use other still-image or motion graphics software (such as Adobe Photoshop or Adobe After Effects) to create a still-image or moving (traveling) matte and apply it to a clip in your Premiere Pro project. A mask works like a film negative; black areas are transparent, white areas are opaque, and gray areas are semitransparent—darker areas are more transparent than lighter areas. You can use shades of gray to create feathered (soft-edged) or graduated masks.

Alpha channel Color in an RGB video image is stored in three color *channels*—one red, one green, and one blue. An image can also contain a mask in a fourth channel called the *alpha channel*. By keeping an image together with its mask, you don't have to manage two separate files. (Sometimes, however, saving a mask as a separate file can be useful; such as when creating a track matte effect, because the mask must be placed in a separate track in Premiere's Timeline.

A 32-bit frame has four 8-bit channels: red, green, blue, and an alpha channel mask.

Programs such as Adobe Photoshop and Adobe After Effects let you paint or draw a mask and use the alpha channel to keep the mask with the image or movie.

Premiere uses the alpha channel for compositing.

Photoshop image (left) contains an alpha channel mask (center), which Premiere Pro uses to composite the subject against another background (right).

Keying Finds pixels in an image that match a specified color or brightness and makes those pixels transparent or semitransparent. For example, if you have a clip of a weatherman standing in front of a blue-screen background, you can *key out* the blue and replace it with a weather map.

Opacity Allows you to control the degree of overall transparency for a clip. You can use opacity to fade a clip in or out.

With Premiere Pro, you can combine the opacity options described here. For example, you can use a matte to remove the background from one clip and superimpose it over a second clip, and then use opacity to fade-in the first clip's visible area.

Using audio in a video

Audio can play an equally important role to imagery in telling your story. In Adobe Premiere Pro, you can adjust audio qualities in the Timeline window, or use the Audio Mixer with greater flexibility and control when mixing multiple audio tracks. For example, you might combine dialogue clips with ambient background sounds and a musical soundtrack. Mixing audio in Premiere Pro can include any combination of the following tasks:

• Fading (increasing or decreasing), the volume levels of audio clips over time.

• Panning/balancing monophonic audio clips between the left and right stereo channels. For example, you may want to *pan* a dialogue clip to match a person's position in the video frame.

• Creating sophisticated surround sound effects using the 5.1 audio support.

• Using audio effects to remove noise, enhance frequency response and dynamic range, sweeten the sound, or create interesting audio distortions such as reverb.

• Directly recording an audio track (such as a voice-over) to the Timeline while watching the video.

• Editing audio clips at the sub-frame, audio-sample level, with a precision of up to 1/96,000 of a second.

• Combining up to 99 audio tracks into a rich array of music, dialogue, and sound effects.

When you import a video clip that contains audio, the audio track is *linked* to its video track by default so that they move together. Adobe Premiere Pro allows you to adjust and mix audio while you watch the corresponding video in Real-Time. The Audio Mixer window, like an audio mixing console in a professional sound studio, contains a set of controls for each audio track; each set is numbered to match its corresponding audio track in the Timeline. When you edit superimposed video tracks, remember to consider the effects of your edits on the audio tracks.

For more information, see "Mixing Audio" in the *Adobe Premiere Pro User Guide* and Lesson 12, "Audio," in this book.

Understanding digital audio

You hear sounds because your ear recognizes the variations in air pressure that create sound. *Analog audio* reproduces sound variations by creating or reading variations in an electrical signal. *Digital audio* reproduces sound by sampling the sound pressure or signal level at a specified rate and converting that to a number.

The quality of digital audio depends on the sample rate and bit depth. The *sample rate* is how often the audio level is digitized. A 44.1 kHz sample rate is audio-CD-quality, while CD-ROM or Internet audio often uses a sample rate of 22 kHz or below. The *bit depth* is the range of numbers used to describe an audio sample; 16 bits is audio-CD-quality. Lower bit depths and sample rates are not suitable for high-fidelity audio, but may be acceptable (though noisy) for dialogue. The file size of an audio clip increases or decreases as you increase or decrease the sample rate or bit depth.

Note: DV camcorders support only 32 or 48 kHz audio; not 44.1 kHz. So, when capturing or working with DV source material, be sure to set the audio for 32 or 48 kHz.

Keeping audio in sync with video

Be mindful of audio sample rates in relation to the timebase and frame rate of your project. The most common mistake is to create a movie at 30 fps with audio at 44.1 kHz, and then play back the movie at 29.97 fps (for NTSC video). The result is a slight slowdown in the video, while the audio (depending on your hardware) may still be playing at the correct rate and, therefore, will seem to get ahead of the video. The difference between 30 and 29.97 results in a synchronization discrepancy that appears at a rate of 1 frame per 1000 frames, or 1 frame per 33.3 seconds (just under 2 frames per minute). If you notice audio and video drifting apart at about this rate, check for a project frame rate that doesn't match the timebase.

A similar problem can occur when editing motion-picture film after transferring it to video. Film audio is often recorded on a digital audio tape (DAT) recorder at 48 kHz synchronized with a film camera running at 24 fps. When the film is transferred to 30 fps video, the difference in the video frame rate will cause the audio to run ahead of the video unless you slow the DAT playback by 0.1% when transferring to the computer. Using your computer to convert the sample rate after the original recording doesn't help with this problem. The best solution is to record the original audio using a DAT deck that can record 0.1% faster (48.048 kHz) when synchronized with the film camera.

Older CD-ROM titles sometimes used an audio sample rate of 22.254 kHz; today, a rate of 22.250 kHz is more common. If you notice audio drifting at a rate accounted for by the difference between these two sample rates (1 frame every 3.3 seconds), you may be mixing new and old audio clips recorded at the two different sample rates.

Creating final video

When you have finished editing and assembling your video project, Adobe Premiere Pro offers a variety of flexible output options. You can:

• Record your production directly to DV or analog videotape by connecting your computer to a video camcorder or tape deck. If your camera or deck supports device control, you can automate the recording process, using timecode indications to selectively record portions of your program.

• Export a digital video file for playback from a computer hard drive, removable cartridge, CD-ROM, or DVD. Adobe Premiere Pro exports Advanced Windows Media, RealMedia, AVI, QuickTime, and MPEG files; additional file formats may be available in Premiere Pro if provided with your video-capture card or third-party plug-in software.

• Use Advanced RealMedia, or Advanced Windows Media export options to generate properly encoded video files for distribution over the Internet or your intranet. Adobe Premiere Pro exports QuickTime, RealMedia, and Windows Media formats for download, progressive download, or streaming.

• Output to motion-picture film or videotape if you have the proper hardware for film or video transfer or access to a vendor that offers the appropriate equipment and services.

For more information, see "Producing Final Video" in the *Adobe Premiere Pro User Guide* and Lesson 13, "Output," in this book.

Review questions

1 What's the difference between the timebase and the project frame rate?

2 Why is drop-frame timecode important for NTSC video?

3 How is interlaced display different from progressive scan?

4 Why is data compression important?

5 What's the difference between applying a mask and adjusting opacity?

Answers

1 The timebase specifies the time divisions in a project. The project frame rate specifies the final number of frames per second that are generated from the project. Movies with different frame rates can be generated from the same timebase; for example, you can export movies at 30, 15, and 10 frames per second from a timebase of 30.

2 Counting NTSC frames using a timecode of 30 fps causes an increasingly inaccurate program duration because of the difference between 30 fps and the NTSC frame rate of 29.97 fps. Drop-frame timecode ensures that the duration of NTSC video will be measured accurately.

3 Interlacing, used by standard television monitors, displays a frame's scan lines in two alternating passes, known as fields. Progressive scan, used by computer monitors, displays a frame's scan lines in one pass.

4 Without data compression, digital video and audio often produce a data rate too high for many computer systems to handle smoothly.

5 A mask, also known as a matte in video production, is a separate channel or file that indicates transparent or semitransparent areas within a frame. In Premiere Pro, opacity specifies the transparency of an entire frame.

A Tour of Adobe Premiere Pro

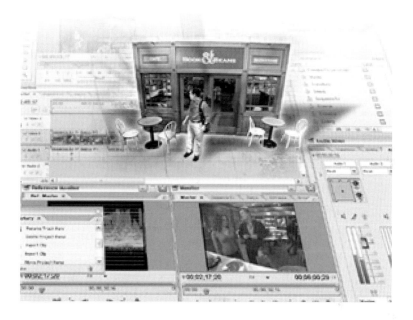

This Tour helps you understand and work with basic concepts and features of the Adobe Premiere Pro program. You'll run through a typical series of steps for creating a video piece, including basic editing techniques, adding transitions, motion, and opacity. Completing this Tour should take approximately one hour.

Over the course of the Tour, you'll create a brief trailer for the short film that you'll edit throughout the rest of the book. You'll be working with video clips, audio clips, and images provided on the DVD-ROM included with this *Adobe Premiere Pro Classroom in a Book*. If you were actually producing this project from the start, you would likely capture clips from the original video tapes and digitize them yourself, using Premiere Pro.

For more information on capturing video and audio, see the previous chapter, "The World of Digital Video," on page 29.

Setting up a new project

To begin, you'll launch Adobe Premiere Pro, set up your workspace, create a new project, and then import the video clips.

1 Make sure you know the location of the files used in this lesson. Insert the *Adobe Premiere Pro Classroom in a Book* disk. Copy the Tour folder to your hard drive. For help, see "Copying the *Classroom in a Book* files" on page 4.

2 Start Premiere Pro.

3 Click on New Project.

4 Under Load Preset > DV – NTSC choose Standard 48 kHz.

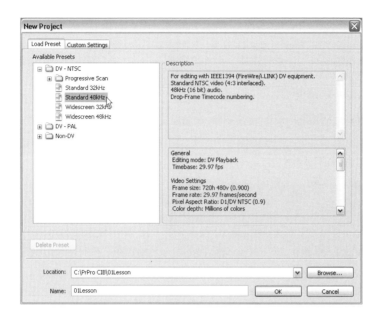

5 At the bottom of the screen, for Location, click Browse, and navigate to the 00Tour Lesson directory you copied to your hard disk.

6 For name, type **00Tour Lesson** and then click OK.

Importing Clips

The trailer you're making is composed of video files, audio files, still image files, and title sequence files.

1 Choose Window > Workspace > Editing to ensure your window layout is in the default editing mode.

2 From the main Premiere Pro menu at the top of your display, choose File > New > Bin.

A new Directory called a "bin," and named Bin 01, appears in the Project window.

3 Deselect the name field of Bin 01 by clicking a blank spot in the Project window.

4 Click on Bin 01 and choose File > Import.

5 Hold down the Control key as you click on the following files: Defeat.prtl, Despair.prtl, Doorslam.wav, Dreamzoom.avi, EXexit.avi, Fear.prtl, Gods1.avi, Gods2.avi, Gods3.avi, Heroexit.avi, Hope.prtl, HseesD.avi, Hwatches.avi, Logo.psd, Nevermind.avi, Rejection.prtl, Storefront2.psd, and Tourmusic.wav. Then click Open.

6 You'll be prompted if you want to Import the Layered File Storefront 2.psd. The default options should be fine, so click OK.

Bin 01 now contains all the files you've just imported.

7 Save the project before continuing.

Navigating the Premiere Pro Workspace

If you are new to the program, a more complete introduction to the Adobe Premiere Pro Workspace can be found in the next lesson, 01Lesson, "The Workspace," starting on page 77. Of quick special reference here, review the illustrations and descriptions starting at the bottom on page 80. There you'll find out about the windows and palettes and their functions. Familiarity with this information will make your Tour experience more rewarding.

Conforming audio files

When you first import the files, you'll notice an activity bar in the lower right frame of your Premiere window. You've just imported many files, most of which have audio in them. Premiere Pro is conforming all the audio for real-time playback on your system. This process takes up a significant amount of disk space on your system. From time to time, you may need to clear older conformed audio files (CFA), to free up disk space.

Another advantage of this process is that it makes the exporting of audio consistent with most output formats. Over the course of the project, you may import files with several different modes of audio used to capture them. Conforming converts all audio within a project to the project settings for audio you choose at its inception. In this book, you'll be using Standard 48 kHz.

Viewing the Trailer before you start

Another file you may wish to import is Trailer.wmv, which is the film output from the Tour project. You can view this file for reference and use it as a guide.

1 Choose File > Import.

2 Navigate two levels up to the folder that you copied from the DVD to your hard disk. Locate the folder named Movies and click Open.

3 In the Movies directory, you'll find Trailer.wmv. Select it and click Open. Trailer.wmv appears in the Project window.

4 In the Project window, select Trailer.wmv, and then double-click it.

5 Trailer.wmv appears in the left side of the Monitor window, named the Source view.

6 Click the Play button (▶) to review what you'll be building in this lesson.

Rough Cut

The Project window now has a bin called Bin 01 with the files you need to work. Make a rough cut of the trailer by placing a sequence of clips into the Timeline window.

1 Double-click to open the bin and see the resources for this tutorial.

2 Press and hold down the Control key, and at the same time, carefully select the following fourteen clips in the exact order listed here: Rejection.prtl, EXexit.avi, Hwatches.avi, Despair.prtl, Gods1.avi, Gods2.avi, Gods3.avi, Hope.prtl, HseesD.avi, Dreamzoom.avi, Fear.prtl, Nevermind.avi, Defeat.prtl, and Heroexit.avi.

3 Choose Project > Automate to Sequence.

4 Use the following illustration to input the following settings in the Automate to Sequence box: for Ordering, choose Selection Order; for Placement, choose Sequentially; for Method, choose Insert Edit; and set Clip Overlap to **0** Frames. Leave all four check boxes unchecked.

5 Click OK.

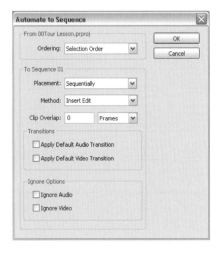

The clips are laid out in the order selected on the Sequence 01 Timeline.

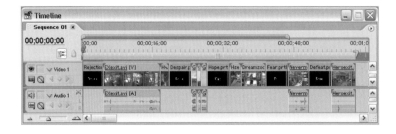

6 Click on the Timeline to make it the active window.

7 Adjust the amount of time displayed in the Timeline by dragging the end of the slider at the top of the Timeline window to the left.

You can dynamically set the time unit for the window by dragging the right or left ends. Dragging the middle changes what portion of the sequence is visible in the Timeline window.

Dynamic time zoom control bar. Experiment with it to become comfortable with its functions.

See Lesson 1 for more information and exercises using the Timeline on page 95.

Previewing in the Monitor window

To see how your work is progressing, you can preview one or more clips in the Monitor window. The Dual View Monitor window displays Source and Program views.

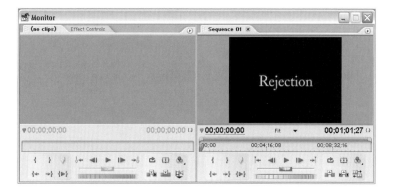

Source view (on the left side of the window) Lets you preview a clip, trim it, and then insert it into the Timeline window. This view can store many clips at a time, but you can view and trim only one clip at a time.

Program view (on the right) Lets you preview your entire video program, at any time. This view displays the sequence of clips currently in the Timeline window. You can also use the Program view to edit your video program.

1 If the Monitor window is not already open, choose Window > Monitor.

2 In the Monitor window, click the Play button (▶) underneath the Program view, or press the spacebar on your keyboard once to play the rough cut of your video program.

3 To replay your video program, click the Play button again, or click the Loop button (⏏) to play the video program in a continuous loop. To stop the action, click the Stop button (■) or press the spacebar on the keyboard.

Now that you're satisfied with the rough cut of your video program, you'll trim the video clips and add audio, transitions, special effects, and superimposing to create the finished version of the Tour movie.

Trimming Clips

When you shoot footage with your camera, you almost always produce much more material than you'll actually use in your video program. To create scenes, cuts, and transitions, you'll trim your clips to remove the parts you don't need. Trimming clips is an essential part of creating a video program, something you'll do many times. Premiere Pro provides a number of different ways to trim clips, including quick rough-cut tools and more precise frame-by-frame exercises.

Using the trimming tools in the Timeline

The first thing you'll notice in the rough cut is that the titles on the screen are far too long.

1 Click on the first title clip called Rejection.prtl.

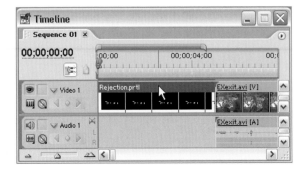

2 Choose Clip > Speed / Duration.

3 Click on the Duration and type **100**, then press Enter.

Premiere Pro converts this to 00;00;01;00, meaning 1 second. You can also click-and-drag on the number to adjust it dynamically. You can do this in Premiere Pro whenever you see this type of blue data value. It is a dynamic text input field, which allows you to click and roll the mouse left to decrease a value and right to increase a value.

4 Click OK

5 Repeat this step for the other four titles: Despair.prtl, Hope.prtl, Fear.prtl, and Defeat.prtl.

Now you need to close the gaps between the clips.

6 Click on the first clip and drag it about 15 frames (or one-half of a second) to the right so the movie will start with half a second of black.

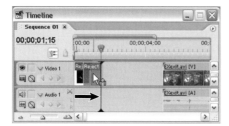

7 To close the gap to the right of this first clip, select the track select tool from the Tools palette.

8 Click-and-drag the second clip to the left to about the 2 second mark of the time code. This tool selects and will move everything that is later in time in the track to earlier in the movie.

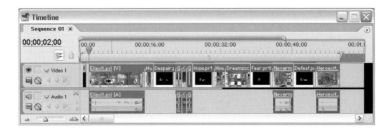

9 Repeat this step for the other four title clips so that they will all be preceded and followed by a half-second of black.

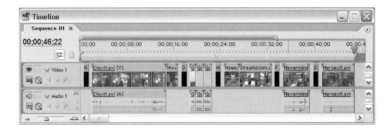

10 Save the project.

Insert versus Overlay editing

Next you need to shorten the initial sequence in which Ex and New Boy leave the shop. You'll do this by inter-cutting with the close-up on the Hero watching them leave.

1 Select the razor tool.

2 Click a little less than half-way through the Hwatches.avi clip to cut it in half.

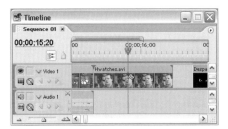

3 Click-and-drag the Edit Line while watching the Program monitor (right-hand view in the Monitor window) to find the part of the EXexit.avi clip just after Ex says, "...some time." This is called scrubbing.

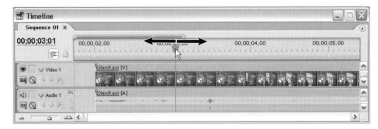

4 Using the selection tool, drag the first half of the Hwatches.avi clip so that its left edge lines up with the edit line.

This is how an Overlay edit operates. Notice how the clip snaps in place, and the edit line turns into an arrowhead. Part of the EXexit.avi clip gets replaced by the Hwatches.avi clip.

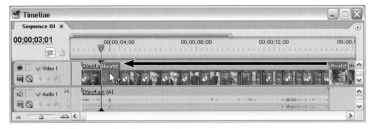

An Overlay edit overwrites the target footage.

5 Now scrub the edit line to a little after Ex says, "...maybe."

6 While holding down the Control key, drag the second half of the Hwatches.avi clip to line up with the Edit Line. When you release the clip, it is inserted, and the rest of the EXexit.avi clip, along with the balance of the project, is moved later in time.

This is the result of an Insert edit. Notice how the clip snaps in place, and the edit line reveals a white triangle in the destination video and audio tracks.

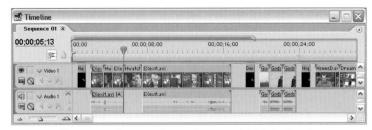

An Insert edit preserves the target footage between which it is placed.

Setting In and Out points in the Source monitor

Now you'll shorten the remaining piece of the EXexit.avi clip to show just the door closing.

1 Double-click on the last piece of the EXexit.avi clip to load it into the Source view of the Monitor window.

2 Using the edit line in the Source view, scrub to just before the door closes.

3 Click the Set In Point button.

4 Scrub to just after the door closes.

5 Click the Set Out Point button.

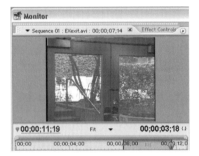

The edits made in the Source view to the third instance of EXexit.avi are updated in the Timeline as you make them.

6 In the Timeline window, drag the edited EXexit.avi clip to the left so that it snaps in place next to the end of the second instance of the Hwatches.avi clip.

Later in this tutorial, you'll replace the ad libbed conversation that Ex and New Boy have as they're walking out the door with a door-closing sound effect.

7 Select the right audio segment of EXexit.avi and choose Edit > Clear to remove it from the Timeline.

8 Finally, using the track selection tool, drag the rest of the sequence from Despair.avi on to the left so that it starts about 15 frames after the end of the door closing.

9 Save the project.

Special effects

The use of Video, Audio, and other computer-generated effects imported from programs like Adobe Photoshop, Adobe After Effects, Adobe Illustrator, Adobe DVD Encore, and Adobe Audition, are the special changes you make to a movie to polish it.

Transitions

Now you'll create a dissolve from when Hero sees Dreams to the Dreams zoom.

1 First you need to create some tails by shortening the end of the HseesD.avi clip and the beginning of the Dreamzoom.avi clip.

2 In the Tools palette, select the ripple edit tool.

The Ripple Edit tool trims and performs the function of the track selection tool as it trims. You shorten the duration of the clip being trimmed and of the entire sequence. If you trim from the end frame (Out point) toward the start frame (In point), the starting point of the subject clip will not change, but the starting point of all clips later in time will change. Likewise, even if you trim from the In point toward the Out point, the Out point of the subject clip will change, and all clips later in time will move toward the beginning of the sequence. If you Ripple Edit the first clip at the zero point, the project will still start at zero, but the overall duration will decrease by the amount of the trim.

3 Using the Ripple edit tool, drag the right edge (the Out point of the clip) of the HseesD.avi clip slightly more than one second to the left.

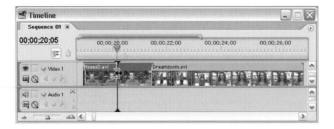

This results in the HseesD.avi being shortened, and the rest of the program being moved toward the start of the movie at the same time.

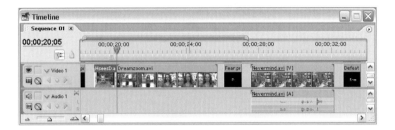

4 Drag the left edge (the In point of the clip) of the Dreamzoom.avi clip slightly more than 1 second to the right.

5 Save the project.

6 Now to add the transition, make the Effects palette active by choosing Window > Effects from the menu.

7 Open the Video Transitions and then the Dissolve folder by clicking on the triangles next to the folder icons.

8 Drag Cross Dissolve from the Effects palette onto the cut between the HseesD.avi and the Dreamzoom.avi clips in the Timeline.

A transition is placed at the cut between two clips.

The result of placing a 60-frame transition on the Timeline.

Now you'll modify the transition so that it starts a little later.

9 Using the selection tool, click on the Cross Dissolve transition.

10 Choose Window > Effect Controls.

11 Set the duration to 1 second if it is not already.

12 Change the Alignment from Center at Cut to Start at Cut.

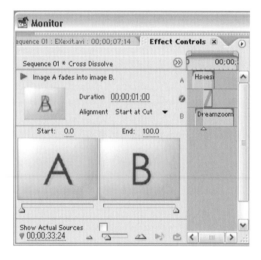

13 Review the Trailer thus far, by setting the timecode or moving the edit line to zero and either pressing the space bar on your keyboard, or by pressing Play (►) in the Program view of the Monitor window.

14 Save the project.

Changing clip speed

To accentuate the zoom effect, you'll speed up the Dreamzoom.avi clip.

1 Using the selection tool ( ), click on the Dreamzoom.avi clip.

2 Choose Clip > Speed/Duration.

3 Change 100% to **125**%. Press Enter and then click OK.

4 Using the track selection tool, drag the rest of the sequence from Fear.avi to about 1 second to the left so that it's one-half second after the end of the Dreamzoom.avi clip.

Adding the Blur video effect

To further accentuate the zoom, you'll apply a blur effect to the Dreamzoom.avi clip.

1 Using the selection tool, click on Dreamzoom.avi.

2 Choose Window > Effects.

3 Choose Video Effects > Blur & Sharpen.

4 Drag Radial Blur onto the clip.

The Radial Blur settings box will appear.

5 For the moment, set the Amount to 80 and the Blur Method to Zoom. Click OK.

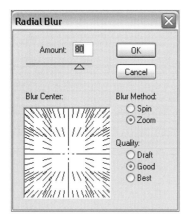

6 Scrub to the beginning of the Dreamzoom.avi clip.

7 Choose Window > Effect Controls, to make the Effect Controls window active.

8 Open the Radial Blur settings by clicking on the triangle next to the name.

9 In the Amount area, click on the stopwatch icon (⏱) to turn on animation. This sets a keyframe of 80 at the beginning of the clip.

10 Scrub to the point in the clip when the camera stops moving forward.

11 Click on the Amount and type **1**. Press Enter. This sets a keyframe at this point.

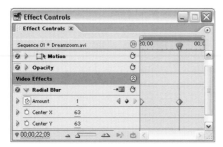

12 Since this blur effect is computationally intensive, you may need to render this section of the sequence to get smooth playback. Press Enter to start the render.

Using a Photoshop File

When Hero exits the store, you'll notice that there are no signs on it. You'll add some signs by placing a Photoshop file over the shot.

Scroll the Timeline so that you can see the clip called Heroexit.avi.

1 Choose Window > Project.

2 Drag the Storefront2.psd clip onto the Video 2 track of the Timeline so that the left edge aligns with the Heroexit.avi clip.

3 Using the selection tool, drag the right edge of the Storefront2.psd clip so that it aligns with the right edge of the Heroexit.avi clip.

If you were to edit the storefront image in Photoshop, that change would automatically appear in Premiere.

Motion Keys

Now you'll make the Books & Beans logo zoom out from above the store entrance to fill the screen.

1 Scrub to when the Hero takes his first step.

2 Choose Window > Project, and drag the Logo.psd clip onto the Video 3 track of the Timeline so that the left edge aligns with the edit line.

3 Choose Clip > Speed/Duration.

4 Change the Duration to **8** seconds (00;00;08;00, that is: 00 hours; 00 minutes; 08 seconds; 00 frames at 30 frames per second).

5 Click OK.

6 Scrub to just before the Hero walks off screen.

7 Choose Window > Effect Controls.

8 Open the Motion parameters by clicking on the triangle next to the name.

9 Change the Y-position from 240 to **180** to move it up a little. Press Enter.

10 Click the stopwatch icon next to Position, Scale and Rotation to create a keyframe for the final position of the logo.

11 Scrub to the first frame of the Logo.psd clip.

12 Change the parameters to the following values: Position: **400, 80**; Scale: **32**;
Rotation: **1**.

13 Play the effect in the Program view or in the Timeline.

14 Save the project.

Fade Out

Now you'll make the scene fade to black as the logo comes forward.

1 Choose Window > Effects > Video Transitions > Dissolve.

2 Drag Cross Dissolve to the right end of the Heroexit.avi clip.

Since there's no clip to cross to, Premiere automatically fades the clip to black.

You'll need to fade the sign, as well.

3 Drag Cross Dissolve from the Effects window to the right end of the Storefront2.psd
clip.

One second seems a bit short for this fade.

4 Select the dissolve on the Storefront2.psd clip.

5 Choose Window > Effect Controls.

6 Change the Duration to 1.5 seconds by clicking on the blue text and typing **115** (this is timecode shorthand for 30 frames + 15 frames, or 00;00;01;15), then press Enter.

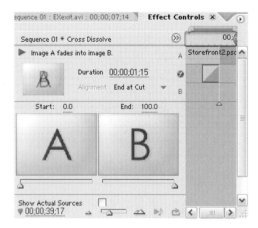

7 Click on the dissolve on the Heroexit.avi clip.

8 In the Effect Controls window, change the Duration to 1.5 seconds.

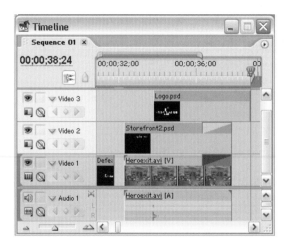

Creating Titles

Now you'll create the final titles for the sequence.

1 In the Timeline, scrub to about 15 frames after the storefront scene has faded completely. You should see only the Books & Beans logo.

2 Choose File > New > Title. This opens the Adobe Title Designer.

3 By default, you should see the Books & Beans logo in the Title Designer's window, and have the Type Tool selected (**T**).

4 Click a little below the B of Books. This places a cursor on the screen.

5 Enter the following text for the title: **A tale about falling in love**.

6 On the right side of the window, under Object Style > Properties, change the Font and Font Size to make the line of type about the same overall width as the entire logo.

You may need to adjust the position of the row of type. You can do this using the Title Designer's selection tool.

7 To center the type horizontally, right-click on the line of type and choose Position > Horizontal Center.

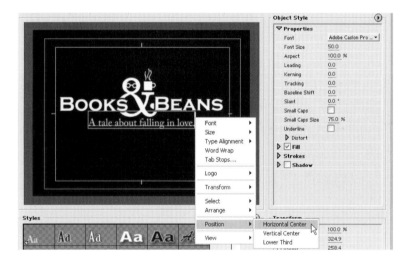

8 Choose File > Save.

9 Navigate to the 00Tour Lesson directory and name your title, such as **Falling.prtl**.

10 Close the Title Designer by clicking on the "X" in the upper right corner of the Title Designer window.

11 Looking in the project window, you'll see that Falling.prtl has automatically been added to the project. Drag Falling.prtl on to the Video 1 track of the Timeline about a second after the Heroexit.avi clip.

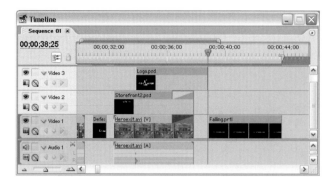

12 Using the selection tool, drag the right end of the Logo.psd clip to the right so that it aligns with the end of the Falling.prtl clip.

To make the last two words of the falling clip appear later, you'll cover them up with black to start.

13 Choose File > Import.

14 Locate the 00Tour Lesson folder and select Blackvideo.psd. Click Open.

15 Drag the Blackvideo.psd clip onto the Video 2 track of the Timeline so that its left edge aligns with the left edge of the Falling.prtl clip.

16 Drag the right edge of the Blackvideo.psd clip to the left to shorten the clip to about 2 seconds in duration.

17 Keeping the Blackvideo.psd selected, choose Window > Effect Controls > Motion.

18 Change the Motion parameters for to the following values: Position: **546**, **290**; Scale: **19**.

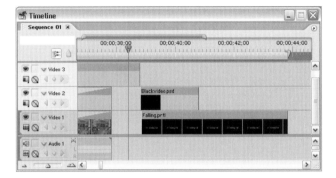

Audio

Here you'll be fixing the audio on the door closing scene.

1 Scroll back through the Timeline so that you can see the third instance of the EXexit.avi clip.

2 Drag Doorslam.wav from the Project window onto the Audio 1 track below the third EXexit.avi clip.

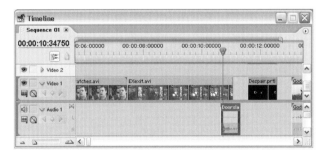

3 You may need to adjust the timing by sliding the audio clip slightly left or right in the Timeline using the selection tool. The audio clip shows a tiny version of the waveform which you can use to help you do this. The highest point on the waveform should align with the moment the door closes. If you need to, you can enlarge the display of the waveform by dragging the bottom edge of the label area of the Audio 1 track down.

Now add a soundtrack.

4 Choose Window > Project.

5 Drag Tourmusic.wav onto the Audio 2 track of the Timeline so that the left edge of the clip snaps to the beginning of the Timeline

Editing audio levels

Although the balance is not bad between the music and voice tracks, you might want to lower the music a little and add a fade at the end. You can adjust the volume and apply keyframes to an entire track at once, or on individual clips. For this tutorial, you'll adjust the volume for the entire music piece on the Audio 2 track.

1 In the Timeline, scroll to the end of the sequence. Scrub the Edit Line to a couple of seconds before the end.

2 Select the music clip in the Timeline.

3 Open the Audio 2 track header area by clicking the triangle next to Audio 2 in the Timeline.

4 Click the Show Keyframes button and choose Show Clip Volume.

5 Click the Add Keyframe button to add a keyframe.

6 Drag the keyframe down to lower the volume for the whole clip. A little window shows you how much you're adjusting the level. Play back the change and adjust to your sensibilities.

7 Scrub to the end of the music clip.

8 Add a keyframe.

9 Drag the keyframe down as far as it will go to set the volume to **0** for the clip.

10 Save the project.

Output

There are many output options in Adobe Premiere Pro. For this tutorial, you export the movie as a DV AVI just like the source clips. For more information on other output options, see Lesson 13, "Output."

1 Activate the Timeline window.

2 Choose File > Export > Movie.

3 Click the Settings button.

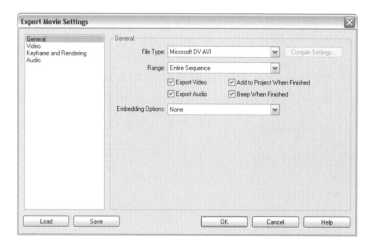

4 Make sure that Microsoft DV AVI is selected for File Type, and Entire Sequence for the Range.

5 Also make sure that the Export Video, Export Audio, and Add to Project When Finished options are selected. The default values for other settings, including those for compression, are fine for this project.

6 Click OK.

7 Choose a file name and a location to save the file.

8 Click Save.

9 Premiere Pro starts making the movie, displaying a status bar that provides an estimate for the amount of time it will take to *render* or *output* the move. The output time always depends on the capabilities of your computer. On most systems, Premiere Pro should finish making the movie within a few minutes. You can cancel the output process at any time by pressing the Escape key.

10 When the movie is complete, it appears as a clip in the Project window.

11 Double click on it to load it in the Source view of the Monitor window.

12 Click the Play button to watch the show.

13 Save the project.

Congratulations on completing the Tour!

Lesson 1

1 | The Workspace

The Premiere Pro workspace organizes editing functions into specialized windows. This gives you the flexibility to arrange a window layout that matches your editing style. Floating palettes give you information and quick access to any part of your video program. You can arrange windows and palettes to make the best use of your computer and television monitors.

In this overview of the Premiere Pro workspace, you'll learn how to do the following:

- Start the Adobe Premiere program.
- Customize your workspace.
- Work with the Project window.
- Work with the Timeline window.
- Work with the Monitor window.
- Navigate to a specific time in your video program.
- Use palettes.
- Discover keyboard shortcuts.

The Workspace in Premiere Pro

Every Adobe Premiere Pro movie starts as a project, and becomes a collection of video clips, still images, and audio organized along a timeline. In this lesson, you'll explore palettes and windows using a new project. Make sure you know the location of the files used in this lesson. For help, see "Copying the Classroom in a Book files" on page 4 of this *Classroom in a Book*.

Starting the Adobe Premiere Pro program

When you start Premiere Pro, the Welcome to Adobe Premiere Pro window appears.

1 Click New Project.

The Project Settings Screen appears.

2 Choose Standard 48 kHz.

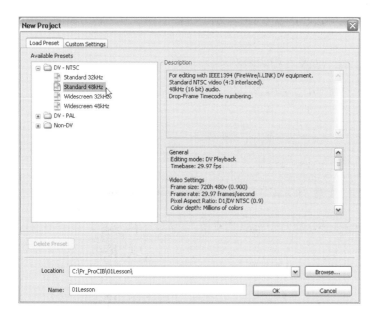

3 Type **01Lesson** in the name field.

4 Click on Browse and locate the directory called C:\Pr_ProCIB\Lessons\01Lesson and click OK to accept the file.

5 Click OK to close the New Project Box and enter the Adobe Premiere Pro Workspace.

*Note: The default file extension for Premiere projects, **prproj**, is added to your filename automatically.*

Note: Premiere Pro remembers the original location of each clip in a project. Because you are using the project file on a computer other than the one that created it, Premiere may prompt you to find some files when you open a lesson project. Locate and select the indicated files and then click OK.

Project settings

Once you start a project, you can check the project settings at any time.

1 Choose Project > Project Settings and you'll see a list of available settings in Premiere Pro.

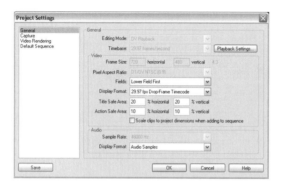

General Provides you with an overview of your project settings, including the Editing Mode, Time Display, and Playback video.

Capture Controls the way in which Premiere Pro transfers video and audio from a camera or deck.

Video Rendering Controls the frame size, picture quality, compression settings, and aspect ratios that Premiere Pro uses when you play back video from the Timeline window.

Default Sequence When you create a new sequence, these settings determine the number of video and audio tracks, plus the type of audio tracks.

💡 *Adobe strongly recommends that if your capture card provides a preset file, you should use the preset provided; manual changes to the settings should not be made. If none of the presets available matches your video, refer to the Adobe Premiere Pro User Guide for assistance in changing the settings.*

Getting to know the Workspace

Once the project is open, the Premiere work area appears. You can use it the way it originally displays, or customize it for your style and efficiency.

View of the Workspace with a sample project in progress: *A. Project window* *B. Monitor window* *C. Info palette* *D. Effects palette* *E. Timeline window* *F. Audio Mixer* *G. Effect Controls palette* *H. History palette* *I. Tools palette*

A new project has the following windows open by default:

Project window This window lets you import, organize, and store references to clips. It lists all source clips you import into a project, although you don't have to use every clip you import.

Monitor window   This window includes the Source view on the left side and the Program view on the right side in the default Dual View mode. In Single View mode the Program view is displayed. Use the Source view to review, edit, and trim an individual video clip, and the Program view to see the current state of the video program being edited in the Timeline.

Timeline window   This window provides a schematic view of your program, including all of the video, audio, and superimposed video tracks. Changes you make appear in the Program view. The Zoom in (⬆)and Zoom out (⬆) buttons located at the bottom left of the Timeline window provide a convenient way to navigate inside the Timeline. You can also navigate with the Time Zoom control bar, located directly above the time ruler at the top of Timeline window.

Audio Mixer window   Choose Window > Audio Mixer to access this window, which acts like a professional mixing console. It provides sophisticated audio mixing technologies that allow you to adjust multiple audio tracks while listening to them and viewing your video in Real-Time. You can control settings such as volume and pan/balance for each audio track from this window.

The palettes are organized in separate windows. All of the palettes are listed in the Window menu.

Effects palette   This palette contains all of the video and audio transitions and effects, which can be applied to clips in the video or audio tracks in the Timeline window. It opens by default and can be docked with the Project window to save space on the desktop.

Tools palette   This palette allows you to perform all of the necessary editing to your video project. It opens by default.

Effect Controls palette   This palette allows you to change effect settings at any time and appears when an effect or transition has been applied to a clip. This palette opens when you choose Window > Effect Controls.

Info palette   This palette provides information about the selected clip, transition, selected area in the Timeline, or operation you are performing.

History palette   This palette lets you go back to any previous state of the project created during the current working session. Each time you make a change, a new state is added to the History palette. You can delete all edits after the selected state, return to your current state, or incrementally restore states.

For more information, see the following sections of the *Adobe Premiere Pro User Guide*, "Using the Info palette", "Using the History palette", and "Working with the Effects window".

You work with clips and assemble your program within the three windows previously described: the Project window, the Monitor window, and the Timeline window, and the Effect Controls palette. Premiere Pro also provides specialized windows for tasks such as capturing video and creating titles. Those windows and their uses are described later in this *Classroom in a Book*, as well as in the *Adobe Premiere Pro User Guide*.

Most windows and palettes in Premiere include menus, and all windows have context menus. The commands found in window menus, palette menus, and context menus are specific to individual windows and palettes. For more information, see "Using window and palette menus" in the *Adobe Premiere Pro User Guide*.

Customizing the Workspace

If necessary, rearrange windows and palettes so they don't overlap. You may want to use the arrangement shown earlier in this section. You can close the Audio Mixer window since you won't be using it during this lesson. You can save this arrangement and use it as a template when you open other projects.

To save your customized workspace:

1 Choose Window > Workspace > Save Workspace.

2 The Save Workspace dialog box appears. Type **My Workspace** for the name.

3 Click Save.

As you open projects throughout this book, you can choose Windows > Workspace > My Workspace. The windows and palettes will adjust to your display in the order in which they were previously saved according to your own preferences.

Working with the Project window

The Project window is where you import, organize, and store references to clips. You can view and add information for every clip in your project. It lists all source clips you import into a project, though you don't have to use every clip you import. You can also expand the size of the Project window.

The filenames in the Project window identify the files imported into the project. Icons next to each filename indicate the file type. Video and audio files are large, so copying each one into a project would waste significant disk space. Instead, a Premiere Pro project stores only references to the clips you import, not the clips themselves. This means that a 5 MB source clip always occupies just 5 MB on your hard disk whether you use it in one project or ten. When you edit your video program, Premiere Pro retrieves frames from the original files as needed.

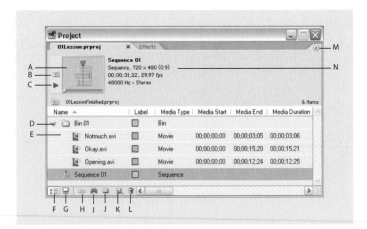

Sample of a Project window in the List view with thumbnails (your view may differ): **A.** *Thumbnail viewer* **B.** *Poster Frame* **C.** *Play Button* **D.** *Bins* **E.** *Clips* **F.** *List View* **G.** *Icon View* **H.** *Automate to Sequence* **I.** *Find* **J.** *Bin* **K.** *New Items* **L.** *Clear* **M.** *Project window menu* **N.** *Clip information*

Working with bins

You can organize clips in a project using *bins*, which resemble folders on your hard drive. Bins are useful for organizing a project that contains a large number of clips; you can even organize bins within bins. A Project window includes a *Bin area*, which shows the bins that have been added to the project. The Bin area appears on the left side of the Project window, and can be resized or hidden. When the bins in the Bin area contain other bins, the hierarchical structure appears, much like the graphical view of folders and subfolders in your operating system. When you import clips, they are added to the currently selected bin.

Let's begin by creating a bin. Do one of the following:

• Click the menu triangle button at the top right corner of the Project window and choose New Bin.

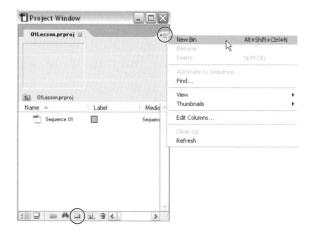

• Click the Bin icon () at the bottom of the Project window.

Bin 01 appears after the Sequence 01 folder.

Importing clips and image files

Now you'll add files to the Project window.

1 Click the triangle next to Bin 01 to open it.

2 To import the movie clips you will need, choose File > Import. Then open the 01Lesson folder you copied or installed from the Classroom in a book DVD-ROM disk. Hold down the Control key and then select the Notmuch.avi, Okay.avi, and Opening.avi movie files (but not the Final folder). Now click Open.

3 The video files are added to the Project window in Bin 01.

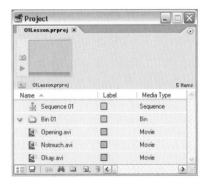

Now, you'll save the project.

4 Choose File > Save.

Viewing and changing poster frames

At the top of a Project window or Bin area is the *thumbnail viewer*, which you can use to preview individual clips. When you select a clip in the Project window, the icon view displays the *poster frame* associated with that clip; that is, the frame used for the icon view of the clip and as a sample frame for titles. By default, the poster frame is the first frame of a clip, but you can change the poster frame to any frame in the clip.

Now, let's view a clip and its information in the Project window:

1 Click the Icon button (⬜) at the bottom of the Project window.

2 Select the Opening.avi clip in Bin 01. The clip's information appears beside the thumbnail viewer in the upper left corner of the Project window.

A. *Thumbnail preview* B. *Poster Frame button*
C. *Play button*

3 View the clip by pressing the Play button (▶·) on the thumbnail viewer. Press the Stop button (■) to stop playback.

4 Click the List View button (⦂≡) to change the view of the clips in Bin 01. Use the Resize button in the lower right corner of the Project window to expand the size of the file area, or scroll along the right side of the window to see all of the columns of information.

Now let's change a clip's poster frame.

5 Select the Opening.avi clip in the Project window if it is not already selected.

6 Press the Play button (▶) until the frame you want to use as the new poster frame is displayed, then press the Stop button (■) to stop the clip at this point. Alternatively, drag the play slider on the thumbnail viewer in the upper left corner of the Project window to the frame you want to use.

7 Click the Poster Frame button (▣) in the thumbnail viewer.

8 Click the Icon view button (▱) at the bottom of the Project window to see thumbnails of the contents.

9 Double-click the Bin 01 icon in the Project window to view the contents of Bin 01, and click on Opening.avi to see the new poster frame you have selected.

10 Create a second bin by clicking the Bin icon (▱) at the bottom of the Project window. Bin 02 appears. To make the Bin area higher or wider, you may need to first make the Project window larger.

11 Do one of the following:

• Drag the Opening.avi clip to the Bin 02 icon.

• Right-click on Opening.avi and choose Cut. Then click the Bin 02 icon and choose Paste.

12 Now, you will delete Bin 02. If you moved a video clip from Bin 01 to Bin 02 that you want to retain, move the clip back to Bin 01 before deleting Bin 02. Then, select Bin 02 and click the Clear button (🗑) at the bottom of the Project window.

Views in the Project window

By default, Premiere uses the List view to display information about the clip files in the Bin area of the Project window. The number of fields available in Premiere Pro includes columns for media start/end, video and audio in and out points, off-line properties, scene, and many more. You can customize the way the list appears, and settings can be unique for each window.

1 Click the menu triangle button in the upper right corner of the Project window and choose Edit Columns.

A list of fields appears. If there is a check mark next to an item, that information is displayed in the Bin area.

2 Select the fields that you want to appear in the Bin area and deselect any fields that you don't want displayed. Click OK.

3 Drag the lower right corner of the Project window to the right to reveal the columns selected.

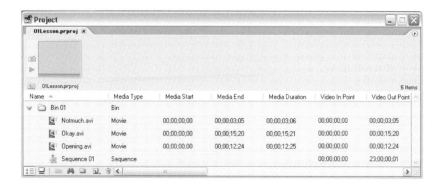

4 Click the Icon button (🖵) at the bottom of the Bin area.

Labels and comments don't appear in Icon view, but you can quickly see them by changing back to the List view.

Note: In Icon view, Premiere displays thumbnails in an orderly grid. You can easily rearrange the thumbnails by dragging them into a new order.

5 Click the List View button at the bottom of the Project window.

In List view, you can change the sort order directly. Now, you'll sort this list by name.

6 Click the Name heading just under the Thumbnail Viewer area to sort it by name.

Adding thumbnails

You can also add thumbnails in the List view by following these steps:

1 Click the menu triangle in the upper right corner of the Project window and choose Thumbnails.

2 Deselect Off if it is selected. (If a check mark appears next to Off, then it is selected. Click on it to deselect it.)

3 To change the size of the thumbnails, click the menu triangle again and choose Thumbnails > Medium or Large as the icon size.

The Icon View with medium thumbnails. Click at the bottom left of the Project window to change the view.

The techniques you've learned for changing the Project window and Bin area options allow you to use these windows to manage source clips. However, you don't use the Bin area and Project window to edit the actual video program. In the following sections, you'll learn about the windows that you use for editing.

> **Using libraries from previous versions of Premiere**
>
> *In previous versions of Premiere, you could create containers called libraries, which were used to store clips from one or several projects. A library was stored as a separate file apart from any project. Although Premiere Pro doesn't support libraries, you can open a library created in a previous version of Premiere. When you open it in Premiere Pro, the library will be converted into the Bin system we've just examined.*
>
> - *To import a library, choose File > Open. Locate and select the library (.PLB) file, and then click Open. The library will be converted to a bin.*
>
> - *If you want to store a set of clips from a library so they are available for other projects in Premiere Pro, save the new bin that contains the clips.*

Saving and autosaving a project

Saving a project saves your editing decisions, references to source files, and the most recent arrangement of the program's windows. Protect your work by saving often. If you prefer, Premiere Pro can save your project automatically at specified intervals. Premiere Pro can either save the project to the same file each time or to a new file. For example, you can set Premiere Pro to save a new archive of your project every 15 minutes.

Saving at fixed intervals produces a series of files that represent the state of your project at each interval. In this way, automatic archiving can serve as an alternate form of the Undo command, depending on how much the project changed between each save. Because project files are quite small compared to source video files, archiving many iterations of a project consumes relatively little disk space. Adobe recommends saving project files to the same drive as your application. Archived files are saved in the Project-Archive folder inside the Adobe Premiere Pro folder. For more information, see "Saving a project manually or automatically" in the *Adobe Premiere Pro User Guide.*

Working with the Monitor window

With Premiere Pro, the *Monitor* window displays a wide array of media, including still images, audio, color mattes, and titles. You can assemble and edit clips in the Monitor window. Depending on how you want to work and the specific tasks you have to accomplish, you can choose from a few different view options for the Monitor window.

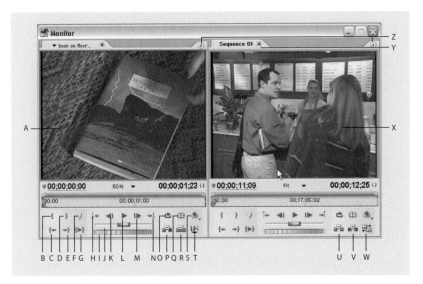

Monitor window in Dual View: **A.** *Source view* **B.** *Set In Point* **C.** *Go to In Point*
D. *Set Out Point* **E.** *Go to Out Point* **F.** *Set Unnumbered Marker* **G.** *Play In to Out*
H. *Go to Previous Marker* **I.** *Jog* **J.** *Shuttle* **K.** *Step Back* **L.** *Play/Stop button* **M.** *Step Forward*
N. *Go to Next Marker* **O.** *Loop* **P.** *Insert* **Q.** *Safe Margins* **R.** *Overlay* **S.** *Output*
T. *Toggle Take Audio and Video* **U.** *Lift* **V.** *Extract* **W.** *Trim* **X.** *Program view*
Y. *Clip/Sequence Tab* **Z.** *Menu buttons*

The default for the Monitor window is the *Dual View* mode, which displays the *Source view* and the *Program view* side-by-side. It can be helpful to think of the Source view as a viewer for the Project window and the Program view as a viewer for the Timeline.

The Dual View mode   Displays both the Source and Program views. This is the default window display when you open a new project.

Source view   Displays the source clip with which you are currently working. When you first open a project session, the Source view is blank because you have not yet worked with any source clips. You use the Source view to prepare a clip for inclusion in the video program or to edit a clip you've opened from the video program.

Program view Displays the current state of the video program you are building. When you first open a project session, the Program view displays the first frame in the Timeline, if at least one clip was placed there in a prior session. When you play the video program in Premiere Pro, it appears in the Program view. You can think of it as an alternate view of the Timeline—the Timeline displays a time-based view of your video program, and the Program view displays a frame-based view of your video program.

In addition to Dual View mode, you can select *Single View* for the Monitor window if you want to see only the Program view. You can change views by clicking the menu triangle in the upper right corner of the Program view and selecting either Dual View or Single View.

The Single View mode Displays only the Program view. Individual clips open in individual Clip windows.

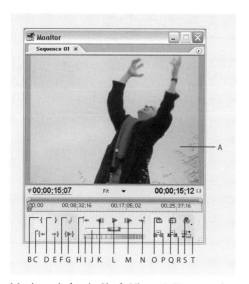

Monitor window in Single View: **A.** *Program view*
B. *Set In Point* **C.** *Go to In Point* **D.** *Set Out Point*
E. *Go to Out Point* **F.** *Set Markers* **G.** *Play In to Out*
H. *Go to Previous Edit Point* **I.** *Jog* **J.** *Shuttle*
K. *Step Frame Back* **L.** *Play button* **M.** *Step Frame Forward*
N. *Go to Next Edit Point* **O.** *Loop* **P.** *Lift button*
Q. *Safe Margins* **R.** *Extract button* **S.** *Output* **T.** *Trim*

1 Click the menu triangle button in the upper right corner of the Monitor window to familiarize yourself with the available settings.

New Reference Monitor
Gang to Reference Monitor

✔ Composite
Alpha
All Scopes
Vectorscope
Waveform
YCbCr Parade
RGB Parade
Vect/Wave/YCbCr Parade
Vect/Wave/RGB Parade

✔ Highest Quality
Fastest Quality
Automatic Quality

Loop
Audio Units
Safe Margins

Dual View
✔ Single View
Trim   Ctrl+T

Playback Settings...

The Source view displays the clip you selected with a double-click in the Project window. Double-clicking a clip in the Project window displays the uncut clip as it appears before any editing. However, if you double-click a clip in the Timeline, you see only those frames that are included in your video program. You'll try that now.

2 In the Project window, double-click the Opening.avi icon. Review the results in the Source view of the Monitor window.

3 In the Project window, select Opening.avi, Okay.avi, Notmuch.avi and drag them to the Program view of the Monitor window. This action inserts these clips onto the Timeline.

4 In the Timeline window, double-click the file Okay.avi.

Now this clip is displayed in the Source view. You'll do this when you want to make changes to a clip that you previously added to the Timeline.

You've viewed two clips in the Source view in this session, and Premiere Pro remembers them in the clip tab in the Source view of the Monitor window.

5 Position the cursor over the clip tab at the top of the Source view and hold down the mouse button. The two clips you've viewed in this session are listed so that you can go back to them while you have this project open.

Because the Program window and the Timeline window offer different views of the same video program, you can edit a video using either window. If you're learning how to edit video, you may find it easier to edit in the more graphical Timeline window. Editors experienced in using high-end video editing systems may be able to edit faster and more precisely using the Source view and Program controllers instead.

Working with the Timeline window

The *Timeline* is a time-based representation of your program. You assemble and edit your video in the Timeline window. When you start a new project, the Timeline is empty.

With Premiere Pro, you can create and nest multiple timelines in a single project. This feature allows you to assemble scenes on different timelines and then nest them on the master timeline. You could also create different versions of your video project by copying the original timeline several times and then applying different visual effects and cuts without affecting the original version. You'll learn about nesting timelines in later lessons. In this lesson, you'll learn how to locate controls for navigating time and for editing.

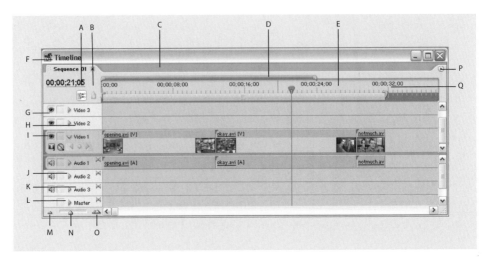

Timeline window: **A.** *Snap* **B.** *Set Unnumbered Marker* **C.** *Time Zoom Level* **D.** *Edit line* **E.** *Work area bar* **F.** *Sequence tab* **G.** *Toggle Track Output* **H.** *Video track* **I.** *Set Display Style* **J.** *Collapse/Expand Track* **K.** *Audio track* **L.** *Master Audio track* **M.** *Zoom Out button* **N.** *Slider* **O.** *Zoom In button* **P.** *Menu triangle button* **Q.** *Time Ruler*

The Timeline window displays time horizontally. Clips earlier in time appear to the left, and clips later in time appear to the right. Time is indicated by the *time ruler* near the top of the Timeline window.

The Time Zoom controls at the lower left of the Timeline allow you to zoom in or zoom out of the time scale. You can change the time scale when you want to view time in more detail or see more of the video program. There are two ways to zoom.

1 Click the title bar of the Timeline window to make it active.

2 Click and hold on the Time Zoom level bar and drag it to the left to zoom in or click the Zoom in button. Zooming in allows you to make very precise edits in the Timeline, but you can't see very much of the video program at once.

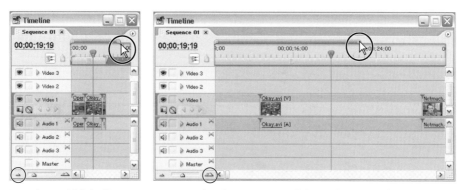

Zooming In (right) allows you to see more detail. Zooming out (left) displays more of the video program. The time ruler reflects the changes in time as you zoom in or out.

3 Click and hold the scroll arrow at the bottom right of the Timeline window to see parts of the video that are later in time. Because you're now using a highly magnified time scale, scrolling through the Timeline takes longer.

4 Click and hold on the Time Zoom level bar at the top of the Timeline and drag to the right to zoom out or click the Zoom Out controls on the bottom left of the Timeline.

5 Click the right end of the Time Zoom level bar and drag to the left to zoom in.

As you zoom in or zoom out of the Timeline, the time ruler reflects your changes.

Note: *Premiere provides keyboard shortcuts for zooming in and out of the edit line. Type an equal sign (=) to zoom in one step per keystroke; type a minus sign (–) to zoom out from the edit line one step per keystroke. Type a backward slash (\) to fit the entire program in the Timeline window.*

Working with tracks

The Timeline window consists of *tracks* where you arrange clips. Tracks are stacked vertically. When a video clip is above another, both clips play back simultaneously.

Tracks are divided into three sections:

• The Video 1 track, located in the center of the window, is the main video editing track.

• All tracks above the Video 1 track become superimposed on a direct frame-by-frame basis over the Video 1 track.

• All tracks below Video 1 are audio tracks. They are combined in playback, and the audio track order is irrelevant.

The Video 1 track includes collapsed or uncollapsed display options. When Video 1 is collapsed, all clips are combined on one track. The Video 2 track is available for superimposing clips over the Video 1 track, and you can add more tracks for additional layers of superimposed video. The highest numbered track is the most "in front." Unless the superimposed tracks numbered 2 and above are made transparent in some way, they completely cover all the tracks that lie below for their run length.

Understanding the Audio track

1 Click the Collapse/Expand triangle (▶) to the left of the Audio 1 track header area.

The Audio 1 track now displays the following settings, Set Display Style (◼), Show Keyframes (◢), and Add/Remove Keyframes (◇).

2 In the Audio 1 track header area, click on the Show Keyframes button (◢).

3 Choose Show Track Keyframes.

A white line appears on the Audio 1 track bisecting the left and right channels.

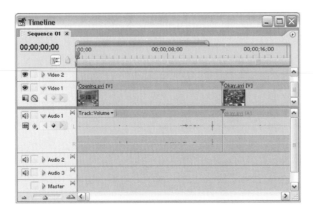

Note: To change the name of a track, double-click the track name and then type a new name in the text box that appears.

4 Click the Collapse/Expand track triangle to the left of the Audio 1 track label to collapse the track.

Changing the height of tracks

With Premiere Pro, you can expand the height of a track in the Timeline window for better viewing and easier editing of your projects. Track heights can be varied independently. As the track enlarges, it displays more information, such as opacity and speed. Now you'll adjust the height of the Video 1 track.

1 To expand the height of a track, click on the Collapse/Expand triangle next to the Video 1 track.

2 When the pointer changes into two parallel lines with two arrows ($\updownarrow$) (known in some programs as the mover tool), click on the top grey border line of a video track and drag upward. The pointer must be positioned in the label area of the track to change the height.

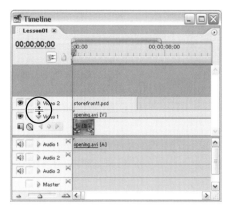 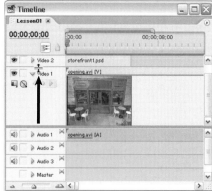

3 To shorten the height of the track, click on the line between Video 1 and Video 2 at the top of the Video 1 track. When the pointer turns into two lines with two arrows, drag downward.

You can adjust the heights of the tracks in the Timeline window in whatever way is most comfortable for you to edit and work on your video projects.

Changing the track format

The *track format* allows you to change the way in which clips in a track are represented in the Timeline window. Tracks in the Timeline can be formatted independently from each other.

1 Click the Collapse/Expand triangle next to the Video 1 track in the Timeline to expand the track if it is collapsed.

2 In the Timeline window, click the Set Display Style icon ( ) to the left of the Video 1 track label.

The track format menu appears listing the four different ways in which movie clips can be displayed in the video tracks.

3 Choose Show Head and Tail.

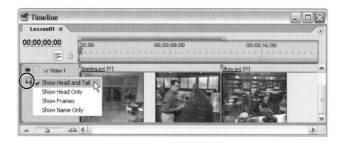

• Choosing Show Head and Tail displays thumbnails at the start and finish of a clip. The Set Display Style icon changes to a ( ) icon.

4 Click the Set Display Style icon again, but this time choose Show Head Only.

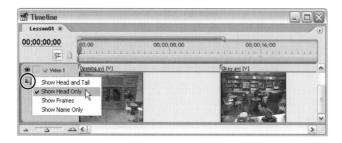

• Choosing Show Head Only displays a thumbnail just at the head of a clip and changes the Set Display Style icon to an ( ) icon.

5 Click the Set Display Style icon again; this time choose Show Frames.

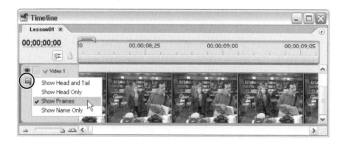

• Choosing Show Frames displays thumbnails for all frames in a clip. The Set Display Style button changes to an (🖿) icon.

6 Click the Set Display Style icon again, but this time choose the last option, Show Name Only.

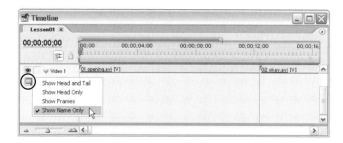

• Choosing Show Name Only displays only the filename without the graphic image. The Set Display Style icon changes to a plain box (🖵).

For the remainder of this lesson, this *Classroom in a Book* will work with the Show Head Only track option. You can choose whatever track format is best for you.

Navigating to a specific frame in the Timeline and Program view

The *edit line* in the Timeline window is a mirror track for the current frame displayed in the Program view of the Monitor window. The current frame in the Program view is indicated by a light blue triangle, or current time indicator (CTI).

The CTI indicates the point in time when the next edit will be applied, when you use a command or a control in the Monitor window.

Top: *The Timecode display below the Program view changes to represent the current frame indicated by the current time indicator (CTI).*
Bottom: *The edit line in the Timeline window.*

The current timecode field can be used to quickly move the edit line to a precise moment in time. For instance, in the Program view, click in the timecode display and type **1421**, then press Enter. The edit line in the Timeline window reflects this change.

Go to the Timeline window and use the time zoom controls to see the current frame at the edit line.

The jog and shuttle controls, located beneath the Play button in the Monitor views, are both tools that allow you to scroll through and to identify precise frames or timecodes in the video project.

Video editors use the *jog* control to move a video tape forward or back a very short distance (one frame at a time) in order to find just the right frame to edit.

With the *shuttle* control, video tape moves forward or reverse more rapidly. Video editors use the shuttle when scanning for edit points.

Using labels

Premiere uses colored labels as a way to identify media in the Project and Timeline windows. With Premiere Pro, you can accept the default label color assigned to a particular media type or change the label color.

To assign a different label color to a clip:

1 In the Project window, select the Opening.avi clip.

2 Choose Edit > Label and select violet.

The label color for the Opening.avi clip changes to violet. We changed it back to cyan, which is the default label color for the remainder of this lesson.

3 Choose Edit > Label and select cyan.

To edit the color of a label:

4 Choose Edit > Preferences > Label Colors.

5 Click on the color to edit and select a color.

Using palettes

Adobe Premiere Pro provides several palettes to display information and to help you modify clips. By default, most of the palettes are open. You can open, close, or group palettes to best suit the way you like to work. If your operating system supports a multiple-monitor desktop and you have more than one monitor connected to your system, you can drag palettes to any monitor. Note that the palettes in Premiere Pro work the same way as the palettes in Adobe Photoshop, Illustrator, and PageMaker®.

You can change the arrangement and display of palettes and palette groups to make the best use of space on your monitor. For more information, see "Using window and palette menus" in the *Adobe Premiere Pro User Guide.*

Using the Tools palette

Premiere Pro contains a comprehensive list of tools for editing your project. Display the Tools palette by choosing Window > Tools. The Tools palette is displayed by default when you open a new project.

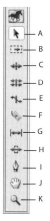

A. Selection tool
B. Track Select tool
C. Ripple Edit tool
D. Rolling Edit tool
E. Rate Stretch tool
F. Razor tool
G. Slip tool
H. Slide tool
I. Pen tool
J. Hand tool
K. Zoom tool

You'll learn more about the Tools palette as you begin editing your project in the next lessons.

Using the Effect Controls palette

1 Display the Effect Controls palette by choosing Window > Effect Controls.

2 Click the Effect Controls menu triangle button, located near the upper right corner of the palette. Note that the menu button for a specific palette identifies only the functions for that palette.

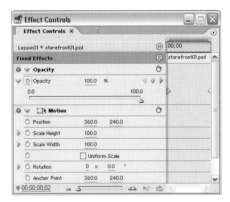

For enhanced editing, you can *dock* the Effect Controls palette with the Source view in the Monitor window. Docking provides easy access to the controls in the Effect Controls palette and places them next to the Program view in the Monitor window.

3 To reposition the Effect Controls palette, click the tab in the Effects palette and drag it to the gray area above the movie clip tab in the Source view of the Monitor window. As you drag, the pointer changes into a little fist. When the fist changes back to a pointer, release the mouse.

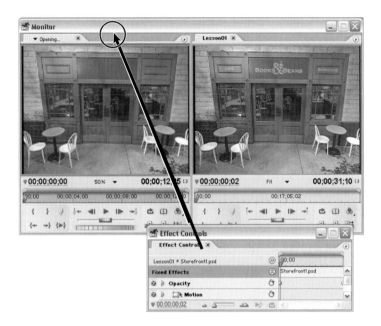

The Effect Controls palette now appears in front of the movie clip in the Source view.

Note: To undock, click on the Effect Controls palette and drag it outside of the Source view.

Using the Info palette

The Info palette displays information about a selected clip. The information displayed in the Info palette may vary depending on the media type and the current window. The Info palette can be helpful in identifying the many kinds of content you can include in your project and the attributes of that content.

1 Make sure the Info palette is visible. To see it, choose Window > Info or press the Tab key once. (The Tab key shows/hides only three palettes: Info, History, and Tools.) You may need to click the Info tab in the window if the History palette is active.

2 Click the video clip Opening.avi in the Timeline. The Info palette now displays the clip's name, type, duration, and audio attributes; its location in the Timeline; and the position of the cursor.

3 In the Timeline window, drag the video clip Opening.avi to the right. After you drag it, the Info palette updates the clip's new position.

4 Choose Edit > Undo Move to return the video clip to its original position.

💡 *If you dragged the clip multiple times, just choose the Undo command multiple times until it returns to its original position. Alternatively, you can use the History palette to return to the state you choose.*

Using the History palette

Use the History palette to jump to any state of the project created during the *current working session.* Each time you apply a change to some part of the project, the new state of that project is added to the History palette.

For example, if you add a clip to the Timeline window, apply an effect to it, copy it, and paste it in another track, each of those states is listed separately in the History palette. You can select any of these states, and the project will revert to how it looked when the change was applied. You can then modify the project from that state forward.

1 Choose Window > History to display the History palette if it is not already open.

2 Click the name of the desired action or change in the History palette to display a state of the current project.

3 Drag the slider or the scroll bar in the palette to move up or down in the History palette.

Use any of the following commands from the History palette menu by clicking the menu triangle button at the top right of the History palette:

Step Forward This command allows you to move forward through the project states listed in the History palette.

Step Backward This command allows you to move backward through the project states listed in the History palette.

Delete Use this to delete *only one* project state in the History palette menu.

Clear History This command clears *all* states in the History palette menu.

Premiere Help Use this to access Adobe Premiere Pro Help.

Customizing keyboard shortcuts

The Keyboard Shortcuts editor in Premiere Pro enables video professionals to customize keyboard shortcuts to suit their individual editing preferences. Some professionals work faster using the keyboard rather than the mouse. In this section, you'll learn how to find and edit the keyboard shortcuts you need.

1 To use the keyboard shortcuts, go to Edit > Keyboard Customization. The Keyboard Customization dialog box appears.

2 Using the second pull-down menu, you can choose shortcuts for applications, tools, or windows. Choose Tools.

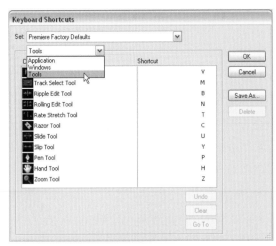

A list of keyboard shortcuts for tools appears in the right column.
For example, the keyboard shortcut for the Zoom tool is Z.

Click OK.

Now, you'll practice editing a keyboard shortcut. In this example, you'll edit the Sequence window shortcut, but you can edit any of the shortcuts in this same manner.

3 Go to Edit > Keyboard Customization, and click on the triangle next to File.

4 Click on the triangle next to New.

5 Click on Sequence. Click in the Shortcut column and type **Shift + S**.

6 Click OK.

7 Try using your new shortcut, by typing **Shift + S**. The New Sequence window appears.

Note: *To delete a shortcut, go to Edit > Keyboard Customization. Click on the shortcut and then press Clear.*

8 To save your keyboard shortcut preferences, go to Edit > Keyboard Customization and click Save As.

9 In the Name Key Set dialog box, type **My shortcuts** or whatever name you want.

10 Click Save and then click OK.

Note: To use your file of customized keyboard shortcuts in other projects, go to Edit > Keyboard Customization. In the Set area, select My shortcuts.

Note: A complete listing of keyboard shortcuts appears on the Quick Reference Card, included in the Adobe Premiere Pro software package.

Review questions

1 What can you do with the Source view in the Monitor window?

2 What can you do with the Program view in the Monitor window?

3 What does a Project window Bin area show?

4 How can more than one video track be made visible?

5 What are two ways to see finer increments of time in the Timeline window?

6 How can you customize a keyboard shortcut for a command?

Answers

1 You can view a clip from a Project window or Bin area, prepare a clip for inclusion in the Timeline, or edit a clip you opened from the Timeline.

2 It is used primarily for playing and reviewing an edited project in the Timeline. You can also edit the Timeline.

3 You can organize clips in a project using Bins. When you import clips, they are added to the currently selected Bin area. A Project window includes a Bin view, which shows the Bins that have been added to the project.

4 A superimposed track, a track that is numbered two or higher, can be made transparent. Thus, whenever it is transparent, the Video1 track will be visible.

5 Along the top of the Timeline window, you can use the Time Zoom level menu or press the equal sign key (=). Also, you can click the Zoom-in button or drag the magnification slider at the bottom of the Timeline window.

6 Add a command to the Commands palette and then assign a keyboard shortcut to that command.

Lesson 2

2 | Sequencing and Basic Real-Time Editing

Editing a video program is at the heart of the work you do with Adobe Premiere. Adobe Premiere Pro makes it easy to arrange clips into sequences, trim video and audio clips, titles, graphics, images, or other source files. You can then assemble the polished result for output to and playback on a variety of media.

In this lesson, you'll learn about different ways to use Adobe Premiere Pro to develop your video. You'll use these basic editing techniques:

- Preparing Sequences for the Timeline.

- Real-Time editing and preview.

- Refining the rough cut.

- Trimming clips in the Timeline.

- Pretrimming, overwriting, and inserting clips.

- Previewing the video program with Real-Time Preview.

- Fine-tuning in the Timeline using In and Out points, razor cut, ripple edit, and rolling edit.

- Exporting the Timeline as a movie.

Getting started

For this lesson, you'll create a new project and then import additional clips. Make sure you know the location of the files used in this lesson. Insert the Adobe Premiere Pro *Classroom in a Book* DVD-ROM disk if necessary. For help, see "Copying the Classroom in a Book files" on page 4 of this book.

1 Launch the Premiere Pro software.

When you start Premiere, the Welcome to Adobe Premiere Pro window appears.

2 Click New Project.

3 Click on Browse and locate the directory called C:\PrPro_CIB\Lessons\02Lesson and click OK.

4 In the Name field, type **02Lesson** and click OK.

5 Before importing files, you should close the palettes that you don't need right now. Click the close box in the upper right corner of the Effects palette, the Info palette, and the History palette.

6 Create a new bin by either clicking the Bin icon (▬) at the bottom of the project window or clicking the menu triangle button at the top right corner of the Project window and choosing New Bin.

7 In the Project window, click on the Bin 01 folder icon.

8 Choose File > Import.

9 Navigate to the 02Lesson folder and click OK.

10 Select Opening.avi, Okay.avi, and Notmuch.avi while holding down the Control key.

11 Click Open.

Viewing the finished movie

To see what you'll be creating, you can take a look at the finished movie.

1 Create a new bin.

2 Type **Resources** to name the new bin.

3 Choose File > Import and select the 02Final.wmv file in the Finished folder, inside the 02Lesson folder. Click Open.

The 02Final.wmv file is now located in the Resources bin.

4 Double-click the 02Final.wmv file so that it opens in the Source view of the Monitor window.

5 Click the Play button (▶) in the Source view of the Monitor window to watch the video program.

6 You can either delete the Resources bin and the 02Final.wmv movie by clicking the Clear button (🗑) at the bottom of the Project window, or you may decide to keep it as a reference.

The Real-Time editing experience

Editing a video program requires a lot of previewing. You need to know how the video program looks in its current state so that you can determine any necessary changes. Or you might make a change, preview it, and then decide to undo the change because the video program looks better without it. Adobe Premiere Pro plays back full-resolution frames, including titles, transitions, effects, color corrections, and motion paths in the Program monitor or on an external video monitor without waiting for sequences to render. Rendering calculates all the frames needed to be played, stores them, and then streams them from RAM for smooth playback.

Throughout the lessons in this book, you'll preview your projects using Real-Time Preview. Keep in mind that you are working in full-frame digital video format, which is 720:480. For more information see, "Previewing a sequence" in the *Adobe Premiere Pro User Guide.*

Various conditions existing in your system may affect the picture quality of your playback. In Lesson 1, you explored the quality and magnification settings located inside the Program view menu triangle button.

Experiment with the quality and magnification settings to adjust the smoothness of playback on your system.

Real-Time Preview

Real-Time Preview is a boon to computer-based video, because, until now, most programs and computers were unable to take advantage of it. Real-Time plays previews instantly in fully rendered final quality without requiring additional hardware. With render-free editing, you can review editing decisions as you make them and experiment more freely.

Note: Real-Time Preview is designed for Pentium 4 systems, 3GHz and faster. Playback frame rates and quality may degrade on less powerful systems.

Methods of working in Premiere Pro

Premiere provides several ways to perform tasks so that you can work the way you prefer. Just as there are different ways to import a clip, there are many ways to edit a video in Premiere Pro.

Adding clips to the Timeline

A clip in your project is not actually part of your video program until you add the clip to the Timeline window. Earlier in the Tour of this *Classroom in a Book*, you added clips to the Timeline window by positioning the hand tool on clip icons and dragging them directly from the Bin area of the Project window to the Timeline window. In this lesson, you will use other methods to add clips to the Timeline window:

• Developing a sequence of clips and using the Automate to Sequence command to add them to the Timeline.

• Selecting your clips in a bin in the Project window in a specified order and using the Automate to Sequence command to add them to the Timeline.

• Pretrimming clips and then using the Source view of the Monitor window to add them to the Timeline window.

Developing a sequence and using Automate to Sequence

Before assembling a rough-cut of a video program, editors often create a *sequence*. A sequence is a visual outline of the project—a collection of sketches or still shots, which, in combination with descriptions, indicates the flow of the story.

In Adobe Premiere Pro, you can easily and quickly organize a set of clips into a *sequence*, which is similar to using a storyboard. When you are satisfied with a sequence, you can move the entire sequence into the Timeline window, using the Automate to Sequence command to create a rough-cut video.

Note: The poster frames, which are the thumbnail images that represent clips in the Timeline window, are the same images used to represent those clips in the Icon view of the Project window. In the middle of your projects, it can be very useful to choose poster frames for new clips that clearly differentiate them in a sequence and distinguish similar clips from each other. See "Viewing and changing poster frames" on page 86 of this book.

Now, let's create a new sequence.

1 Choose File > New > Sequence.

Note: The New Sequence dialog box appears with Sequence 02 as the Sequence name. (This is because whenever you open a new project in Premiere, Sequence 01 automatically appears in the Project window by default.)

2 Rename the new sequence from Sequence 02 to **Sequence Ex** to signify the Ex-girlfriend's scene and click OK.

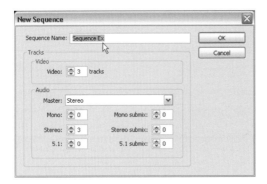

Sequence Ex is now the foremost sequence on the Timeline.

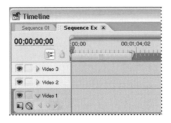

ADOBE PREMIERE PRO | **121**
Classroom in a Book

3 From Bin 01 of the Project window, select the Opening.avi clip and drag it to the beginning of the Video 1 track in the Timeline.

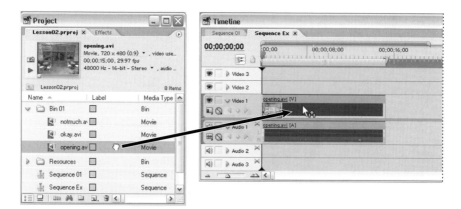

4 Make sure Snap is selected in the Timeline beneath the timecode area.

5 From Bin 01 of the Project window, select the Okay.avi clip and drag it to the Video 1 track so that its beginning point snaps to the end point of Opening.avi. A vertical black line and a pair of triangles appear at the snap point indicating that the clips are butted up against each other.

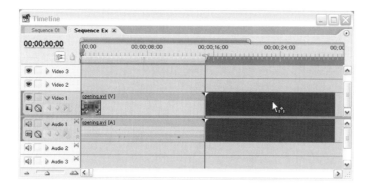

This type of edit is called an insert edit, because the entire contents of the clip are placed on the Timeline without changing the contents of any of the clips.

Note: *Dragging a clip to the left in the Sequence makes it occur earlier in time; dragging it to the right makes it occur later.*

Note: *The filename extension for a project is ".prproj".*

There are several methods to remove the contents of Sequence Ex. First, you'll experiment with a method that uses the History palette.

6 Choose Window > History. The History palette appears.

7 Click on Create Sequence Ex.

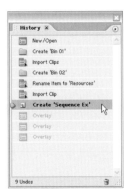

The steps for adding clips to the sequence are undone with just one click of the mouse. You can also use the following methods to remove the contents of Sequence Ex:

• Click on the Timeline to activate it and choose Edit > Select All to select all of the clips on the Timeline. Then choose Edit > Clear.

• Choose Edit > Undo three times until you've retraced your steps.

Using the Automate to Sequence command

Another way to add clips to the Timeline window is to select them in the Bin area of the Project window in a specified sequence and then use the Automate to Sequence command to move them all at once to the Timeline.

1 Double-click on the Bin 01 icon in the Project window to view the contents of Bin 01.

2 Press and hold down the Control key as you click the icon for the following clips in this order: Opening.avi, Okay.avi, and Notmuch.avi. All three clips are now highlighted (selected) in the bin.

Now, you'll use the Automate to Sequence command to add the clips to the Timeline.

3 Choose Project > Automate to Sequence.

4 Make the following changes in the Automate to Sequence dialog box: In the Ordering field, choose Selection Order; in the Placement field, choose Sequentially. In the Method field, choose Insert Edit; for Clip Overlap, type **15** Frames if it is not already set to that number. Deselect both Apply Default Audio Transition and Apply Default Video Transition. Make sure that there are no Ignore Options selected and then click OK.

Now, look at Sequence Ex in the Timeline window. You will see that the three clips you just added are at the beginning of the Sequence.

5 Choose File > Save to save the project file.

Multiple sequencing

Multiple nestable timeline sequences give you flexibility when creating video projects. For example, different videographers could be assigned to work on different sections of a project to save time. Each separate timeline sequence could be imported, reviewed, and nested into the main Timeline.

The Timeline window contains a separate named tab for each timeline sequence, so you can locate any sequence easily. The Program view of the Monitor window also contains a named tab for each sequence. Clicking on the Sequence tab brings it to the front of the Timeline and Program Monitor windows.

You will work with nested sequences in Lesson 10, "Advanced Editing Two: Nested and Multiple Sequences," of this *Classroom in a Book*, in which the movie will contain several complex compositions for you to edit.

Viewing the rough cut

You've assembled a rough cut out of the first part of Sequence Ex. You can preview your work using a couple of methods, in addition to Real-Time Preview.

Scrubbing in the Timeline ruler

For quick previewing, you can drag the *edit line* in the Timeline window. This method is called *scrubbing* because of the back-and-forth motion you use. This method plays your video program at the rate at which you move your hand, so it's best for a quick check of your changes, rather than as a way to accurately view your video. Another way to preview clips is to press the Enter key in the Timeline window and then view the video in the Program view.

1 With the Timeline window active, position the pointer in the Timeline ruler at the point where you want to start previewing. Notice that the edit line jumps to the pointer location as soon as you click in the Timeline ruler. Now, drag the edit line to scrub. The clips appear in the Program view of the Monitor window as you scrub through them.

2 Continue scrubbing across the clips in the Timeline window until the timecode reads 00;00;23;05 in the Program view of the Monitor window.

💡 *Some steps in these lessons will direct you to make edits at an exact timecode. For convenience, first locate the general area of the Timeline described in the step, then fine-tune the edit point by using the controllers under the Program view of the Monitor window to go to the specific timecode. Using the specified timecode enables you to check your results against the figures illustrated in the procedure.*

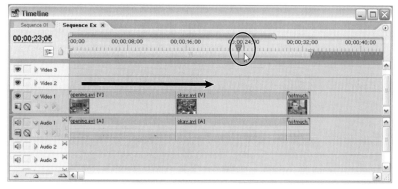

Using the Play button

Some of the controls below the Program view are similar to those for the Source view. You use the Source view to work with individual clips; you use the Program view to work with the complete assembly of clips in the Timeline window. Consequently, clicking the Program view Play button plays the clips in the Timeline window.

1 To start the preview from the beginning of the project, drag the edit line from 00;00;23;05 to the left so that it is positioned at the beginning of the Timeline. (Or, click at the left edge of the timeline ruler to quickly move the edit line to the beginning.)

*Note: Pressing the Home key on your keyboard returns the edit line to the beginning of the Timeline. You can also use the Auto Selection button (▼) in the Program view of the Monitor window to select the timecode and then type **0**.*

2 Below the Program view, click the Play button (▶). The current flow of your video plays in the Program view of the Monitor window.

Refining the rough cut

After you have clips assembled in the Timeline, you can trim them using two different methods:

- Trimming clips in the Timeline window.
- Trimming clips in the Source view of the Monitor window.

In this lesson, you will work with these two methods of trimming clips.

Trimming clips in the Timeline window

Now that you have some clips assembled in the Timeline window, you'll trim the end of Opening.avi to remove extra footage.

1 Scrub in the Timeline ruler to move the edit line through the first part of the Opening.avi clip to where Hero begins to step through the doorway. Position the edit line so that the Program view shows him mid-stride on his third footstep (at approximately 00;00;06;05).

For more precision, you can advance or go back one frame at a time using the Step Forward (▶) and Step Back (◀) buttons under the Program view. Each time you click one of these buttons, the clip backs up or advances one frame. The current frame is indicated by the CTI.

Program view in the Monitor window
A. *Current time indicator (CTI)*
B. *Go to Previous Edit Point*
C. *Step Frame Back button (left arrow)*
D. *Step Frame Forward button (right arrow)*
E. *Go to Next Edit Point*

The edit line marks the last frame of the Opening.avi clip that you want to use in your project. Now you'll trim to this point.

2 Make sure the Timeline window is selected. Choose Sequence > Razor at Current Time Indicator. The Opening.avi clip is cut into two parts at the edit line.

3 Select the tail (the second clip named Opening.avi).

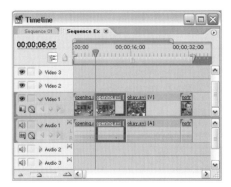

4 Choose Edit > Ripple Delete.

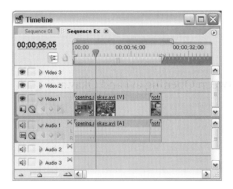

You've just trimmed Opening.avi to the edit line.

Trimming in the Source view of the Monitor window

Simple trimming is easy in the Timeline window. More complex editing, such as precise frame-by-frame adjustments, is easier in the Source view of the Monitor window. The Source view also provides additional tools. First, you'll add some clips to Bin 01.

1 Select Bin 01 in the Project window to make it active and choose File > Import.

2 Go to the 02Lesson folder and press and hold down the Control key as you select Mtntop.avi and Pieplease.avi. Click Open.

Before you trim Pieplease.avi, you'll insert it into the Timeline window.

3 In the Timeline, click the Sequence Ex tab to make it active.

4 Press the Home key to return the edit line to zero.

5 Make sure the Timeline window is selected. Press the Page Down key to move the edit line to the beginning of the next edit, which is the head of Okay.avi.

6 In the Project window, select Pieplease.avi.

7 Choose Clip > Insert.

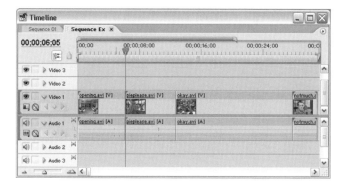

The Pieplease.avi clip is now inserted between Opening.avi and Okay.avi.

8 Double-click Pieplease.avi in the Timeline window, so that it appears in the Source view of the Monitor window.

9 Drag the *shuttle slider* below the Source view or use the Step Forward (▶) and Step Back (◀) buttons to display the frames of Pieplease.avi where Hero starts to stand up, but continues stooping to retrieve his book (at 00;00;06;17).

Source view of Monitor window:
A. Set In Point button B. Set Out Point button
C. Go to Previous Marker button
D. Shuttle slider E. Go to Next Marker button

10 In the Source view, set the Out point by clicking the Set Out Point button (▸).

The Out point icon appears in the current location of the shuttle slider.

You can double-click in the Source view in the location timecode or click the Auto Selection button to the left of the timecode and simply type **617**.

Edits are automatically applied to the clip in the Timeline window.

 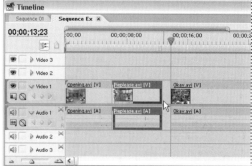

In the Program view of the Monitor window, you can advance or go back to an edit point using the Go to Previous Edit Point (⊢) and Go to Next Edit Point (⊣) buttons. Each time you click one of these buttons, the edit line backs up or advances to the nearest edit point. This is useful as you create more edits in a clip. It's a quicker way to move back and forth between edit points.

11 Click the Go to Previous Edit Point (⊢). The edit line moves backward to the new Out point of Pieplease.avi. You have trimmed one second (00;00;01;00) from it.

12 Click the Go to Next Edit Point (⊣). The edit line moves forward to the In point of Okay.avi.

Trimming Pieplease.avi, however, has left a gap in the Video 1 track. You'll now use the track select tool (⊡), which enables you to select all clips to the right of any clip in a track. Then you'll use the selection tool to move the clips and close the gap between Pieplease.avi and Okay.avi.

13 In the Tools palette, select the track select tool (⊡).

14 Position the pointer anywhere on the Okay.avi clip so that it turns into the track select pointer and click once. Choose the selection tool (▶) and click on Okay.avi. Drag left until the Okay.avi clip snaps to Pieplease.avi.

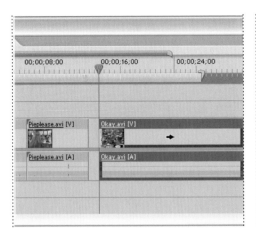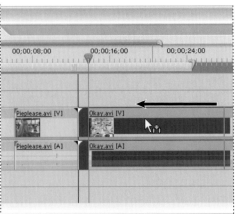

When you release the mouse, all subsequent clips move to the left.

All four clips in the Timeline should now be edge-to-edge, without any gap or space between them.

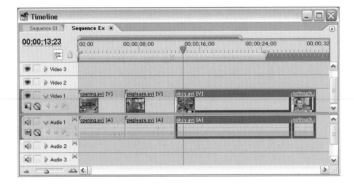

15 Click anywhere in the Timeline window to deselect the clips you just moved.

16 Choose File > Save to save the project.

💡 *It's a good idea to get in the habit of deselecting clips when you are finished with a task so that the next task doesn't affect the previously selected clips.*

Pretrimming clips using the Source view

In the Tour, you added clips to a project by dragging them individually from the Project window into the Timeline. Earlier in this lesson, you added clips to the Timeline from a sequence and from a bin in the Project window using the Automate to Sequence command. In one case, you trimmed a clip after it was added to the Timeline.

Alternatively, you can pretrim clips in the Source view of the Monitor window before you add them to the Timeline. (Remember that clips are actually in a video program and will play back only if they are in the Timeline.)

Dragging clips to the Source view

You'll move a clip into the Source view.

In the Project window, select Mtntop.avi and drag it to the Source view.

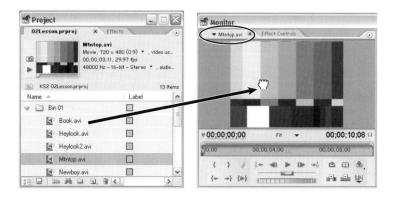

The Mtntop.avi clip is displayed in the Source view of the Project window, and the Mtntop.avi tab is the foremost tab above the clip image area.

Pretrimming and inserting clips

Before you start trimming the clip in the Source view, look at the controls you'll use to add them to the program after they have been trimmed. When working in the Source view, you can add clips in two ways: inserting and overlaying. The Insert button (⊞) and the Overlay button (⊞) are at the bottom right of the Source view panel in the Monitor window.

The Insert button inserts the clip at the specified edit line by splitting any existing material into two parts; none of the existing material is replaced; it is merely displaced. In contrast, the Overlay button places a clip at the edit line by replacing any existing material for the duration of the clip you are placing.

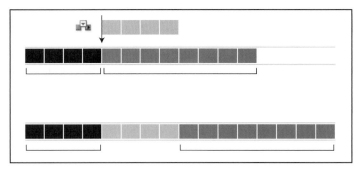

Inserting a clip makes a break in existing material and moves or displaces the existing material.

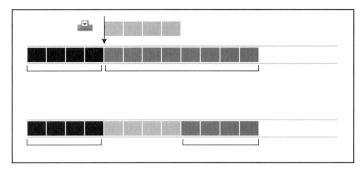

Overlaying a clip replaces a portion of the existing material with an equal amount of new video.

Now that you understand the concepts of inserting and overlaying clips, you'll trim the Mtntop.avi clip that you dragged into the Source view and add it to the video program. Take a look at the clip you're about to trim.

💡 *To move and view one frame at a time in either the Source view or the Program view, use the left and right arrow keys under the image in the appropriate view.*

1 Play the Mtntop.avi clip by clicking the Play button (▶) below the Source view.

You'll be inserting Mtntop.avi near the end of the sequence, but first you'll trim it to remove the color bars at the beginning and extra footage at the end of the clip. Since you don't want the color bars to appear in your video program, you need to trim them.

2 Drag the shuttle slider below the Source view to locate the point in the first part of Mtntop.avi where the color bars end. Locate and display the last frame of the color bars (at 00;00;05;00) using the Step Forward (▮▶) and Step Back (◀▮) buttons, or the left and right arrow keys on your keyboard.

3 Click the Set In Point button (↕) below the Source view to mark this frame as the In point.

Now you'll locate the Out point to remove some extra footage from the end of Mtntop.avi.

4 Click the Play button and view the movie to the point where Hero raises his arms to the gods in the close up view of the scene. He repeats this gesture.

5 Use the Step Forward and Step Back buttons to locate the frame where the Hero's right hand virtually touches the top of the frame for the first time (at 00;00;08;10).

6 Click the Set Out Point button (↕) in the Source view.

Now that you've set the new In and Out points for the Mtntop.avi clip, you'll insert it into your program. This is a common editing decision—one you might make after deciding the program would work better with additional material. His Ex asks Hero what he's been up to lately. The Mtntop.avi clip cuts away from the scene to show his inner thoughts before cutting back to his matter-of-fact answer.

7 In the Program view of the Monitor window, drag the shuttle slider to the right to display the first frame of the Notmuch.avi clip. Or, you can click the Go to Next Edit Point button (⇥) next to the step right button.

By doing this, you have positioned the edit line at the beginning of the Notmuch.avi clip.

8 Before you insert the pretrimmed Mtntop.avi clip, you'll edit Notmuch.avi. Position the edit line just before Hero says, "Not much" (at approximately 00;00;28;19).

9 Go to the Timeline to activate it and choose Sequence > Razor at Current Time Indicator.

10 In the Source view of the Monitor window, click the Insert button (🖥) to place the pretrimmed clip of Mtntop.avi into the Video 1 track in the Timeline window at the specified edit line position between the two parts of Notmuch.avi.

The pretrimmed Mtntop.avi clip is inserted into the program between the two parts of Notmuch.avi in Sequence Ex. You used the Insert button because you didn't want to replace any existing material. Clicking the Overlay button would have replaced some of the second part of the Notmuch.avi clip.

11 Preview the sequence by dragging the edit line to the beginning of the Timeline and clicking the Play button (▶) below the Program view in the Monitor window. Click the Stop button (■) when you are finished previewing.

12 Save the project.

Pretrimming and overlaying clips

The sequence is almost complete. Use the overlay button to perform two cuts with one action. Overlaying replaces footage rather than extending the length of the program.

1 In the Timeline, play Sequence Ex to the frame just after the sound of the book hitting the floor in Pieplease.avi.

2 Scrub in the Timeline to the end of the sound of the book hitting the floor (at 00;00;10;15).

3 Click on the Audio 1 track Collapse/Expand triangle button to reveal the track header area.

4 Click on the Show Keyframes button (◐) and choose Show Clip Volume.

5 Use the Time Zoom controls to zoom in to the maximum amount.

6 In the Program view, use the Step Forward button or the jog control to advance forward until the timecode reads 00;00;11;00. This is the point where Ex looks down at the book on the floor.

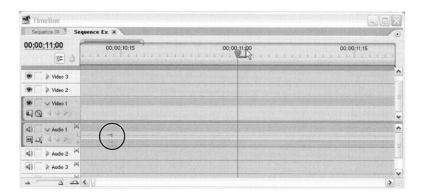

7 In the Timeline window, zoom out so that you can see the entire Pieplease.avi clip.

8 Choose File > Import. Navigate to the 02Lesson folder and click Okay.

9 Select Book.avi and click Open.

10 Make sure Book.avi is selected in the Project window and choose Clip > Overlay. Book.avi replaces all of the frames to the end of Pieplease.avi.

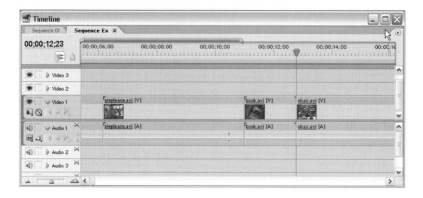

The total running time of the program remains the same, because Book.avi overlaid the first frame of Okay.avi. By using overlay, you've performed two trims with one action.

11 Save the project.

Fine-tuning in the Timeline

You will often need to adjust In and Out points after you've placed a number of clips in the Timeline window. Adjusting any clip that's part of a sequence will affect the entire video program. Special tools in the Timeline window let you specify how your adjustments will affect the other clips.

Performing a ripple edit

In this section, you'll perform what's called a *ripple edit*. A ripple edit adjusts the In or Out point of one clip and shifts other clips in or out accordingly. This method changes the total length of your video program, but preserves the duration of the other clips.

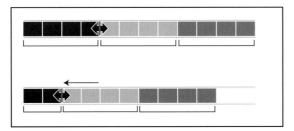

In a ripple edit, all subsequent clips move in response to the change.

To trim the project, you'll shorten Heylook.avi.

Project duration is indicated by the *duration timecode,* the left set of blue numbers accompanied by the autoselect button (▾) under the Program view. If you used the exact timecodes given for edit points in the previous steps, the overall duration of the project at this point in the lesson should be 45:26. Now, you'll trim 77 frames from the head of Heylook.avi.

1   In the Project window, click on Bin 01. Choose File > Import. Locate Heylook.avi in the 01Lesson folder and click Open.

2   Set the edit line to the end of the Timeline.

3   Drag Heylook.avi from the Project window to the edit line in the Timeline.

4 Use the Step Back and Step Forward buttons or the Go to Previous/Next Edit buttons in the Program view to move the edit line to the first frame of Heylook.avi (at 00;00;34;09). The edit line is now at the cut between Notmuch.avi and Heylook.avi.

*A. Go to Previous Edit Point **B.** Step Back button*
*C. Step Forward button **D.** Go to Next Edit Point*

The location timecode (the left set of blue numbers) displayed under the Program view indicates the time at the beginning of Heylook.avi (34:17). You'll determine where to place a new In point for Heylook.avi by adding 77 frames to its current In point by positioning the edit line at the new In point.

The purpose of this exercise is to familiarize yourself with the calculus of 30 frames per second. You could step over 77 frames, one at a time, but it could become time-consuming and less precise.

5 Add 77 frames to 34:09.

An easy way to do this is to convert 77 frames to an equivalent with which you can add to 34:09. Your timebase for this project is 30 fps, so 1 second = 30 frames. Thus, 77 frames converts to 30 fps + 30 fps (2 seconds) + 17 fps, which is written as 00:00:02:17. Now add 2:17 to the current timecode of 34:09. So, 2:17 + 34:09 = 36:26 (36 seconds + 26 frames). This results in a timecode of 36:26 where you'll set the new In point for the early instance of Heylook.avi. (Remember the last two numbers in the timecode represent frames.)

6 In the Program view of the Monitor window, click the location timecode or the autoselect button to highlight it, and then type **3626** and press Enter.

The edit line jumps to 00;00;36;26 in the Timeline.

7 In the Tools palette, select the ripple edit tool (✛).

8 In the Timeline window, move the pointer to the right edge of the cut between Notmuch.avi and Heylook.avi. The pointer changes into the ripple edit pointer. Be sure the ripple edit pointer is over Heylook.avi and not Notmuch.avi. Drag right until the beginning of Heylook.avi snaps to the edit line.

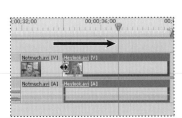

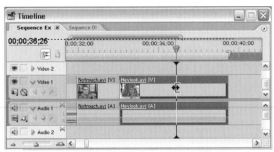

The Heylook.avi clip is trimmed forward in time. With the ripple edit function, there is no gap between Notmuch.avi and Heylook.avi.

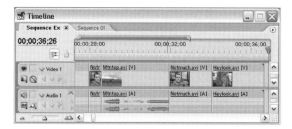

9 Save the project.

In a ripple edit, the total duration of your project changes. The project is now exactly 77 frames shorter in duration.

10 View your changes by clicking the Play button (▶) below the Program view.

Performing a rolling edit

Another editing method that acts on a sequence of clips is called the *rolling edit*. A rolling edit adjusts the In or Out point of one clip and also adjusts the duration of the adjacent clip, keeping the total duration of the two clips the same. As you shorten one clip, the adjacent clip is extended to maintain the total duration of the two clips. Note, however, that you can extend a clip only if the clip was previously trimmed.

Note: *You cannot make a clip longer than its original length as captured or imported—you can only restore frames that were previously trimmed from the clip for the current project.*

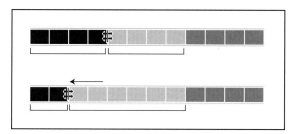

A rolling edit changes two clips at once to preserve the project's duration.

To fine-tune the last two clips, you'll now perform a rolling edit to achieve and then preserve the finished duration of 20 seconds. You don't want to use a ripple edit, as it would change the total length.

1 Click on Bin 01 in the Project window. Choose File > Import. Select Newboy.avi in the 02Lesson folder and click Open.

2 Double-click Newboy.avi so that it appears in the Source view of the Program window.

3 To set the new edit point, you'll look for a visual cue in the clip. Locate the frame where Ex takes New Boy's wrist for the second time and pulls him toward her (at 00;00;02;14 in the Source view).

4 Click the Set In Point button ({).

5 In the Timeline, move the edit line to the end of the program by pressing either the End or Page Down keys.

6 Go to the Source view and click Insert ( ) to insert Newboy.avi at the end of the Timeline.

7 Go to the Out point of Heylook.avi by pressing the Page Up key once or clicking the Go to Previous Edit button once.

8 In the Tools palette, select the rolling edit tool ( ).

9 Position the pointer over the edit point between Heylook.avi and Newboy.avi. The pointer changes into the rolling edit tool. While watching the timecode in the Program view, drag the pointer to the left until it reaches -00;00;00;16. Then release the mouse button.

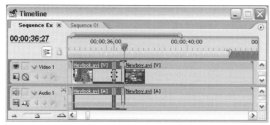

Using Toggle Take Audio and Video with the manual overlay function

Ex is going to introduce a new character into the movie, her New Boy. To set up his appearance in Sequence Ex, you'll use the overlay function interactively on the Timeline.

1 Select Bin 01 in the Project window. Choose File > Import. Navigate to the 02Lesson folder and click OK. Select Heylook2.avi and click Open.

2 In the Project window, double-click Heylook2.avi to display it in the Source view.

You are going to overlay Heylook2.avi onto Heylook.avi, replacing video frames but not audio frames. First, let's take a look at the Toggle Take Audio and Video function.

3 Locate the Toggle Take Audio and Video button (🔳) at the bottom right corner of the Source view. The Toggle Take Audio and Video button toggles three ways:

• Take Video and Audio (🔳).

• Take Video Only (🔳).

• Take Audio Only (🔳).

4 For this exercise, choose Take Video Only.

5 Set the current time indicator (CTI) to the end of Heylook.avi. From the Source view of the Monitor window, drag Heylook2.avi to overlay Heylook.avi, while its Out point snaps to the edit line.

 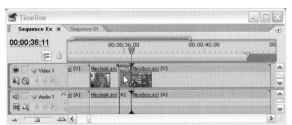

You've now performed a rolling edit on both clips, preserving the total duration.

6 Save the project.

Exporting the Timeline as a movie

To view Sequence Ex as a movie file, you need to export it.

1 Select Sequence Ex in the Timeline window to make it active.

2 Adjust the Timeline view so that you can see the entire sequence. (Type a reverse slash (\) or use the zoom controls.)

3 With the selection tool, double-click the texturedtextured portion at the center of the work area bar so that it conforms to the length of the entire project.

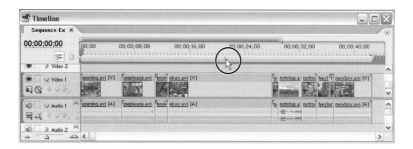

Note: *For more details and exercises about exporting movies from Premiere Pro, see Lesson 13, "Output" in this Classroom in a Book.*

4 Choose File > Export > Movie.

5 In the Export Movie dialog box, click Settings. Make sure Microsoft DV AVI is selected for the File Type and Work Area Bar is selected for the Range. Make sure that the Export Video option and the Export Audio option are selected. Also make sure that Add to Project When Finished and Beep When Finished are selected. The default values for other settings are fine for this project.

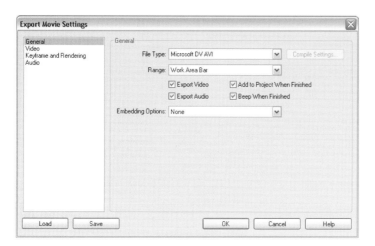

💡 *Use the Save and Load buttons in the Export Movie Settings dialog box to save and later quickly load export settings that you use frequently. Loading saved settings is particularly useful when you create several types of video files (for example, NTSC and Web video) from the same project.*

6 Click OK to close the Export Movie Settings dialog box.

7 In the Export Movie dialog box, type **Sequence Ex.avi** for the name of the video program and click Save.

Premiere Pro starts making the video program, displaying a status bar that provides an estimate for the amount of time it will take.

8 When the video program is complete, it is imported into the Project window.

Grab some popcorn, double-click SequenceEx.avi, and then click the Play button in the Source view to watch what you've just created.

Exploring on your own

Feel free to experiment with the project you have just created. Here are some suggestions:

• Use the buttons at the bottom of the Project window to change the view of clips in the window.

• Use the rolling edit tool to change the edits between clips. You can choose Edit > Undo after each change to undo it.

• Use the shortcuts listed in the Premiere Pro Quick Reference Card and in Premiere Pro Help to position the edit line and the work area bar.

• Open the Timeline window menu by clicking the menu triangle button near the upper right corner of the Timeline window. Experiment with different Timeline attributes.

• Read "Using Monitor window controls" in the *Adobe Premiere Pro User Guide*. Experiment with Monitor window controllers and learn about the various functions, including how to jog or shuttle through frames.

Review questions

1 What are three ways to add clips to the Timeline?

2 What are two ways to create a rough cut?

3 What are three ways to preview clips in the Timeline without rendering?

4 How does the insert function differ from the overlay function?

5 The ripple edit and the rolling edit both affect a sequence of clips in some way. Which one cannot be used with untrimmed clips, and why?

Answers

1 Dragging clips into the Timeline from the Project window, using the Automate to Sequence command, or opening and trimming clips in the Source view and then inserting or overlaying them into the Timeline.

2 Dragging clips into the Timeline from the Project window and using the Automate to Sequence command from the Project window.

3 Scrubbing in the Timeline ruler, pressing the Play button in the Program view of the Monitor window, or pressing the Enter key.

4 Inserting affects the project duration and doesn't trim any material. By contrast, overlaying trims material and preserves the project duration.

5 The rolling edit cannot be used with untrimmed clips because as one clip is shortened, the adjacent clip is extended, which can happen only if the clip has previously been trimmed to shorten it.

Lesson 3

3 | **Transitions**

*Although an instantaneous switch
from one clip to another is the most
common and simple way to combine
video clips, Adobe Premiere Pro also gives
you dozens of options for varying
the change from one clip to another.
Such transitions can provide texture,
nuance, and special effects.*

If you have taken the lessons in order to this point, you have learned to navigate the Adobe Premiere Pro Workspace, develop sequences for the Timeline, insert clips onto the Timeline in a rough cut approach, and then clean up the in and out points for what are called straight cuts. The clips are butted up to one another end-to-end in insert edits. In overlay edits, the front clip's head and tail frames are bracketed by the underlying clip. As the movie plays, it runs through straight from clip to clip.

Thus far, the Hero in the movie has encountered his Ex with her New Boyfriend. In this lesson, you'll add nuance to a later sequence by using *transitions* between clips, special effects, and precisely trimmed clips. The *Classroom in a Book* DVD includes the completed Lesson 3 project in the Lesson 3 folder. You may want to use this completed project as a reference while you work with tools to perform steps in this lesson. Since the subject of the Hero's fantasies and daydreams lends itself well to the use of transitions, you'll use a variety of transitions in interesting ways. Specifically, you'll learn how to do the following:

• Place a transition using the Default transition and the Effects palette.

• Preview transitions.

• Modify transition settings.

• Trim clips to precise timecodes for special transition effects.

• Add a special effect.

Getting started

In this lesson, you'll affect scenes in the movie project by adding transitions in stages. Make sure you know the location of the files used in this lesson. Insert the Adobe Premiere Pro *Classroom in a Book* DVD-ROM disk if necessary. For help, see "Copying the Classroom in a Book files" on page 4.

1 Launch the Premiere Pro software.

2 Click New Project in the Welcome window.

3 Click on Browse and locate the directory called C:\PrPro_CIB\Lessons\03Lesson and click OK.

4 In the Name field, type **03Lesson** and click OK.

5 Create a new bin by either clicking the Bin icon at the bottom of the project window or clicking the menu triangle button at the top right corner of the Project window and choosing New Bin.

6 In the Project window, click on the Bin 01 folder icon.

7 Choose File > Import.

8 Navigate to the 03Lesson folder and click OK.

9 While holding the Control key, select the following files: Approach1.avi, Approach2.avi, Approach3.avi, Approach4.avi, Gaze1.avi, Gaze2.avi, Gaze3.avi, Gaze4.avi, and Sigh.avi.

10 Click Open.

View the finished footage for reference

To see what you'll be creating, you can take a look at the finished movie for this lesson.

1 Create a new bin by either clicking the Bin icon at the bottom of the project window or clicking the menu triangle button at the top right corner of the Project window and choosing New Bin.

2 Rename the new bin by selecting it and double-clicking in the name field to make the field editable. Type **Resources** and press Enter.

3 Click the triangle next to the Resources bin to open it.

4 Make sure the Resources bin is selected. Then choose File > Import and select the 03Final.wmv file in the Finished folder within the 03Lesson folder. Click Open.

The 03Final.mov file is located in the Resources bin.

5 Double-click the 03Final.wmv file, so that it opens in the Source view in the Monitor window.

6 Click the Play button (▶) in the Source view in the Monitor window to watch the video program.

7 You may choose to keep the Resources bin for further reference or you can delete it by selecting the Resources bin and then clicking the Clear button (🗑) at the bottom of the Project window.

About transitions

In the Tour, you were introduced to *transitions* or changes from one scene or clip to the next. The simplest type of transition is the *cut*, in which the last frame of one clip is simply followed by the first frame of the next. The cut is the most often used transition in video and film and is often the most effective. However, you will also use a variety of other types of transitions to achieve effects between scenes.

In Premiere Pro, transitions can be added to a project in a variety of ways. For example, you can select clips in the Bin area of the Project window, or create a sequence in the Sequence window, and then use Automate to Sequence with a default transition. This is useful, for instance, if you want to focus on the general flow of the sequence first, and then adjust or replace some of the transitions as you fine-tune your program. You can also pre-trim clips, add them to the Timeline, and then insert a transition between them. Whichever method you prefer, Premiere makes it easy to replace or modify transitions after adding them to the Timeline.

How clips operate in transitions

Many transitions convey the passage of time, appearing to overlap several frames from the end of one clip with frames from the beginning of the next clip. The frames at the end of the first clip that are used in the transition are called the *tail material*; the frames affected by the transition at the beginning of the next clip are called the *head material*.

The Effects palette

Adobe Premiere Pro includes a wide range of transitions, including 3D motion, dissolves, wipes, and zooms. Transitions are grouped into two main folders in the Effects palette: Audio Transitions and Video Transitions. Within these two main folders, transitions are grouped into subfolders, by type. Each transition is listed with a unique icon to the left of its name.

1 If the Effects palette is not visible, choose Window > Effects. Click the triangle to the left of the Video Transitions folder to see a list of subfolders containing video transitions.

2 Click the triangle to the left of the Dissolve folder to see the types of dissolve transitions available. Notice that the *Cross Dissolve* icon is outlined in red. This indicates that Cross Dissolve is selected as the *default transition*. Then close the triangle to collapse the folder.

You may find it useful to create a separate folder to hold your favorite transitions and effects or filters for easy access.

3 Click the New Custom Bin icon (🖼) at the bottom of the Effects palette or click the menu button at the upper right of the Effects palette and choose New Custom Bin.

Favorites now appears at the bottom of the list. (You may need to scroll down to see it.)

4 Locate your favorite effect or transition and drag its icon to the Favorites folder.

5 Repeat this step whenever you want to add an effect or transition to the Favorites folder.

6 Select the Favorites folder and click the Delete Custom Items icon (🗑) at the bottom of the Effects palette to delete it.

Transition parameters

All transitions have duration, alignment, and direction parameters. Some transitions have additional parameters such as borders, edge adjustments, and softness. The parameters depend on the nature and complexity of the specific transition type.

Duration refers to the number of frames required for the transition. All transitions use frames from the end of the first clip—called *tail material*—and frames from the beginning of the second clip—called *head material*—to create the transition.

Alignment refers to the position of the transition in relation to the cut between the two clips.

Direction indicates how the transition operates on the two clips. Normally, the direction will be from clip A to clip B—from left to right in the Timeline. In most cases, Premiere Pro sets the direction of the transition automatically, and you won't have to worry about it. Later in this lesson, you'll use the Track Selector and other controls to modify the direction of a transition.

About the default transition and default settings

Cross Dissolve is the factory setting for the *default transition* in Premiere Pro because it is so frequently used in video and films. In a Cross Dissolve, one scene "dissolves" into another over a brief duration. You can select another transition as the default at any time. The default transition and the *default effect settings* apply not just to the current project on which you are working but to all your projects.

Working with a default transition is a quick way to insert transitions between clips, until you designate a different transition as the default. You can modify or replace them after you are satisfied with the general flow of the project.

The default effect settings for all transitions specify a duration of 30 frames with the alignment of the transition centered at the cut between the two clips. You can change both the duration and alignment of the transition in the Effect Controls window.

For most transitions, the default direction of the transition is from clip A to clip B (forward in time; left to right in the time sequence). You alter the direction of the transition to move from clip B to clip A by clicking the transition in the Timeline window and making changes to the Track Selector settings in the Effect Controls window. Additional effect parameters, if they pertain to a transition, are also changed in the Effect Controls window for that transition.

Selecting the default transition

Now, you will modify the default effect settings of the Cross Dissolve transition before you add any clips to the 03Lesson.prproj Timeline.

1 In the Effects palette, click the triangle next to the Video Transitions folder, and then click the triangle to open the Dissolve folder and locate the Cross Dissolve transition icon. The icon should be outlined in red to indicate that it is the default transition. Click once on the icon to select the transition.

2 Click the menu triangle button at the upper right corner of the Effects palette, and click Set Default Transition. The Cross Dissolve icon is still outlined in red.

Default Transition settings are modified in the General Preferences dialog box or the Effect Controls window once the transition is placed on the Timeline.

3 To access the Default Transition settings, click the menu triangle button at the upper right corner of the Effects palette and choose Default Transition Duration. The Preferences dialog box appears. Click OK.

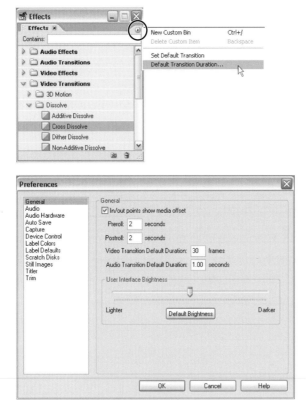

Inserting a transition

You will first use the Automate to Sequence feature to move two clips into the Timeline with the default transition—Cross Dissolve—between them. Later in this lesson, you will use other methods to insert clips and transitions. First you will rename the sequence.

1 In the Project window, rapidly triple-click on the editable field named Sequence 01.

2 Type **Transitions** to rename it.

Using Automate to Sequence and the default transition

1 In the Timeline window, use either of the Time Zoom Level controls to adjust the Timeline so that you can see the action clearly, as it happens.

2 Move the Edit line to the beginning of the Timeline.

*You can also use the plus (+) or minus (-) keys to zoom in or zoom out. If you select the timecode on either the Timeline or Program monitor and type **0** and then press Enter, the edit line moves to the beginning of the sequence.*

3 In the Project window, hold down the Control key as you click on the Gaze1.avi icon and then the Approach1.avi icon in Bin 01 to select both clips. (Make sure to select the clips in this exact order.)

4 Choose Project > Automate to Sequence to bring both clips to the Timeline.

5 In the Automate to Sequence dialog box, change the Ordering setting to Selection Order, and keep Clip Overlap at 15 frames. Verify that Sequentially, Insert Edit, and Apply Default Video Transition are selected. Make sure the Apply Default Audio Transition and the Ignore Options are not selected.

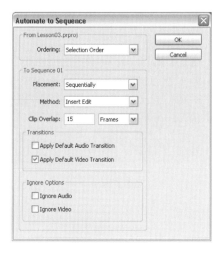

6 Click OK.

The Cross Dissolve transition appears in the Timeline window between Gaze1.avi and Approach1.avi in the Video 1 track.

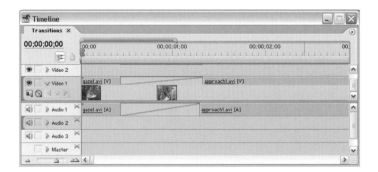

Changing parameters of a transition instance

A transition *instance* refers to an individual occurrence of a transition in the Timeline. The default settings make the transition operate from clip A to clip B. You can change the direction for a specific instance without changing the default. You do this by changing the direction of the transition after it has been inserted into the Timeline. When you click on a transition in the Timeline, the transition's settings appear in the Effect Controls window. You will want to have the Timeline window and the Effect Controls window visible for this lesson.

1 Click the Cross Dissolve transition in the Video 1 track of the Timeline.

2 Go to the Effect Controls window to see the Cross Dissolve settings. (If the Effect Controls window is not open, choose Window > Effect Controls.)

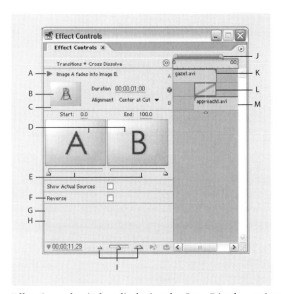

Effect Controls window displaying the Cross Dissolve settings:
A. Preview button B. Transition preview
C. Edge Selector D. Previews E. Start/End sliders
F. Reverse selector G. Border Thickness and Color selector
H. Anti-aliasing I. Time Zoom controls J. Time Zoom slider
K. Clip A (first clip) L. Transition M. Clip B (second clip)

In the Effect Controls window, the selected clip's effects are listed on the left side of the palette. The right side contains a time ruler, edit line, and navigator area similar to those found in the Timeline window. The Video Transition settings area of the Effect Controls window shows the "start" clip and the "end" clip in the middle of the palette display area. By default, "A" and "B" are displayed in these clip thumbnail viewers, but you can display the actual clips instead by clicking the Show Actual Source box below the viewers. (You may need to lengthen the Effect Controls window to view all of its settings.)

Now you'll explore transitions.

3 Click in the Show Actual Sources box to display the starting and ending frames of the clips used in this transition. Gaze1.avi is now displayed as clip A and Approach1.avi is displayed as clip B, because the direction is set for "A-to-B".

Below each clip thumbnail viewer is a *Start/End Slider* that allows you to change the initial and final appearance of the transition. You can adjust the Start sliders separately for different settings, or you can adjust them simultaneously if you want the same setting.

4 Move one of the sliders to 40%. Notice that the other slider maintains its position.

5 Put the Start and End sliders back to the original settings for this transition instance.

Previewing the transition

Two preview options are useful when working with transitions: previewing at the intended frame rate and render-scrubbing in the Timeline.

Previewing the transition at the intended frame rate

To preview transitions (and other effects) at the intended frame rate, you use Real-Time Preview. Premiere Pro then plays this file in the Program view in the Monitor window.

Previewing in Real-Time

Adobe Premiere Pro offers Real-Time previewing of transitions, opacities, titles, and other effects. To preview in Real-Time, without rendering preview files or having jumpy playback from the hard disk, requires a 3 GHz Pentium 4 processing unit. Real-Time Preview is the factory preview mode in Premiere Pro.

To improve playback speed, adjust the magnification and display quality settings found in the Monitor window menu by clicking the upper right triangle button. Viewing with smaller magnification and lower resolution may allow you to view the movie at its intended speed.

Using render-scrub to preview the transition

Render-scrubbing in the Timeline ruler displays the transition effect. Every time you apply a transition, a thin render bar appears above it in the Timeline window, below the work area bar. If the transition has not been previewed, the render bar is red. Once you preview a fully rendered transition, the render bar appears green, as you'll see in the next few steps.

In the Timeline window, notice the render line above the Cross Dissolve transition is red.

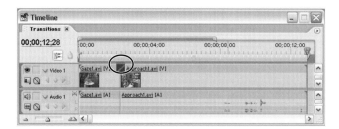

1 Drag the pointer in the Timeline ruler to move the edit line across the transition. The preview plays in the Program view in the Monitor window. You can also preview the transition in the Effect Controls window by dragging it's edit line across the transition.

2 The preview plays in the Monitor window.

Now that the Cross Dissolve transition has been previewed, the render bar below the work area bar in the Timeline window is green.

3 Save the project.

You can also preview a transition in the Timeline window by pressing Enter on the keyboard. This builds, renders, and plays a preview file. As Premiere Pro generates the preview file, the Rendering Preview dialog box displays the status.

When completed, the preview plays in the Program view in the Monitor window. You can replay this preview by positioning the edit line before the transition and pressing Enter.

Pretrimming a clip and adding a transition

Typically, a transition overlaps portions of clips that are not essential to the video program, since these portions are likely to be obscured by the effect of the transition. So, it often makes sense to pretrim your clips to make sure the transition occurs where you want it to. The transition will "borrow" these pretrimmed frames from the tail of clip A and the head of clip B. In the next few steps, you'll pretrim clips, add them to the Timeline, and then insert the transition.

1 Double-click Approach2.avi in Bin 01 of the Project window to view it in the Source view in the Monitor window. Or simply drag the Approach2.avi clip icon to the Source view in the Monitor window.

2 Click the timecode under the Source view (at the left), type **122**, and press Enter to locate a specific frame, where Hero presents flowers to Girl of His Dreams.

Note: For this implementation of the timecode, you'll be in 29.97 Frames per Second Drop Frame (00;00;01;14) format. If necessary, click the Timeline window to make it active. From the title bar, choose Project > Project Settings > General. In the Video Display Format dialog box, the setting is 29.97 fps Drop-Frame Timecode. Click OK.

You can click the triangle button to the left of the timecode to select the entire timecode.

3 Now, click the Set In Point button ( ) under the Source view to set a new In point for the Approach2.avi clip. The Clip Duration shown under the Source view (at the right in black) now indicates that the clip has been trimmed to a total run length of 00;00;05;17. Now the transition will operate with the flowers swinging into view.

4 Use the Page Up or Page Down keys to move the edit line to the end of Approach1.avi clip in the Timeline.

5 In the Project window, select Gaze2.avi and drag it to the edit line.

6 Press the Page Down key to move the edit line to the end of Gaze2.avi.

7 In the Source view, make sure that the trimmed Approach2.avi clip tab is the frontmost clip.

8 Click the Insert button ( ) to insert Approach2.avi at the edit line.

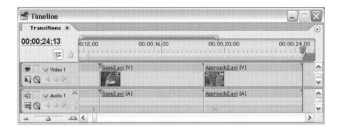

To prepare the next transition, you will borrow frames from Gaze2.avi.

9 Press the Page Up key or click on the Go to Previous Edit button ( ) in the Program view. The edit line should be at 00;00;18;26.

10 Now position the edit line so that it is 15 frames earlier in Gaze2.avi at 00;00;18;11 (18:26 - 00:15 = 18:11).

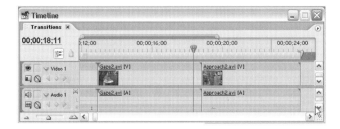

11 In the tools palette, select the ripple edit tool ( ).

12 Place the ripple edit tool on the tail of Gaze2.avi and drag it to the edit line at 00;00;18;11 so that it is 15 frames shorter in duration.

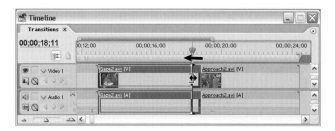

The transition will utilize the 15 frames. To add a transition between Gaze2.avi and Approach2.avi, you will use the Effects palette. But first, check the duration of the default transition.

13 Make sure Cross Dissolve is the default transition in the Effects palette. It should have a red outline. In the upper right corner of the Effects palette, click the menu triangle button and choose Default Transition Duration.

Note: The default transition duration setting applies to all transitions regardless of which one has been selected as the default. This setting remains the same for any transition applied to the Timeline, unless you specify otherwise.

For more information, see "Adding Transitions" in the Adobe Premiere Pro User Guide.

14 In the General Preferences dialog box, make sure the Video Transition Default duration is 15 and click OK.

15 Save the project.

Adding a transition using the Effects palette

1 The position of the edit line in the Timeline is at the end of Gaze2.avi (at 00;00;18;11).

2 In the Effects palette, expand the Video Transitions folder and scroll down and open the Zoom subfolder.

3 Click the Cross Zoom icon to select it.

💡 *To find a transition quickly, click the Video Transitions folder in the Effects palette. In the Contains area, type in the name of the transition. Premiere will locate the transition and highlight it.*

4 Drag the Cross Zoom transition icon to the Video 1 track at the edit line in the Timeline window, where Gaze2.avi ends and the trimmed Approach2.avi begins.

5 Preview the Cross Zoom transition in your project.

Note: *The final movie uses all Cross Dissolve transitions. Later you can replace the transitions with the Cross Dissolve transition if you want to match the 03Final.wmv movie. Experiment on your own to obtain the look and feel that's right for you.*

6 Save the project.

Changing the attributes of transitions

You can modify all of the various parameters or settings for a transition, including the transition duration, alignment, direction, start and end values, border, and softness. Frequently, you will want to modify a specific instance of a transition in your video program. In many cases, you may insert a particular transition into your video project, and then want to replace it with another transition.

Modifying a transition instance

The Cross Zoom you just added to the sequence allows you to set the focal point in each clip where the zoom begins. You'll do that now.

1 Using the selection tool, click the Cross Zoom transition in the Timeline to activate it.

2 Check the Cross Zoom settings in the Effect Controls window.

3 Dock the Effect Controls window with the Source view of the Monitor window so that they are side by side. Use the Program view to guide you as you set the focal point.

4 Set the edit line to 00;00;18;01.

5 The Clip A and Clip B thumbnails each contain white circles that allow you to adjust the focal point of the zoom in each clip.

6 Click on the white circle in the center of the Clip A thumbnail and drag it to the upper point of the letter "A" in the Clip A thumbnail.

If you scrub with the edit line in the Effect Controls window, the Program view will reflect the movements of your mouse.

7 Click on Show Actual Sources in the Effect Controls window.

8 Adjust the focal point circle for Clip A, so that Hero's face fills the screen. You do this by clicking on points in the Clip A window until it adjusts to what you intend.

Note: *The Program view changes whenever you release the mouse.*

9 Move the edit line four frames forward to 00;00;18;05.

10 In the Effect Controls window, click on the Clip B thumbnail. Click on the focal point (the white circle located in the center of Clip B) and drag it to the upper right so that Hero's face is the center, especially his smile.

11 Play the transition or render scrub and then save the project.

Modifying transition settings

As you develop your own video style, you may want to modify the settings of some transition types so that they have your customizations as their default settings in the Effect Controls window. You'll customize Swing In now.

1 Open the 3D Motion subfolder within the Video Transitions folder in the Effects palette and locate the Swing In transition.

2 Click the Swing In transition icon and drag it to the edit line replacing the Cross Zoom transition.

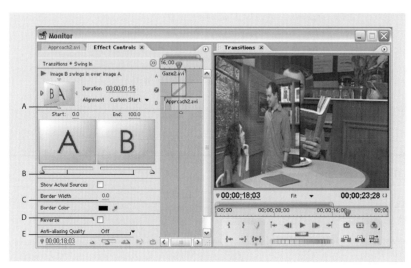

*A. Direction selector arrow **B.** Start/End sliders **C.** Border Width **D.** Forward/Reverse selector*
E. Anti-aliasing Quality menu

3 Adjust any or all of the following settings:

• To change the initial and final appearance of the transition, use the Start and End sliders. Hold down the Shift key to move the Start and End sliders together.

• To adjust the width of the optional border on the transition, click on the hot text controls (the underlined numbers in blue) or select the width area and type a number.

• To select a border color, click the color swatch and select a color from the color selection window.

• To change the orientation of the transition, click a Direction selector on the transition's thumbnail. The Direction selectors are black arrows that border the transition icon and face north, south, east, and west.

• To make the transition play backward, check the Reverse box in the lower left corner of the transition's settings. If the box is not selected, the transition will play forward.

• To adjust the anti-aliasing (pixel smoothness) of the transition, click the Anti-aliasing menu button in the lower part of the settings and choose either low, medium, or high.

Note: Not all of these settings parameters are available in all transitions.

Replacing a transition instance

You replace a transition instance by simply dropping the new transition icon on top of the old one in the Timeline. When you replace a transition instance, the *default effect settings* (duration and alignment) that apply to all transitions are preserved. However, the *transition-specific settings* (direction, borders, edges, softness, and so on) are replaced by the transition-specific default settings of the new transition.

1 With the Effects palette active, click the triangle next to the 3D Motion subfolder within the Video Transitions folder to expand the folder, if it is not already open.

2 Select the Cube Spin transition in the 3D Motion subfolder, drag its icon to the Timeline window, and place it on top of the Cross Dissolve transition between the Gaze1.avi and Approach1.avi clips.

The Cross Dissolve transition has been replaced with a Cube Spin.

3 In the Timeline, click the Cube Spin transition you have just inserted. The Cube Spin settings now appear in the Effect Controls window.

4 Choose Edit > Undo to restore the transition to the Cross Dissolve, in order to reproduce the 03Final.wmv movie.

Adding multiple transitions at one time

You can have some fun with the movie by choosing transitions that go with the mood of the scenes. First, you'll add some more clips to the Timeline.

1 Make sure the edit line is at the end of the footage (at 00;00;23;28).

2 In the Project window, select the following clips in this order while holding down the Control key: Gaze3.avi, Approach3.avi, Gaze4.avi, and Approach4.avi.

3 Click the Automate to Sequence button (🎞) at the bottom of the Project window to insert the four clips with the default transition between them. The Automate to Sequence dialog box appears. Click OK.

Three more transitions are added to the Timeline at one time. One of them breaks the pattern of having them lead from Hero's gaze into his fantasies.

4 In the Timeline, locate the transition between Approach3.avi and Gaze4.avi (at 00;00;37;27) and select it by clicking on it.

5 Choose Edit > Clear.

6 Select the third transition between Gaze3.avi and Approach3.avi.

7 In the Effects palette, locate the Swing In transition, which is in the 3D Motion subfolder within the Video Transitions folder. Drag its icon to the third transition, overlaying the default Cross Dissolve transition and replacing it.

8 Click on the Swing In transition so that its settings appear in the Effect Controls window.

9 In the Effect Controls window, click the direction selector arrow pointing south of the transition icon so that the transition moves from South to North.

10 Select the default transition between Gaze4.avi and Approach4.avi.

11 In the Effects palette, locate the Curtain transition in the 3D Motion subfolder within the Video Transitions folder. Drag the Curtain icon to the default transition and overlay it to replace the Cross Dissolve transition.

12 Play the Sequence or render-scrub to review your new work.

Now the sequence consists of a Cross Dissolve, followed by reciprocating Swing In transitions, and then a Curtain going up on Hero's fantasy of introducing himself to the girl of his dreams.

13 Save the project.

Transitions used as special effects

Experiment with the transitions thus far. To achieve the look of the Lesson 3 Final movie, simply use Cross Dissolve for all of the transitions. In this exercise, you'll finesse a transition and add a new one to create nuances that serve as special effects.

Modifying a transition in a sequence

Adjustments are made to transitions in the Effect Controls window. The first Cross Dissolve lets the audience know that Hero is daydreaming about ways to meet the girl of his dreams. To indicate to the audience that the next scene also takes place in his mind, you'll extend the Cross dissolve, so that it lingers in Clip A as it dissolves into Clip B.

1 In the Timeline, select the first transition at 00;00;02;04.

2 Move the edit line back 22 frames to 00;00;01;12.

3 In the Tools palette, select the Ripple Edit tool (⊷).

4 Select the tail of Gaze1.avi and drag it to the left to the edit line.

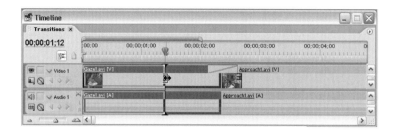

5 Move the edit line to the end of the Cross Dissolve transition (at 00;00;01;19).

6 Now, move the edit line 23 frames forward to 00;00;02;12.

7 Using the ripple edit tool, select the head of Approach1.avi and drag it to the edit line.

You've just trimmed a total of 45 frames (2.5 seconds). This will allow you to create a lingering Cross Dissolve transition of that length.

8 In the Timeline, click on the Cross Dissolve transition with the selection tool so that its settings appear in the Effect Controls window.

9 In the Effect Controls window, click on the duration and type **215**.

10 Preview the project and then save it.

Using a transition as a special effect

Now, you'll have some fun inserting a transition at the point in the project where Hero covers himself with a bouquet of flowers.

1 In the Timeline, press the Page Down key or use the Go to Next Edit Point in the Monitor window to locate the cut between Approach2.avi and Gaze3.avi.

2 Move the edit line backward 15 frames.

3 Using the ripple edit tool, select the tail of Approach2.avi and drag it to the edit line.

4 Move the edit line forward 15 frames.

5 Using the ripple edit tool, select the head of Gaze3.avi and drag it to the edit line.

6 Use the Page Up key to locate the previous edit between Approach2.avi and Gaze3.avi. Now, you'll learn a new method for adding a transition.

7 In the Effects palette, type **iris round** in the Contains area to locate the Iris Round transition and then select it.

8 Click on the menu triangle button in the upper right corner of the Effects palette and choose Set Default Transition. Notice that Iris Round is now outlined in red to signify that it is the default transition.

9 Select the Timeline window to make it active and then choose Sequence > Apply Video Transition.

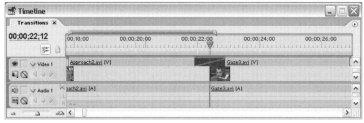

Adjusting and fine-tuning a transition

To embellish the humor of the scene, you'll change the direction of the Iris Round transition.

1 In the Sequence called Transitions, select the Iris Round transition, which is the last transition you added to the Timeline.

2 In the Effect Controls window, click inside the Reverse box.

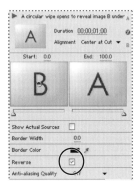

Reversing the Iris Round transition causes Clip A to shrink away from Clip B.

3 In the Effect Controls window, scrub through the transition. Notice how the Iris Round shrinks.

Now you'll adjust the focal point of Clip A so that the Iris Round closes around the flowers.

4 Click on Show Actual Sources to make this next adjustment easier.

5 Adjust the right slider so that the End field is set to 68. This allows you to see the next focal point adjustment.

6 Go to the Effect Controls window and click on the center white circle inside the Clip A thumbnail. Drag the focal point to the right and downward a short distance. The movements of the mouse are reflected in the Program view.

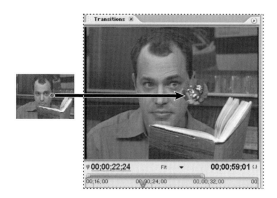

7 Add a border width of 2 by clicking on the Border Width hot text controls or selecting the Border Width area and typing **2**.

8 Change the Border Color to green by doing one of the following:

• Click on the Border Color swatch and select green from the color sample area.

• Use the eyedropper to select a color from the Program view of the footage. For example, choose Hero's shirt.

Note: To use the eyedropper, click on it and then drag it to the area in the Monitor display containing the color sample that you want. As the eyedropper rolls over different colors, the color swatch changes to whatever color the eyedropper touches.

9 Click on the Anti-aliasing Quality menu triangle and choose High. This blends the border smoothly into the surrounding pixels.

10 Playback or scrub to review the Iris Round transition in reverse with a border.

11 Save the project.

Completing the Lesson 3 project

One last transition needs to be added to the project, although it's not a Premiere Pro one. Indeed, it's a psychological transition. Hero gives up and leaves the bookstore cafe.

1 In the Timeline, move the edit line to the end of the sequence.

2 In the Project window, select Sigh.avi from the Bin 01 folder and drag it to the edit line.

💡 *You can also use the keyboard shortcut for inserting a clip at the edit line in the Timeline by clicking on the Sigh.avi icon in the Project window and typing a ";" (comma).*

3 Preview the project and then save it.

Exporting the movie

To view Sequence Transitions as a movie file, you need to export it.

1 Select the Transitions sequence in the Timeline window to make it active.

2 Adjust the Timeline view so that you can see the entire sequence. (Type a reverse slash (\) or use the zoom controls.)

3 Double-click on the textured portion at the center of the work area bar so that it conforms to the length of the entire project.

Note: For more details and exercises about exporting movies from Premiere Pro, go to Lesson 13, "Output," in this Classroom in a Book.

4 From the title bar at the top of your screen, choose File > Export > Movie.

5 In the Export Movie dialog box, click Settings. Make sure Microsoft DV AVI is selected for the File Type and Work Area Bar is selected for the Range. Make sure that the Export Video option and the Export Audio option are selected. Also make sure that Add to Project When Finished and Beep When Finished are selected. The default values for other settings are fine for this project.

💡 *Use the Save and Load buttons in the Export Movie Settings dialog box to save and later quickly load export settings that you use frequently. Loading saved settings is particularly useful when you create several types of video files (for example, NTSC and Web video) from the same project.*

6 Click OK to close the Export Movie Settings dialog box.

7 In the Export Movie dialog box, type **Transitions.avi** for the name of the video program and click Save.

Premiere Pro starts making the video program, displaying a status bar that provides an estimate for the amount of time it will take.

8 When the video program is complete, it is imported into the project.

Double-click SequenceEx.avi and then click the Play button in the Source view to watch what you've just created.

Congratulations on completing the Transitions Lesson!

Exploring on your own

Feel free to experiment with the project you have just created. Here are some suggestions:

• Change the direction of a transition (click the Track Selector), and then preview the results.

• Click on one of the transitions in the Timeline to view its settings/options in the Effect Controls window. See how the options affect the transition.

• Look at the differences in the appearance of transition icons when you change the height of the track.

• Practice using the shortcuts listed on the Premiere Pro Quick Reference Card and in Premiere Pro Help to preview in the Monitor window and the Timeline window.

Review questions

1 What are four ways to preview transitions?

2 What does the Track Selector button do in a transition?

3 What is the purpose of the Anti-aliasing feature available in a number of transitions?

4 What does the Reverse selector do in a transition?

5 What are two ways to get more information within the Effects palette about the function of a specific transition?

Answers

1 Use Real-Time Preview, render-scrub in the Timeline ruler, render-scrub in the Effect Controls window, and play back the work by clicking the Play button in the Program view.

2 The track selector tool sets the direction of the transition between the two clips.

3 Anti-aliasing smooths the edges of an effect, reducing the rough appearance of the edge. This can be useful for transitions that have angled or curved edges.

4 The Reverse selector sets the direction of the effect used in the transition in the opposite direction. For example, in the Zoom transition, Clip A zooms in and Clip B zooms out. Upon reversal, Clip B zooms in and Clip A zooms out.

5 Select the transition and view the Info palette; in the Effect Controls window a description is displayed by the Play icon.

Lesson 4

4 | **Color and Opacity**

When color correction becomes necessary in projects, Adobe Premiere Pro has tools to balance footage from multiple sources. Using the Timeline, you can create up to 98 different video tracks for countless combinations of layered movies and stills. With the generous selection of opacity keys, you can key out (remove) specific areas of a movie and create customized effects.

In this lesson, you'll learn about color correction and opacity, which is the basis for layering. You'll use the superimpose tracks feature in the Timeline to create opacity blends fades, and other special effects. Specifically, you'll learn how to perform these tasks:

- Work with Waveforms and Vectorscopes in a Reference Monitor.
- Color correct clips with split screen previews of the changes.
- Adjust clips shot with different cameras.
- Implement keyframes to fine-tune effects.
- Apply opacity key types and adjust settings.
- Work with Matte channels.

Getting started

For this lesson, you'll continue the movie project you began in Lesson 2 and add one more nuance related to opacity for the Transitions sequence you created in Lesson 3. Make sure you know the location of the files used in this lesson. Insert the Adobe Premiere Pro *Classroom in a Book* CD-ROM disk if necessary. For help, see "Copying the Classroom in a Book files" on page 4 of this *Classroom in a Book*.

1 Launch the Premiere Pro software.

2 In the Premiere Pro Welcome window, click Open Project.

3 In the Open Project dialog box, locate the 04Lesson folder that you copied into your hard drive from the DVD-ROM.

4 Locate the 04Lesson.prproj file in the 04Lesson folder and click Open. (You can also double-click on the 04Lesson.prproj file to open it.)

5 Choose Window > Workspace > Color Correction.

The Color Correction workspace is adapted. You'll see the default Reference Monitor in front of the Monitor window in single view. The Reference monitor is used to view comparisons between the behaviors of color correction steps.

You'll be superimposing still clips with transparent areas in the footage that will affect color and opacity in the project. The color management and correction features in this lesson along with the opacity settings will best display at Highest Quality in the Monitor window. In the Timeline, if you prefer to work with larger icons, adjust the height of the track or tracks to display larger icons.

Viewing the finished movies

To see what you'll be creating, you can look at the final movies.

1 Click the triangle next to the Resources bin to open the bin. Make sure the bin is still selected.

2 Choose File > Import. Open the Finished folder and select 04Final.wmv, Chromafinal.avi, Bluescreenfinal.avi, and Trackmattefinal.avi inside the Finished folder, within the 04Lesson folder. Click Open.

The final movie clips for this lesson are located in the Resources bin.

3 Double-click the movie files you wish to review so that they open in the Source view of the Monitor window.

4 Click the Play button (▶) in the Source view of the Monitor window to watch the video programs.

5 You can either delete the Resources bin and the movies by clicking the Clear button (🗑) at the bottom of the Project window. Or you may decide to keep them as references as you proceed through the exercises in this lesson.

Color management and correction

The color correction features in Premiere Pro give video editors precise controls for monitoring color from clip to clip. Premiere Pro provides built-in waveforms and vectorscopes to ensure that your color adjustments are within the legal broadcast limits.

By default, the Source and Program views display video as it would ordinarily appear on a video monitor. However, you can also display the video's *alpha channel*, or transparency information. In addition, you can evaluate the video's brightness and color by running several iterations of measurements and displaying them with a Vectorscope or a Waveform Monitor.

Understanding the waveform monitor and vectorscope

The waveform monitor is used primarily to display the levels of luma and chroma components of the video signal. With the waveform monitor, you can see the level of a pixel, plus determine the brightest and darkest levels in the video signal.

The vectorscope tool displays precisely the color content of a video signal, including hue and saturation. A specific point on the vectorscope represents a specific color with its corresponding hue and saturation points. The distance from the center of the display represents the saturation; the counter-clockwise rotation from the center of the display represents the hue.

The Luma key creates transparency for darker values in the image, leaving brighter colors opaque. Use the Luma key to create a subtle superimposition or to key out dark areas. The width and height of the waveform correspond to the width of a video scan line and amplitude of the video signal, respectively.

Chroma is judged by an area that appears to be white. Videographers use the chroma key to set the white point for their camera, so that no bright spot will be brighter than the chroma calibration. It is the whitest white in view.

1 Click on the menu triangle button in the upper right corner of the Program view and choose New Reference Monitor.

You'll use the Reference monitor to view waveforms and vectorscopes. You can have only one reference monitor open at a time per sequence.

*A. Gang to Program Monitor **B.** Output*

2 To have the Reference Monitor track the playback of the Program monitor with color and levels information, select the Gang to Program Monitor button ( ).

3 Dock the Reference Monitor to the Source view of the Monitor window by dragging its tab into the tab area of the Source view.

Reference monitor docked with Source view with Gang to Program Monitor option on to track the Program view playback.

4 To view the waveform of Sequence Ex, click the menu triangle button in the upper right corner of the Reference view in the Monitor window and choose Waveform.

5 To view the waveform version of Sequence Ex, click the play button in the Program view of the Monitor window. You can view the changes by scrubbing.

Notice the differences in luma and chroma intensities in the two images in step 4. Throughout this lesson and the *Classroom in a Book*, you can check the waveform or vectorscope displays in the Reference monitor to see the effects of your color corrections.

Applying the Color Corrector video effect

With the powerful color correction tools available in Premiere Pro, you can control the look of every clip in your production. The 3-point color correction tools allow you to adjust the hue, saturation, and lightness of clips to make sure all of the shots in a scene match. These tools make it easy for you to accurately adjust the color of your video images and correct exposure, color-balance, and lighting.

You'll adjust the Mtntop.avi clip, which was shot outdoors in grey weather conditions. The rest of the movie was shot with a different camera, either indoors with studio lighting or outdoors in bright weather conditions.

1 In the Timeline window, set the edit line to the head of Mtntop.avi (at 00;00;28;26).

2 In the Effects palette, open the Image Control subfolder within the Video Effects folder and locate the Color Corrector effect. Or, you can type **color corrector** in the Contains area and the program will find the effect for you.

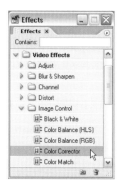

3 Drag the Color Corrector effect to the Mtntop.avi clip in the Timeline window.

4 In the Timeline window, click the Mtntop.avi clip so that the Color Corrector video effect will appear in the Effect Controls window.

Note: If the clip is selected in the Timeline window, and the Effect Controls window is open, you can drag the effect to the Effect Controls window.

5 In the Effect Controls window, click the triangle next to the Color Corrector effect.

The Color Corrector effect combines several color correction tools so that you can easily adjust the color of video clips. It displays the following settings:

Setting Keys Saves or loads your settings from the hard disk.

Split Screen Preview Displays the right half of the image as the corrected view and the left half of the image as the uncorrected view.

Black/White Balance This is the first adjustment that should be applied to any image. It establishes proper black, white, and gray points.

Total Range Definition Use this to alter the colors in an image area, such as the highlights, midtones, or shadows.

HSL Hue Offsets These controls adjust the hue and saturation values by using four different color wheels corresponding to the master, shadow, midtone, and highlight controls.

HSL Use these controls to adjust an image in the HSL (Hue-Saturation-Lightness) color space. Controls for changing Tonal Range, Hue, Saturation, Brightness, Contrast, and Contrast Center are included. You can make adjustments based on whether an area is a shadow, midtone, or highlight.

RGB With these controls, you can manipulate the gamma, pedestal, and gain of each of the red, green, and blue color channels in the RGB (Red-Green-Blue) color model. These controls allow you to make adjustments based on whether an area is a shadow, midtone, or highlight.

Curves The Curves correction pane allows you to create complex color adjustments by placing control points on curves and adjusting the curves. The curves can have up to 16 control points.

Video Limiter These controls allow you to prepare video that falls within broadcast and other regulatory limits.

With the Color Corrector video effect, you can accurately adjust the color of your video images.

Note: The Color Corrector performs its image processing operations in the order that the settings appear in the list, from top to bottom. This may be useful when analyzing the correction results or applying multiple corrections to the same image.

6 In the Effect Controls window, select Split Screen Preview to view the before and after effects of your changes during playback.

White triangles appear at the top and bottom of the clip in the Program Monitor view.

7 In the Effect Controls window, click on the triangle next to the RGB settings.

You can use the RGB controls to adjust gamma, pedestal, and gain of each of the RGB channels separately or simultaneously. For example, you might want to make the mountain scene a little more brooding.

8 Click on the triangle next to the Pedestal settings.

The pedestal is a small DC voltage step within the video signal indicating a picture's black level. It is used as the reference in a standard video signal for white and gray levels.

Most of the adjustments in the Color Corrector and in many of the effects in Premiere Pro can be made in three ways: editable text fields, Hot Text Keys controls, and sliders.

9 Using one of the three methods, reduce the Mtntop.avi clip Pedestal to **-0.08**.

10 Preview the results by scrubbing in the Effect Controls window.

The changes in the clip's RGB values are reflected in the Program view of the Monitor window.

Experiment with the other settings in the Color Corrector effect. For example, if you click on HSL hue offsets, the adjustment tools are color wheels. Explore how adjustments to the color wheels affect the scene in the clip. To use the color wheel, click on a wheel and drag it clockwise or counter-clockwise. The color wheel spins as you drag.

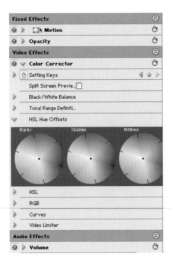

The changes in the clip's hue are reflected in the Program view of the Monitor window.

Note: To make fine adjustments using the color wheel, hold the Shift key while you click and drag. This increases the precision by a factor of ten.

• Click the Saturation controls to adjust the strength of the color. The default value is 100, which does not alter the saturation. Change the setting to zero, and all color is removed.

• Click the Contrast and Contrast Center controls. The contrast curve gives a more natural look to the adjustments you make.

11 Close the Reference Monitor window by clicking on the "X" on its tab.

12 Save the project.

Using the Color Match video effect

The Color Match video effect allows you to match the colors of one video clip to another clip. This is especially useful if the footage was shot with different cameras. For example, if you're combining shots of a sunny day with shots of a fluorescent-lit office, you may want to remove the green hues in the latter clips. Or, if you're creating graphics for a corporate video, you may need to match them to the colors in the company logo. For a description of the Color Match effect and its settings, see the online Help. In this exercise, you'll learn how to replace a color throughout a clip.

1 In the Project window, click on the triangle next to the Resources bin to open the bin and choose File > New > Bin.

2 A new bin appears within the Resources bin. Rename this new bin **Color**.

3 Select the Color bin and choose File > Import.

4 In the 04Lesson folder, hold down the control key and select Faceadj.avi, Faceadj2.avi, Faceorig.avi, and Faceorig2.avi. Click Open.

5 In the Project window, double-click Sequence 01, making it the active Timeline. You'll use Sequence 01 as an experimental workspace.

6 From the Color bin, select Faceadj.avi and then Faceorig.avi, and drag them to the Video 1 track on Sequence 01.

Faceadj.avi and Faceorig.avi now appear on the Sequence 01 Timeline.

7 In the Sequence 01 Timeline, scrub with the edit line to the middle of Faceorig.avi (at approximately 00;00;10;11).

8 Click on the menu triangle button in the Program Monitor and choose New Reference Monitor.

9 Dock the Reference Monitor with the Source view of the Monitor Window.

10 Change the viewing mode of the Reference monitor to Composite if it displays waveforms.

Faceorig.avi becomes the model for your color adjustments to Faceadj.avi.

11 Position the edit line in the Timeline or adjust the time code field so that the Program view displays the frame at 00;00;04;26.

The Monitor window now displays the two frames from the separate clips side by side. The Reference Monitor is on the left where the source view is displayed, and the Timeline Sequence is on the right in the Program view.

The two clips, Faceadj.avi and Faceorig.avi, were both shot in identical conditions with the same camera. As Faceadj.avi was being shot, however, the sun peeked out from behind a cloud at several points in the scene, causing Hero's face to "burn out" in some highlight areas.

Now you'll use the Color Match video effect to remove some of the glare from the highlights and midtones in Hero's face in Faceadj.avi. This will make it look closer in tone to Faceorig.avi.

12 In the Effects palette, open the Image Control subfolder within the Video Effects folder and locate the Color Match effect.

13 Drag the Color Match effect icon onto Faceadj.avi on Sequence 01 in the Timeline.

14 Click on Faceadj.avi in order for the Color Match settings to appear in the Effect Controls window.

15 In the Effect Controls window, click on the triangle next to the Color Match effect to display its settings. In the Method area, click on the menu triangle to the right of HSL and choose RGB.

16 Click and hold the Master Sample eyedropper. The cursor changes to the eyedropper icon (✎).

17 Drag the eyedropper across the Program monitor onto the bright spot in Hero's forehead.

18 Release the mouse button to capture the color of the bright spot. That color will show up in the color field of the Master Sample area of the Color Match effect.

You don't want the brightness of Hero's face at any one point to exceed that of the brightest area on Hero's face in the target frame of Faceorig.avi 00;00;10;11 in the Reference Monitor. You, therefore, need to locate the bright color in the target frame.

19 In the Effect Controls window, choose the Master Target eyedropper.

20 Drag the eyedropper across the Reference monitor to the brightest spot on the back of Hero's neck above his collar.

21 Release the mouse button to capture the color on the back of his neck. This color will show up in the color field of the Master Target area of the Color Match effect.

Now that you have made your selections, you will apply the effect.

22 In the Color Match effect, click the triangle next to the Match settings at the bottom of the list.

23 Click Match.

24 Make the Timeline active and preview the Color Match effect.

Note: You can also scrub in the Effect Controls window to preview your changes.

The glare in Faceadj.avi has been toned down.

25 Close the Reference Monitor window by clicking on the "X" in its tab.

26 Save the project.

Using the Color Match video effect with clips from different cameras

Now, you will use the Color Match effect with two clips that were shot with different cameras under different lighting conditions.

1 Make the Timeline active. Choose Edit > Select All.

2 Choose Edit > Clear to prepare the Timeline for new editing.

3 Restore the edit line to the beginning of the program by pressing the Home key.

4 From the Color bin in the Project window, drag Faceadj2.avi and Faceorig2.avi to the Timeline.

5 Double-click Faceorig2.avi to make it active in the Source view.

Notice the lighting and color differences between the two clips. You'll remove the rosiness from Faceadj2.avi and brighten it a little.

6 From the Effects palette, locate the Color Match effect in the Image Control folder within the Video Effects folder and drag it onto Faceadj2.avi in the Timeline.

7 In the Timeline window, click the Faceadj2.avi clip so that the Color Match effect appears in the Effect Controls window.

8 In the Effect Controls window, click the triangle next to Color Match effect to view its settings.

9 In the Method area, click on the menu triangle to the right of HSL and choose RGB.

10 In the Effect Controls window, choose the Master Sample eyedropper.

11 The Program view displays Faceadj2.avi. Drag the eyedropper across Hero's forehead to the bright spot on his right forehead.

12 Release the mouse button to capture the color of his skin. This color will show up in the color field in the Master Sample area of the Color Match effect.

13 Select the eyedropper for the Master Target area in the Color Match settings.

14 Drag the Master Target eyedropper to the Source view to the bright spot just above the arch in Hero's right eyebrow.

15 Release the mouse button to capture this color, which will show up in the Master Target area of the Color Match.

Now that your selections are made, you will apply the effect.

16 In the Color Match effect, click on the triangle next to Match at the bottom of the list.

17 Click on the Match button.

18 Make the Timeline active and preview the Color Match effect.

19 Save the project.

Native YUV processing

Adobe Premiere Pro provides native support for YUV color, ensuring higher color quality in your final productions. With YUV support, the native color space of the original video material is preserved.

Premiere preserves the native color space of the source clip when processing effects to avoid any loss of quality caused by converted colors. Effects in Adobe Premiere Pro use either RGB or YUV color, depending on the color space of your media. DV video uses the YUV color space; most computer-generated graphics use the RGB color space. Although most color conversions are generally not noticeable, DV images lose some information when converted to RGB. This is because the RGB color palette does not include all of the colors represented in the YUV color palette.

The value of keyframe techniques

To change an effect over time, you'll use a standard technique known as *keyframing*. This form of adjustment helps to enliven and animate your program.

When you create a keyframe, you specify the value of an effect property for a specific point in time. When you apply different values to keyframes, Adobe Premiere Pro automatically calculates the values between the keyframes, a process called *interpolation*.

For example, suppose that you wanted to use the Gaussian Blur effect and have it increase and then decrease over time. In this case, you would need to set three keyframes: the first with no blur; the second with more significant blur; and the third with no blur. Because Adobe Premiere Pro automatically interpolates the blur values between each keyframe, the blur gradually increases between the first and second keyframes and then gradually decreases between the second and third keyframes. Some Adobe Premiere Pro effects cannot be animated with keyframes.

You can set keyframes for most standard effects within the clip's duration. You can also animate clips by setting keyframes for fixed effect properties, such as position and scale. You can move, copy, or delete keyframes and change the interpolation method of a keyframe.

Keyframing in the Effect Controls window

Many of your keyframe adjustments will take place in the Effect Controls window. Keyframe values for spatial properties, such as the Position property for the Motion effect, can be adjusted in the Program view of the Monitor window by directly manipulating the clip. You can also adjust keyframe values in the Timeline window. Each keyframe icon indicates the keyframe's position in time. In the Effect Controls window, the shape of the keyframe also indicates how values between keyframes are interpolated.

In this lesson and throughout the remainder of this *Classroom in a Book*, you'll use keyframing to create changes, effects, and animations over the run-length or over a portion of the clips in your projects.

For more information, see Lesson 5, "Motion Paths," and Lesson 6, "Special Effects: Using Effect Controls" in this *Classroom in a Book*.

Opacity

To obtain layered effects that depend on transparency levels of clips in Premiere Pro, opacity adjustments are made in tracks above the Video 1 track. This is called *superimposing*.

Superimposing (often called *matting* or *keying* in television and film production) means playing one clip on top of another. In Premiere Pro, you can add clips to the superimpose tracks (Video 2 track and higher). Then you can add opacity or fades so that the clips placed in lower tracks in the Timeline appear partially as well. If you don't apply opacity to the clip in the highest track, the clips directly below will not appear when you preview or when you play your final movie.

Clips in superimpose tracks with various transparencies applied

Premiere Pro provides a broad variety of *keys* (methods for creating opacity) that allow you to vary the type and intensity of opacity applied to different areas of a clip. When superimposing, you can designate *matte* (specified area) to be totally transparent, or you can apply opacity based on a color or color quality, such as brightness.

It is always best to plan ahead for superimpositions, before you make your video captures. For example, if you videotape a person talking and you want to superimpose a different background behind the person, tape the person in front of a solid-color background, such as a blue screen or seamless background paper. Otherwise, keying out the background will be difficult, if not impossible.

Creating a split screen

A split screen is one of the effects you can create using the opacity settings in Premiere Pro. A split screen displays a portion of a clip on one part of the screen, and a portion of another clip on the other part of the screen.

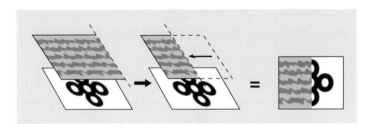

Opacity applied to upper clip; split-screen effect

In this exercise, you'll create a split screen that displays half of one clip on the top and half of another clip on the bottom. But first you'll import the first two clips and add them to Sequence 01.

1 Make sure the CTI is set at zero.

2 Go to the Timeline and select Sequence 01. Choose Edit > Select All. Then choose Edit > Clear to delete all of the clips from Sequence 01 before you start this exercise.

3 With Bin 01 active in the Project window, choose File > Import. Navigate to the 04Lesson folder and click OK.

4 While holding down the Control key, select Split1.avi and Split2.avi and click Open.

5 Drag Split1.avi from the Bin area in the Project window to the Video 1 track, placing its In point at the very beginning of the Timeline.

6 Preview the first clip before applying opacity.

7 Drag Split2.avi from the Bin area in the Project window to the Video 2 track, aligning it at the very beginning of the Timeline as well.

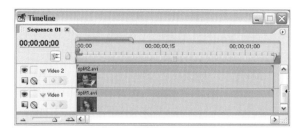

8 Scrub through the Timeline ruler to preview both clips before applying opacity.

Notice that only Split2.avi appears in the Program view in the Monitor window. Without opacity, nothing below this clip displays.

You cannot apply opacity to a clip in the Video 1 track, so you'll apply it to Split2.avi in the Video 2 track. Because Split1.avi is located directly below Split2.avi, after you apply opacity to Split2.avi, Split1.avi will reappear.

9 Select Split2.avi in the Timeline and then go to the Effect Controls window.

10 Click the triangle to the left of the Motion settings to reveal the settings.

When you create a split screen, you don't use an opacity key type; instead, you adjust aspects of the clip, such as position, height, and width.

11 In the Position area, type **470** for the Vertical position (the right-hand set of numbers in the Position field) or drag the slider to 470.

You can see the effect of the split screen in the Program view.

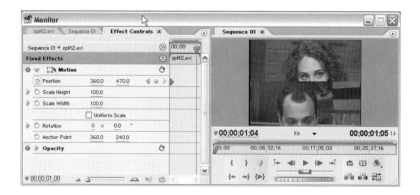

Now you can see Split2.avi in the bottom half of the Program view and Split1.avi in the top half.

Note: You can create vertical, horizontal, or diagonal split screens by adjusting rotation, position, and other fields of the clip appropriately.

12 Use Real-Time playback or render-scrub to preview the split screen.

13 Save the project.

Applying the Blue Screen opacity key

The two most commonly used opacity keys are Blue Screen and Green Screen. These keys are generally used to substitute the background of one video clip with another. They are favored because they do not interfere with skin tones. For example, TV news programs regularly use blue screens to display footage of the current topic behind the newscaster.

If you use a blue or green background when videotaping footage and plan to key it out using the Blue or Green Screen key, make sure everything that is to remain opaque is a color other than your key color. For example, if you film a newscaster in front of a blue backdrop and the newscaster is wearing a blue tie, the tie will become transparent along with the background when you apply the Blue Screen key to the footage.

Blue Screen opacity with blue tie and with white tie

Now you'll add a clip to the Video 2 track and apply the Blue Screen key and the Chroma key.

1 In the Project window, double-click Sequence Ex to make it active in the Timeline.

2 Select the Color bin and choose File > Import. Select Storefront1.psd and click Open.

3 The Import Layered File dialog box appears. Select Choose Layer.

4 In the Choose Layer menu choose Bluescreen. Click OK.

5 Insert Bluescreen/Storefront1.psd at the beginning of the Video 2 track in the Timeline.

6 Make the duration equal to the duration of Opening.avi (00;00;06;05) by selecting Bluescreen/Storefront1.psd, choosing Clip > Speed/Duration, typing **605** in the duration field, and clicking OK.

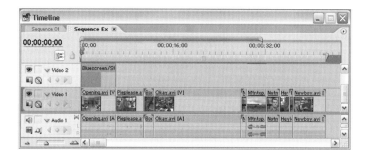

7 Scrub in the Effect Controls window to see that Bluescreen/Storefront1.psd covers Opening.avi.

8 Go to the Effects palette and type **blue** in the Contains area. The Blue Screen Key effect appears. (Or, expand the Keying folder within the Video Effects folder and locate the Blue Screen Key effect.)

9 Select the Blue Screen Key effect and drag it to Bluescreen/Storefront1.psd in the Video 2 track of the Timeline window.

10 Click on Bluescreen/Storefront1.psd in the Timeline and then go to the Effect Controls window.

11 Click the triangle next to the Blue Screen Key effect to view its settings.

The Threshold and Cutoff sliders in the Effect Control palette alter the shadows and the extent of color selected and removed.

12 Scrub in the Effect Controls window, to see how much of the blue background has been keyed out.

Notice how the blue background carries over slightly. To enhance the appearance of the clip by removing all of this blue background, you'll adjust the Threshold slider.

13 Click in the box next to the Threshold area and type **83.0** or drag the Threshold slider to 83.0.

Notice how the background colors become saturated and more true. This is because you're removing more of the lingering blue value from the selected clip. You can see the effect in the Program view.

14 Preview the blue screen opacity effect by using Real-Time playback or by scrubbing through the Timeline.

15 Save the project.

Applying the Chroma key

The Chroma key lets you select any color as the transparent area. If you can't videotape footage using a blue or green background because of conflicting colors in your clip (such as the color of someone's clothes), you can use any solid color background and then use the Premiere Pro Chroma key to make that color represent your transparent area.

Now, you'll use the Chroma key on a clip with a range of grey in its background.

1 Make the Sequence 01 Timeline active, by double-clicking Sequence 01 in the Project window or by clicking on the Sequence 01 tab in the Timeline.

2 Choose Edit > Select All.

3 Choose Edit > Clear.

4 From Bin 01 of the Project window, insert Notmuch.avi at the beginning of the Sequence 01 Timeline.

5 In the Project window, double-click Mtntop.avi so that it appears in the Source view of the Monitor window.

6 In an Earlier lesson, you trimmed the In point of Mtntop.avi to 00;00;05;00 and its Out point to 00;00;08;12. The duration of Notmuch.avi is 00;00;03;06. In the Source view for this exercise, set the In point marker to 00;00;05;07 and the Out point to 00;00;08;12 so that the duration of Mtntop.avi is equal to the duration of Notmuch.avi.

7 Click on the Toggle Take Audio and Video button (🎬) and make sure it is set to Take Audio and Video.

8 Drag Mtntop.avi from the Project window to the Video 2 track, aligning its In point with the beginning of the Timeline.

9 Scrub through the Timeline to preview the movie before applying the Chroma Key effect.

10 Go to the Effects palette and type **chroma** in the Contains area. The Chroma Key effect appears.

11 Select the Chroma Key effect and drag it to Mtntop.avi in the Video 2 track of the Timeline window.

12 Click on the Mtntop.avi clip in the Timeline window and then go to the Effect Controls window.

13 Click on the triangle next to the Chroma Key effect to view the settings.

Notice that the Color box in the Chroma Key Settings area now displays white. You can click the white box to either select a color or assign a key color from the Color Picker. For this exercise, you'll assign the blue sky color from the last frame.

14 Click on the Color box in the Chroma Key effect.

The Color picker opens. Premiere Pro allows you to assign color in five different ways.

15 In this exercise, type **168** for the Red (R) value; **190** for the Green (G) value, and **204** for the Blue (B) value and click OK.

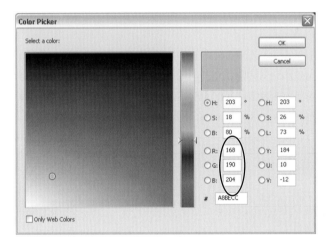

The cloudy background in Mtntop.avi is dithered (not a solid color). You'll need to use the Blend settings to make this clip's background transparent. The Blend settings blend the edges of the image with the background by gradually changing the opacity where the color pixels meet.

16 In the Effect Controls window, click in the box next to the Blend area and type **40**. Notice how the edges between the image and background lose their sharpness.

Note: Another way to adjust the Blend settings is to use the Blend slider. Click the triangle next to the Blend area to reveal the slider. Drag the slider to 40.

The Threshold and Cutoff settings do not apply to this clip; however, it is good idea to clean up the edges and the blending by using the Smoothing controls.

17 Click on the menu triangle to the right of the Smoothing area and select High.

18 Preview the clips using Real-Time preview or by scrubbing through the Timeline. Notice how the Mtntop.avi clip now appears on-screen with no clouds in the sky.

19 Save the project.

Applying the Track Matte opacity key type

Premiere's Track Matte Key effect lets you customize and layer movies. When you apply this key effect, you can play one movie through the matte of another while yet another movie plays in the background.

When you create a track matte effect, the order of your clips is important. Applying the Track Matte Key effect to different clips and different video tracks results in a wide range of effects. You'll see some of those effects in this lesson.

Use the Track Matte Key to superimpose one clip over another, using a third file as the matte that integrates the two. Areas of white in the matte create opaque areas in the superimposed clip, preventing underlying clips from showing through. Black areas in the matte create transparent areas, and gray areas make partially transparent areas. To retain the original colors in the superimposed clip, use a grayscale image for the matte. Any color in the matte removes the same level of color from the superimposed clip.

You can create mattes in various ways:

• Use the Title window to create text or shapes (grayscale only), save the title, and then import the file as your matte. For more information about the Titler and Title window, see Lesson 11 "Titles and Credits" in this book.

• Create a matte from any clip using the Chroma, RGB Difference, Difference Matte, Blue Screen, Green Screen, or Non-Red key. Then select the Mask Only option.

• Use Adobe Illustrator or Adobe Photoshop to create a grayscale image, import it into Adobe Premiere Pro, and then (optionally) apply motion settings to the image.

In this section, you'll apply the Track Matte effect using the Sequence 01 Timeline.

1 In Sequence 01, select Mtntop.avi so that the Chroma key is active in the Effect Controls window.

2 In the Effect Controls window, click on the Chroma Key name and deselect it by toggling the Effects icon ( ) to off. It is located to the left of the triangle next to the Chroma Key. This will allow you to go back to experiment with it later.

3 In the Project window, select Bin 01 and choose File > Import.

4 Select Trackmatte.psd in the 04Lesson folder and click Open.

The Import Layered File dialog box appears.

5 Select Choose Layer and make sure Document Size is selected for the Footage Dimensions.

6 Click OK.

7 In the Project window, click Layer1/Trackmatte.psd in Bin 01 and choose Clip > Speed/Duration.

The Clip Speed/Duration box appears.

8 Change the Duration to 3.06 to match the Mtntop.avi and Notmuch.avi clips.

9 Click OK.

10 Insert Layer1/Trackmatte.psd onto the Video 3 track at the beginning of Sequence 01 so that it is superimposed over Mtntop.avi and Notmuch.avi.

11 In the Effects palette, locate the Track Matte Key video effect.

12 Drag the Track Matte Key to the Mtntop.avi clip on the Video 2 track.

13 In the Timeline, select Mtntop.avi to make the Track Matte Key active in the Effect Controls window.

14 In the Effect Controls window, click on the triangle next to the Track Matte Key to expand its settings.

15 From the Matte field menu choose the Video 3 track.

Other aspects of this effect are Composite Using and Reverse. Select Matte Alpha to composite using the values in the alpha channel of the track matte. Select Matte Luma to composite using the image's luminance values instead. Reverse inverts the values of the track matte.

16 For Composite Using choose Matte Alpha.

17 In the Timeline select the Video 3 track.

18 Choose Clip > Enable to toggle it to Disabled (unchecked). This is done so that the Trackmatte.psd image is not part of the composite; only its opacity values will be used.

19 Preview the effect.

Results with Video 3 track disabled for the final Track Matte effect

20 Save the project.

Exporting the movie

It's time to generate a movie file.

1 If you turned off audio previewing earlier in the lesson, make sure you turn it on again by clicking the icon in the track header area of each audio track so that it changes to the speaker icon ( ).

2 Choose File > Export > Movie.

3 In the Export Movie dialog box, click the Settings button. In the General settings, make sure that File Type is set to Microsoft DV AVI.

4 Select Entire Sequence for the Range.

5 Make sure that Export Video, Export Audio, Add to Project When Finished, and Beep When Finished are selected.

6 In the Audio section, choose 48000 Hz for Sample Rate, 16-bit for Sample Type, and Stereo for Channels.

7 Click OK to close the Export Movie Settings dialog box.

8 In the Export Movie dialog box, specify the 04Lesson folder for the location and type **04Done** for the name of the movie. (Premiere Pro will add the AVI extension.) Click Save.

While Premiere Pro is making the movie, a status bar displays the time remaining to complete the process. When the movie is complete, it appears in the Project window.

9 Double-click the movie to open it in the Source view of the Monitor window.

10 Click the Play button to play the movie you've just created.

Exploring on your own

Feel free to experiment with the project you just created. Here are some suggestions:

- Change the opacity key for the various effects to see the different effects.

- Use the Wipe transition to create a split screen between Split1.avi and Split2.avi.

- See what other opacity keys will remove the background of clips.

Review questions

1 How do you create a split screen?

2 What is the difference between the Blue Screen key and the Chroma key?

3 Which key lets you customize and layer movies by playing one movie through the mask of another?

4 When would you use the Color Match video effect and how is it helpful?

5 What is the difference between the Similarity slider and the Blend slider?

Answers

1 By changing the position setting in the Effect Controls window.

2 The Blue Screen Key only lets you key out the color blue. The Chroma Key lets you key out any color you choose.

3 The Track Matte Key effect.

4 Use the Color Match video effect to match the colors of one video clip to another clip. This is especially useful if the footage was shot with different cameras or different lighting.

5 The Similarity slider increases the range of colors that the Opacity Key keys out. The Blend slider blends the color pixels around all edges where the transparent pixels meet the opaque pixels.

Lesson 5

5 | Motion Paths

Motion enhances and enriches the effect of still image files in a video program. The Adobe Premiere Pro Motion feature lets you move, rotate, distort, and magnify a variety of still image and video files.

In this lesson, you'll have some fun with flying logos and learn the basics of animation with Premiere Pro. In particular, you'll learn how to do the following:

- Develop techniques for creating, applying, and transforming keyframes.
- Set and change a *motion path.*
- Adjust the Motion along the Effect Controls window timeline.
- Adjust the scale and rotation settings.
- Load a saved motion path and adjust it.
- Create a traveling matte from a still image.

Getting started

For this lesson, you'll continue working with the existing project from Lesson 4 in which the necessary files are already imported. Then, you'll apply different motion and transparency settings to the clips. Make sure you know the location of the files used in this lesson.

To keep the exercises within the structure of this lesson, locate the 05Lesson.prproj file and open it. Insert the DVD-ROM disk if necessary. For help, see "Copying the Classroom in a Book files" on page 4.

1 Launch the Premiere Pro software and click Open Project.

2 Double-click the existing project 05Lesson.prprj in the 05Lesson folder to open it.

3 If necessary, rearrange windows and palettes so that they don't overlap, by choosing Window > Workspace > My Workspace. Make sure the Effect Controls window is open for this lesson.

Viewing the finished movies

If you'd like to see what you'll be creating, you can open and play the finished movies.

1 Click the Resources bin in the Project window. Click the triangle next to the Resources bin to open the folder.

2 Choose File > Import. Locate the Finished folder within the 05Lesson folder and select the Linearfinal.avi, Nonlinearfinal.avi, Scalerotatefinal.avi, and Travmattefinal.avi movie files while holding down the Control key. Click Open.

The final movie files are located in the Resources bin.

3 Double-click the movie files you wish to review so that they open in the Source view of the Monitor window.

4 Click the Play button (▶) in the Source view to watch the video programs.

5 You can either delete the Resources bin and the movies by clicking the Clear button (🗑) at the bottom of the Project window, or you can keep them as references as you proceed through this lesson.

Creating animation in Premiere Pro

An *animation* is different from a video, in that the motion is generated synthetically, not by shooting live action. With animation you create movement over time, giving the visual effect of motion. You can import animation clips into Premiere Pro from other software programs such as Adobe After Effects. There are also a number of ways to create animations right in Adobe Premiere Pro.

You can move, rotate, scale, and transform a still image or video clip in Premiere. But note that you can add motion only to the entire clip; you cannot animate individual elements within the clip. Yet with the use of keyframes, opacity, and other image manipulations, you can achieve some movement over time.

The motion settings in Premiere Pro let you create a motion path along which to animate any still image or video clip. Small white squares represent keyframed positions. You can specify the path to be completely within the visible area, or to extend beyond the visible area so that the clip appears to enter and exit the frame at the boundaries.

In this lesson, you'll animate a still image in several ways by creating a variety of motion paths. You'll also learn how to use motion controls along with opacity filters to enhance the animation.

Applying a motion path to a still image

Here you'll add a simple linear motion path to Logogold.psd, a layered Photoshop file that contains an alpha channel. As you may recall from Lesson 4, an alpha channel is a fourth channel in an RGB image that contains a mask (also known as a matte). The mask defines the parts of the image that are opaque, transparent, or semitransparent.

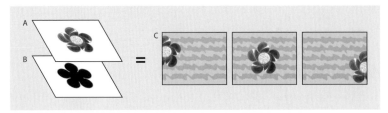

A. Photoshop file B. Alpha channel in Photoshop file
C. Alpha channel key and motion applied

You'll explore the basic aspects of motion using Sequence Ex from the previous lessons. These exercises serve as a primer for adding titles and credits, which you'll expand upon in Lesson 11, "Titles and Credits" in this *Classroom in a Book*.

1 In the Project window, double click Sequence Ex to make it the active Timeline.

2 Make sure the edit line is at 0.

3 Select Bin 01 in the Project window. Choose File > Import.

4 Locate Logogold.psd within the 05Lesson folder and click Open.

5 Click OK in the Import Layered File dialog box.

6 Drag Logogold.psd to the beginning of the Video 3 track. The still image is superimposed over a portion of Bluescreen/Storefront01.psd on the Video 2 track and Opening.avi on the Video 1 track.

7 Using the Selection tool, drag the tail of Logogold.psd, so that it snaps to the end of Opening.avi (at 00;00;06;06). This is an easy way to change the duration of a still image.

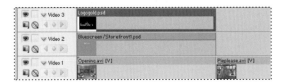

8 Make sure Logogold.psd is still selected in the Timeline so that the Motion controls are active in the Effect Controls window.

9 In the Effect Controls window, click on the Motion effect (⌷▸).

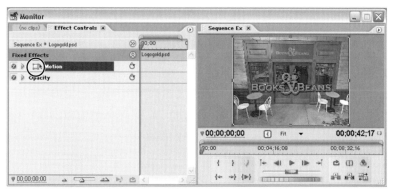

*Clicking on the Motion **icon** to the left of the Motion area or clicking on the word Motion selects the Motion effect.*

Notice that the clip appears in the Program view with handles in the corners and along the sides. These handles allow you to adjust the clip's scale, rotation, and position. These properties are calculated from the anchor point located at the clip's center. You can adjust the motion controls in the Effect Controls window or by directly manipulating the clip handles in the Program view.

10 Click on the triangle to the left of the word Motion to expand the Motion settings.

Logogold.psd is superimposed over the underlying clips in the center of the frame in the Program view, which is the default position.

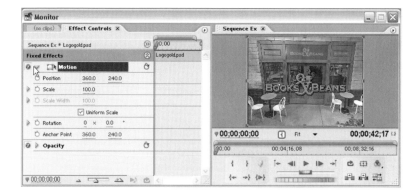

Now you'll graphically depict the motion parameters.

11 Click on the Position Toggle Animation button (⏱) to establish a keyframe at the beginning of the program.

12 First you'll move Logogold.psd off-screen and to the left by doing one of the following:

• In the Position area of the Motion settings, type -**268.8** in the first field, which represents the horizontal motion or the x coordinate.

• Click on the x coordinate and drag the hot text controls to the left until Logogold.psd reaches -268.8.

• In the Program view, drag the handles of the rectangular structure that outlines the frame to the left while holding down the Shift key until Logogold.psd is off screen.

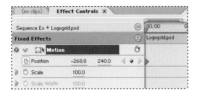

13 In the Effect Controls window, scrub the edit line to the end of the clip.

14 Click on the Add/Remove Keyframe button (◆) to set a keyframe on the last frame of the clip.

15 In the Position area, set the x coordinate to **990.1** so that Logogold.psd moves off screen and to the right.

Spacing between dots in the handles in the Program view indicates the speed between keyframes. If the spacing is wide, then the motion is slow. If the spacing is tight, then the movement is fast.

16 In the Effect Controls window, scrub through the clip to view the effect.

17 In the Timeline window, preview in Real-Time the motion effect you have just created.

Logogold.psd starts off screen from the left and travels off screen to the right.

18 Save the project.

Applying a nonlinear path to a still image

You will add a little warp or curve to the flying logo that you've just created.

1 Set the CTI to 00;00;01;09.

2 In the Effect Controls window, set the *x* coordinate to approximately **160,** which adds a keyframe. Now you have created three keyframes.

3 Click on the Motion effect ( ).

4 In the Program view, drag Logogold.psd down toward the bottom left of the frame.

5 Position the edit line in the Effect Controls window to a later point in the clip, for example, 00;00;03;28.

6 Click the Add/Remove Keyframe button ( ).

7 In the Program view of the monitor window, drag Logogold.psd toward the upper right of the frame.

Now there are four keyframes in the clip.

8 In the Effect Controls window, position the edit line at 0.

9 Render the file and preview the curve that you've just created.

10 Save the project.

Scaling, rotating, and opacity transformations in a nonlinear motion path

In this exercise you will make the Logogold.psd image appear to fly onto the wall and merge with the sign on the front of the store.

1 Make sure the Logogold.psd clip is selected in the Timeline.

2 In the Effects Control palette, click on the Go to Next Keyframe button (▶) until you locate the last keyframe on the edit line.

3 Click on the Add/Remove Keyframe button to remove the last keyframe in the clip.

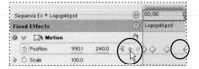

There are now three keyframes.

4 Click on the Go to Previous Keyframe button (◀).

5 Click on the Motion effect (▱▸).

6 In the Program view, position Logogold.psd so that it is centered over the sign on the storefront at approximately 365.0 in the x direction and 59.6 in the y direction.

7 In the Effect Controls window, click on the Scale Toggle Animation button (⟳) to set a keyframe for the scale transformation. It will appear beneath the position keyframe.

8 Click on the triangle to the left of the Scale Toggle Animation button to reveal the scale slider.

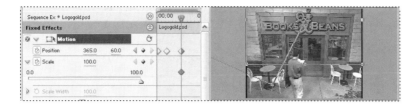

9 Drag the scale slider to the left, reducing Logogold.psd to the width of the logo on the storefront (approximately 37.6%).

10 Click on the Motion effect (⊡) and, in the Program view of the Monitor window, adjust the position of Logogold.psd until it is virtually covering its counterpart on the wall of the store.

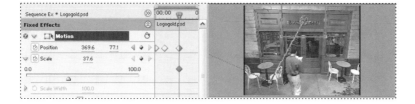

11 In the Position area, click on the Go to Previous Keyframe button to set the edit line at the middle keyframe.

12 Click on the Rotation Toggle Animation button to establish a rotation transformation.

13 Click the triangle next to the Rotation area to reveal the rotation dial.

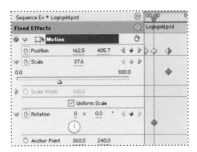

14 Use the rotation dial to twist Logogold.psd to 48.0°.

15 In the Scale area, click the Go to Next Keyframe button to locate the final keyframe, which was previously scaled to 37.6%.

16 In the Rotation field, restore the angle to 0 for the keyframe at 00;00;03;28.

17 In the Position area, click on the Go to Previous Keyframe button, twice to locate the starting frame of the clip.

18 In the Scale area add a keyframe at the beginning of the clip.

19 Drag the scale slider to 100%.

20 While still in the Scale area, click on Go to Next Keyframe button which will take you to the third keyframe.

21 In the Effect Controls window, locate the opacity controls.

22 Click on the triangle to the left of the Opacity area to reveal its settings.

23 Click on the Opacity Toggle Animation button to add an opacity keyframe in line with the third keyframe in the clip (at 00;00;03;28).

24 Drag the edit line in the Effect Controls window to the end of the clip (at 00;00;06;05).

25 Drag the opacity slider to 0.0, which will add an Opacity keyframe at the end of the clip.

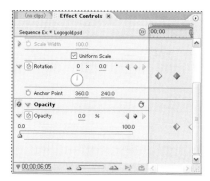

26 Preview the scale and rotation transformations.

Notice how the logo flies in, rotates, and seems to disappear into the sign on the store.

27 Save the project.

Adjusting multiple keyframes

Keyframe techniques are a very important aspect of video editing and production. In the following section you will explore three techniques for adjusting a large number of keyframes. You will use an existing project file, called Keyframe.prproj.

1 Choose File > Import.

2 Browse to the 05Lesson folder and select Keyframe.prproj. Click open.

When you open the keyframe project, a bin named Keyframe, containing the Keyframe Sequence, appears in the project window. The Keyframe Sequence contains numerous embedded keyframes in both the Position and Scale properties of the Motion settings. You will work with them now.

3 In the Project window, open the Keyframe bin.

4 Double-click the Keyframe Sequence to activate it on the Timeline.

The Keyframe Sequence displays the "Motion: Position" keyframe curve.

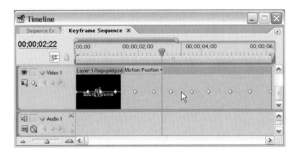

Note: *If your Timeline settings are not displaying the keyframes in the Video 1 track header area, click the Show Keyframes button. It may be useful to enlarge the track height for better viewing and easier workflow.*

5 Select the clip in the Video 1 track of the Keyframe Sequence to activate it in the Effect Controls window.

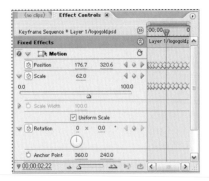

6 In the Effect Controls window, click on the Motion effect ( ). The position and scale attributes are displayed in the Program view of the Monitor window.

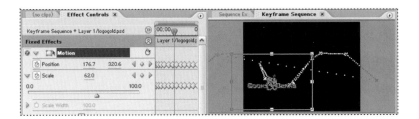

You can manipulate the position keyframes and scale keyframes interactively in three places: the Keyframe Sequence in the Timeline, the Effect Controls window, and the control points in the Program view of the Monitor window.

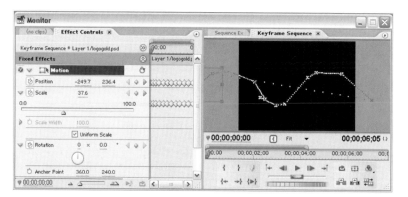

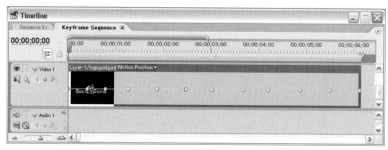

Make adjustments to some of the points along the position curve. Change the scaling along the scale path. Render, scrub, or preview as you go to edit, change, and transform these effects.

7 Save the project.

Creating a traveling matte

A matte containing motion is called a *traveling matte* or *moving matte*. The matte may consist of motion footage, such as a blue-screen silhouette, or you can animate a still image matte by applying the Motion effect in Adobe Premiere Pro. When you animate a still image, you might consider making the matte frame size larger than the project frame size so that you don't see the matte edges. In the following exercise, however, you'll need to choose the actual document size.

Because the Track Matte key can be applied to a video clip, the matte can change over time. You can create a traveling matte by using a still image with applied motion or by using a black-and-white or grayscale video clip. The motion applied to a still image can be as simple as a zoom or it can be complex, involving rotations, distortions, and delays.

Applying transparency to a traveling matte

In in this exercise, you'll apply the Track Matte Key filter to a moving image and create a traveling matte effect. In Lesson 10, you'll also apply several kinds of superimposed opacity effects in combination with virtual and duplicate clips.

When creating a track or traveling matte transparency effect, always apply the Track Matte Key to the clip located below the matte in the Timeline. Here you'll apply the Track Matte Key to Mtntop.avi so that Notmuch.avi shows through the black area (matte area) in Trackmatte.psd, which is superimposed above it.

Now you will make the matte move over time. To apply effects like Motion to the matte image (a travelling matte), you'll use a nested sequence. You'll create a new sequence and then place the matte image on a track inside that sequence for the traveling matte to function properly in Adobe Premier Pro.

1 Choose File > New > Sequence.

The new sequence dialog appears.

2 Name the sequence Travel Matte and click OK.

3 In the Project window, double-click the Travel Matte Sequence to activate it on the Timeline.

4 Choose File > Import. Locate Trackmatte.psd within the 05Lesson folder and click Open. Click OK in the Import Layered dialog box.

5 From the Project window, insert Trackmatte.psd at the start of the program on the Video 1 track.

A quick way to insert one clip into the timeline at the edit line position is to select it in the project window and type a "," (comma).

6 In the Travel Matte Sequence, click on Trackmatte.psd to activate it in the Timeline and in the Effect Controls window.

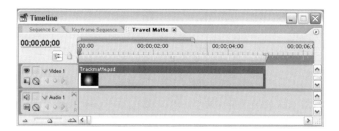

7 Choose Clip > Speed/Duration.

8 Change the clip's duration to 00;00;03;05 and click OK.

9 In the Effect Controls window, position the edit line to 0.

10 Click the triangle next to the Motion properties area.

11 Click the Position Toggle Animation button to set a keyframe at 0.

12 Click on the Scale Toggle Animation button to set a scale keyframe at 0.

13 Scale the keyframe to 150.

14 Click on the Motion effect (⬚).

15 In the Position area set the *X* coordinate to **236**.

16 Position the edit line at the end of the clip (at 00;00;03;05).

17 Click on the Add/Remove Keyframe button to add a keyframe at the last frame in the Travel Matte Sequence.

18 In the Position area, set the *x* coordinate to **524.2**.

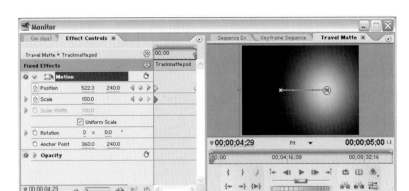

19 Preview the new Motion and Scale properties of Trackmattte.psd.

20 Save the project.

Replacing a still clip with an animated one

Now you'll replace the still track matte clip with the motion Track Matte Sequence.

1 Go to the Project window. Choose File > Import.

2 Select the TrackAnimation.prproj file in the 05Lesson folder and click Open.

The TrackAnimation project appears as a bin in the Project window.

3 Click the triangle next to the TrackAnimation bin to open it.

4 Double-click on the TrackAnimation Sequence to make it the active sequence.

5 Select Trackmatte.psd on the Video 3 track.

6 Choose Edit > Clear to remove Trackmatte.psd from TrackAnimation Sequence.

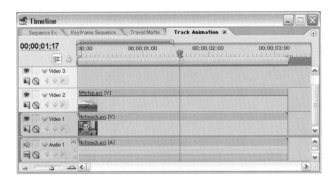

7 From the Keyframe bin in the Project window, select the TravelMatte Sequence.

8 Insert the TravelMatte Sequence at the beginning of the program on the Video 3 track.

9 In the TrackAnimation Sequence, select TravelMatte to activate it.

10 Choose Clip > Speed/Duration.

11 Type **306** for the duration if it is not already set and click OK.

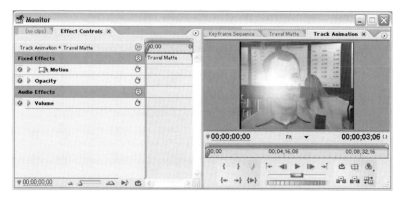

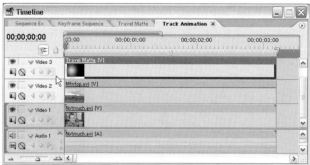

12 Choose Clip > Enable to toggle the clip to its disabled state. (Enable is deselected.)

13 Preview the Travel Matte Sequence.

14 Save the project.

In the next two lessons, you'll continue to explore the effect controls.

Exporting the movie

Now that you've finished your editing, it's time to generate a movie file.

1 If you turned off audio previewing earlier in the lesson, make sure you turn it on again by clicking the icon in the track header area of each audio track so that it changes to the speaker icon (◀)).

2 Choose File > Export > Movie.

3 In the Export Movie dialog box, click the Settings button. In the General settings, make sure that File Type is set to Microsoft DV AVI.

4 Select Entire Sequence for the Range.

5 Make sure that Export Video, Export Audio, Add to Project When Finished, and Beep When Finished are selected.

6 In the Audio section, choose 48000 Hz for Sample Rate, 16-bit for Sample Type, and Stereo for Channels.

7 Click OK to close the Export Movie Settings dialog box.

8 In the Export Movie dialog box, specify the 05Lesson folder for the location and type **05Done** for the name of the movie. Click Save.

While Premiere is making the movie, a status bar displays the time remaining to complete the process. When the movie is complete, it appears in the Project window.

9 Double-click the movie to open it into the Source view of the Monitor window.

10 Click the Play button (▶) to play the movie you've just created.

Exploring on your own

Take a few minutes to experiment with the project and try out some of your new skills. Here are some suggestions:

• Change the motion path for Logogold.psd so that it continually rotates along the path. Save the path as a file.

• At different keyframes along Trackmatte.psd's motion path, set the Motion to Accelerate and Decelerate and notice the effects.

Review questions

1 Under what circumstances would you need to use the Fill Color setting in the Motion settings?

2 When should you accelerate a motion path?

3 How do you set a keyframe on the Effect Controls timeline that matches a specific time in the clip

4 What are three different ways to add keyframes to a motion path in the Effect Controls window?

5 How do you convert a track matte to a traveling matte?

6 How do you adjust the time between two keyframes on the motion path?

Answers

1 When your clip has a colored background, such as blue.

2 When your image zooms in to a larger size.

3 First set the timecode in either the Timeline or Program view of the Monitor window.

4 Click on the Add/Remove Keyframes button; click the Toggle Animation button; change a value of a setting.

5 Add motion to the clip that has the track matte applied.

6 Move the keyframe on the Effect Controls window timeline. The farther the keyframes are from each other, the longer the time between them.

Lesson 6

6 Special Effects: Using Effect Controls

Adobe Premiere Propro provides a broad range of video and audio effects that you can use to solve problems and to enhance your video projects. When applied in nuanced and well-integrated ways, they form a wide spectrum of power at your fingertips, ready to do your magic.

To learn about using effects in Adobe Premiere Pro, you'll create a short promotional spot for the fictional bookstore cafe featured in the movie that you are editing in these lessons. Specifically, you'll learn how to do the following:

- Apply video and audio effects.
- Change effects and settings.
- Use multiple effects and change their order.
- Change effects over time using keyframes and transitions.
- Copy effects and settings from one clip to another.
- Apply an effect to part of an image.
- Use Scale together with the ZigZag effect.

Getting started

For this lesson, you'll work with an existing project in which the necessary files and the Bookstore sequence are already imported. Make sure you know the location of the files used in this lesson. For help, see "Copying the Classroom in a Book files" on page 4.

1 Launch the Premiere Pro software and click Open Project.

2 Double-click the existing project 06Lesson.prprj in the 06Lesson folder to open it.

3 Choose Window > Workspace > Effects. This lesson is practiced in the Effects Workspace.

Viewing the finished movie

To see what you'll be creating, you'll first take a look at the finished movie.

1 Create a new bin by clicking on the Bin icon (🗀). Name the bin Resources.

2 Choose File > Import. Select the Effectsfinal.wmv, Swirlfinal.avi, and Tintfinal.avi files in the Finished folder within the 06Lesson folder. Click Open.

3 Double-click the final movie that you would like to view, so that it appears in the Source view.

4 Click the Play button (▶) in the Source view in the Monitor window to watch the video program. When the movie ends, the final frame will remain visible in the Source view in the Monitor window.

5 You can either delete the final movies by selecting the Resources bin and clicking the Clear button, or you can keep it as a reference.

Why use effects?

Video and audio *effects* (known as "filters" in previous releases of Premiere) serve many useful purposes. You can use them to fix defects in video or audio material, such as correcting the color balance of a video clip or removing background noise from dialogue. Effects are also used to create qualities not present in the raw video or audio, such as softening focus or giving a scene a sunset tint, or adding reverb or echo to a sound track.

You can add an effect to a clip at any time, and even apply the same effect multiple times to a single clip with different settings. By default, when you apply an effect to a clip, the effect is active for the duration of the clip. However, by using keyframes, you can make the effect start and stop at specific times, or make the effect more or less intense over time.

🖳 *For more information, see "Applying Effects > Video effects" or "Applying Effects > Audio effects" on the Adobe Web site at* (www.adobe.com).

Many of the video and audio effects in Adobe Premiere Pro are different from those included in earlier releases of the software. In fact, to enhance compatibility, many of the older versions' effects (filters) have been replaced with effects developed for Adobe After Effects software.

After Effects is another professional video production program from Adobe. Premiere Pro shares many software filters with After Effects that add powerful dynamics to any project.

Getting to know the Effects workspace

The Effects mode is designed for easy access to both audio and video effects. You'll begin by opening the Effects workspace and becoming familiar with its components.

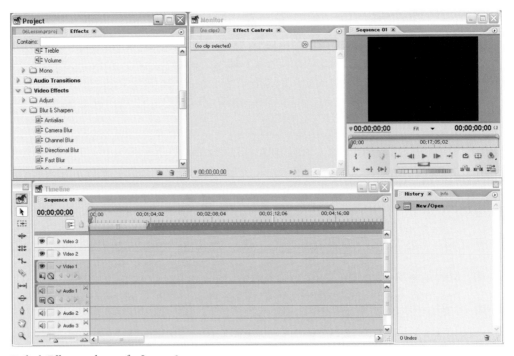

Default Effects workspace for Lesson 6

When you choose Window > Workspace > Effects, Premiere Pro sets up the following conditions:

• In the Monitor window, Single View is displayed. Clips open in a separate Clip window.

• The Info palette and the Effect Controls window are grouped into one palette window.

• The Navigator, History, and Commands palettes are grouped into another palette window.

• The Video Effects, Audio Effects, and Transitions palettes are grouped into a third palette window.

How effects are organized

All effects are stored in the Audio Effects palette and the Video Effects palette, grouped by type. For example, all video effects that create a blur are grouped within a Blurs folder in the Video Effects palette. You can customize the palettes by creating new folders. For instance, you can group effects that you use frequently or group effects that you rarely use. You can also change settings to show or hide a folder or an effect.

Note: You use the same tools to organize or manipulate folders in either palette.

Using effects from other Adobe programs

Adobe Premiere Pro includes many effects from Adobe After Effects in the Effects palette. With practice, you can turn these effects (filters) and plug-ins into powerful development tools for your productions. You'll also be using files created in Adobe Photoshop and Adobe Illustrator.

The next lesson is made up of exercises for integrating these external programs into Premiere. In this lesson and throughout this entire *Classroom in a Book*, there are many instances of this integration.

For more information on special effects, see Lesson 7 of this book or the *Adobe Premiere Pro User Guide*.

Applying effects

An effect can be added to a clip that is already in the Timeline window, or the effect can be dragged to the Effect Controls window if the clip is selected in the Timeline. Effects can be added to clips or removed at any time. You apply video effects and audio effects in the same way: you select the clip and you apply a selected effect. Video effects are listed in the Video Effects dialog box; audio effects are listed in the Audio Effects dialog box. A clip that has an effect applied to it appears with a blue-green bar at the top of it in the Timeline window. An effect can be modified after it has been applied. For instance, it is easy to make adjustments after you preview an effect.

After you've applied effects to a clip, you can temporarily turn off one or all of those effects to concentrate on another aspect of your project. Effects that are turned off do not appear in the Program window and are not included when the clip is previewed or rendered. Turning off an effect does not delete the keyframes created for any of the effect's settings; all keyframes remain until the effect is changed or deleted from the clip.

In this exercise, you'll apply effects to create a monochrome appearance, using a brown tint that will be applied to a number of clips. Three video effects are used to achieve this result: Black & White, Color Replace, and Tint. You'll start by applying the Tint effect to the Pie.avi clip.

Before you begin working on effects for this project, mute the audio tracks to avoid the distraction of audio while previewing the video effects.

1 In the Project window, double-click the Tint Sequence to make it the active sequence on the Timeline.

2 Click the speaker icon ( ) on the left side of the Audio 1 track so that the speaker icon disappears. The blank box indicates that the audio is muted for that Audio track.

Audio 1 track is muted;
Audio 2 track is not.

3 Double-click Pie.avi in the Timeline to open it in the Source view, and then click Play to preview it.

For this project, you want this clip to resemble an old photograph, using a brown tint to simulate the sepia tone of early photographic prints. As you apply effects to the clip, it will be helpful to keep the original clip displayed in the Source window so that you can compare it to the preview image in the Program view.

4 In the Contains field of the Video Effects palette, type **Tint**. The Tint effect is located and displayed.

5 Drag the Tint effect to the Pie.avi clip in the Timeline window. Or, if the Pie.avi clip is selected in the Timeline window, drag the Tint effect to the Effect Controls window.

6 Click on the triangle next to Tint to reveal its settings.

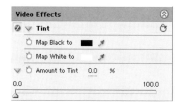

7 In the Effect Controls window, click the Map Black Color box to open the Color Picker dialog box.

8 Select a medium-dark brown color for your tint or type in the following values to match the final movie: (Red: **85**, Green: **42**, and Blue: **0**). Click OK to close the Color Picker dialog box.

9 Do one of the following to set the Tint Amount to 93%:

• Drag the Level slider to 93%.

• In the Effect Controls window, click in the text field, type **93**, and click OK.

10 Preview or render-scrub to preview this effect by dragging in the Timeline ruler while holding down the Alt key.

11 Save the project.

When compared to the original image in the Source view of the Clip window, you should see a brown tint applied over a color image in the Program view of the Clip window, especially in white areas. Notice the blue-green bar along the top of the clip indicator in the Timeline. This indicates that an effect has been applied to the clip.

Applying effects in the correct order

When you apply multiple effects to one or more clips, the order in which you apply them can affect the final result. If a clip has multiple effects applied, the Effect Controls window identifies them in an ordered list. They are rendered from this list, in order, from the top to the bottom. You can reorder the list to change the sequence in which the effects are rendered. In this exercise, you'll change the render order.

Now, you'll add an additional effect to the Pie.avi clip. You'll apply the Black & White effect to strip out the original color from the clip, making it look more like an early black-and-white photograph.

1 In the Contains field of the Video Effects window, type in **Black & White**.

The Black & White effect is located and displayed.

2 Drag the Black & White effect to the Pie.avi clip in the Timeline window, or if the Pie.avi clip is selected in the Timeline window, drag the Black & White effect to the Effect Controls window.

3 Play back or render-scrub to preview the result of both effects by dragging the edit line in the Timeline ruler while holding down the Alt key.

Now, instead of seeing the brown tint over a black-and-white image, you see only the black-and-white image. This is because the Black & White effect removed all color from the image. Ordering the effect sequence is important. It's easy to put these effects in the right order.

4 With Pie.avi still selected, click the triangle next to each effect to collapse the settings in the Effect Controls window.

5 In the Effect Controls window, click the Tint effect and drag it to its new location on the list, below the Black & White effect.

6 Play back or render-scrub to preview the result of both effects by dragging the edit line in the Timeline ruler while holding down the Alt key.

This time when you preview the clip, you see a brown tint over a black-and-white image. This is just what you want. Now, you'll add the last effect to this clip. You'll change highlights of a color by applying the Color Replace effect.

Customizing an effect

Some Premiere effects can be customized. If an effect can be customized, the Setup option appears next to the effect. You can click Setup for that effect to open its specific Settings dialog box. The settings you choose here apply to the first keyframe of a clip (if you change settings for other keyframes in the same clip) or apply to the entire clip (if you make no changes to a keyframe).

Note: If you use effects in a Premiere Pro project that are created in After Effects, that effect must be customized in the Effect Controls window, not in the Audio Effects or Video Effects palette.

1 In the Contains field of the Video Effects palette, type in **Color Replace**.

2 The Color Replace effect is located and displayed.

3 Drag the Color Replace effect to the Pie.avi clip in the Timeline window. Or, if the Pie.avi clip is selected in the Timeline window, drag the Color Replace effect to the Effect Controls window.

4 The Setup option (⇥▣) appears next to this effect, indicating that the Color Replace effect can be customized. Click Setup to open the Color Replace Settings dialog box.

The settings you choose in the Color Replace Settings dialog box apply to the entire clip if you make no changes to any keyframe later in the clip. Alternatively, the settings you choose here apply to the first keyframe if you change the effect settings for other keyframes in the clip.

To establish which color you'll replace, you'll use the eyedropper tool (🖊) in the Color Replace Settings dialog box.

5 Position the pointer in the Clip Sample image so that it turns into the eyedropper icon (🖊). Move the eyedropper over the bright area in the pie plate. Click to capture the color.

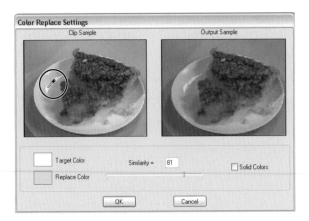

6 Now, click the Replace Color swatch to access the Color Picker. Then, click a light golden color. Or type in these values: Red: **255**, Green: **178**, Blue: **115** to replace your first color selection. Click OK.

Now, you'll set the Similarity slider to indicate the range of colors to be replaced, based on their similarity to the color you selected. This setting determines the smoothness of the transition from original colors to the replaced color.

7 Using the Similarity slider in the Color Replace Settings, set Similarity to about **83**. Click OK to close the Color Replace Settings dialog box and to apply the settings.

8 Preview the cumulative color effects of the effects you just applied. Play back or render-scrub to preview the result of all three effects by dragging the edit line in the Timeline ruler while holding down the Alt key.

9 Save the project.

Copying effects, keyframes, and settings

Once you have set up and applied one or more effects to a clip, you may want to use the same effects and settings on other clips. Doing this manually would be a lot of work, but there is a much easier way. Using the Paste Attributes command, you can apply identical effects and settings to any number of clips. You'll use this technique to copy the effects from Pie.avi in the Tint Sequence to Bookstore.avi and apply them to Bookstore2.avi, Bookstore3.avi, and Bookstore3-split.avi.

1 Make sure Pie.avi in the Tint Sequence is still selected in the Timeline. Choose Edit > Copy.

2 Double-click the Bookstore Sequence to make it the active Timeline.

3 In the Timeline window, hold down the Shift key and select Bookstore.avi and Bookstore2.avi and choose Edit > Paste Attributes.

4 Click Paste.

5 Preview Bookstore.avi and Bookstore2.avi by render-scrubbing in the Timeline ruler while holding down the Alt key.

The effects you originally applied to Pie.avi are now also applied to Bookstore1.avi and Bookstore2.avi, along with the settings you selected. You also need to apply the same effects to Bookstore3.avi and Bookstore3-split.avi.

6 In the Timeline window, drag the selection tool over Bookstore3.avi and Bookstore3-split.avi in the Timeline to select them, or click on them while holding down the shift key.

Because you have not used the Copy command since you copied Bookstore.avi, the Paste Attributes command still contains the effects and settings from that clip. You can simply use the Paste Attributes command to reuse these settings.

7 Choose Edit > Paste Attributes.

The effects and settings from Bookstore.avi have been applied to the clips you selected, so the last four clips in the project now have identical effects and settings.

8 Preview the project, or render-scrub in the Timeline ruler while holding down the Alt key.

9 Save the project.

Changing effects over time

Some Premiere effects change dynamically; some change over time. Effects that change dynamically use *keyframes* to tell them when to make changes. Effects that don't have settings associated with them, such as the Black & White effect, don't need or use keyframes, so they can't be changed in this way.

For effects that don't use keyframes, you can often create change over time using transitions, although this technique is not as flexible nor as precise as using keyframes.

Changing effects using keyframes

A keyframe is a marker in time that contains a video effect's settings for a specific point in a clip. By default, Premiere Pro creates a beginning and ending keyframe when you apply an effect to a clip. But, you can change the keyframes to have the effect change gradually over time.

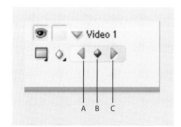

A. Go to Previous Keyframe
B. Add/Remove Keyframe
C. Go to Next Keyframe

Each effect has a default keyframe at the beginning and end of the clip, indicated by half-diamonds on the keyframe line in the Timeline window. If an effect has adjustable controls, you can change the start or end time of the effect or add additional keyframes to create an animated effect. If you don't make any changes to the default keyframes, the settings for the associated effect apply to the entire clip.

After you add an effect to a clip, the effect is listed in the effect properties menu that appears after the name of the clip in the Timeline window. This menu displays each of the applied effects. If the effect has adjustable controls, you can set keyframes for it in the keyframe line. The keyframe line for an audio file can display effect, volume, or pan keyframes. To display effect keyframes for either type of clip, click the Show Keyframes button ( ) in the track header area and choose Show Keyframes for video or Show Clip Keyframes for audio.

When you add more than one effect to a clip, a menu of effects that have been applied to it appears at the right of the name of the clip on the Timeline.

Applying the Replicate effect

Now you'll use the Replicate effect to add an effect to Bookstore3-split.avi, and use keyframes to indicate when the effect starts and what its settings are at that point. Then, you'll use another keyframe to change the effect again at a different point in time.

1 Select Bookstore3-split.avi in the Timeline window and make sure the Effect Controls window is showing.

2 In the Contains field of the Video Effects palette, type in **Replicate**.

3 The Replicate effect is located and displayed.

4 Drag the Replicate effect to the Bookstore3-split.avi clip in the Timeline window, or if the Bookstore3-split.avi clip is selected in the Timeline window, drag the Replicate effect to the Effect Controls window.

5 The Setup option appears next to the Replicate effect on the Effect Controls window. Click Setup to open the Replicate Settings dialog box.

The settings you choose in the Replicate Settings dialog box apply to the first keyframe (if you change settings for other keyframes) or to the entire clip (if you make no changes to any keyframe).

6 In the Replicate Settings dialog box, drag the slider to see the different effects created by varying the settings for this effect. Set the slider back to the 2-by-2 format as shown here, and then click OK to close the dialog box.

To create and position keyframes and edit their settings in Premiere Pro, you use the keyframe line in the Timeline window or the timeline representation in the Effect Controls window. The appearance of a keyframe icon depends on where it is on the track. The default (first and last) keyframes are white rectangles (□) that rest at the edges of the clip. By default, the first and last keyframes are active when you select an effect. Once you add additional keyframes (◇), the initial keyframes become white half-diamonds. Once you move the keyframes from the edges, they become full diamonds. The first keyframe is gray on the left half (◈), and the last keyframe is gray on the right half (◈).

Because you want the effect to start near the head of the clip, you'll add the first keyframe on the keyframe timeline at that point. Then you'll add a new keyframe and change its effect settings. Finally, you'll change the settings for the last keyframe.

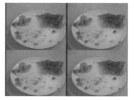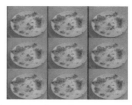

The Replicate effect will change at keyframes along the keyframe timeline, from one image to four to nine.

7 In the Timeline window, click the triangle to the left of the Video 1 track label to expand the track and display the keyframe line.

8 Position the edit line at the first frame of Bookstore3-split.avi.

9 Click on the Count Toggle Animation button ( ) to add a keyframe there for the count of **2**.

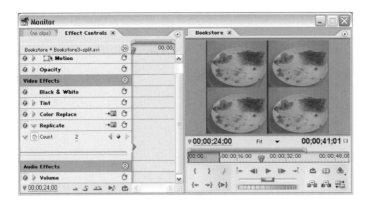

Next, you'll create a new keyframe and set the Replicate effect value for that keyframe.

10 Position the edit line about two-thirds of the way toward the end of the clip at about 00;00;29;12.

11 Click the Add/Remove Keyframe button ( ) in the Count field to create a keyframe there.

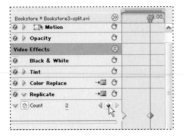

12 In the Effect Controls window, click the Setup button to open the Replicate Settings dialog box. The Replicate Settings dialog box opens with the same settings as the previous keyframe.

13 Drag the slider so that the preview shows the 3-by-3 format, and then click OK.

Once you insert a keyframe for an effect other than the beginning or the end keyframes, the Effect Enabled icon (⊘) appears next to the effect name in the Effect Controls window, and the beginning and end keyframe symbols change into triangles. A grey triangle points in the direction where there is no effect established.

14 Preview this effect, or scrub in the Timeline, while holding down the Alt key.

The Replicate effect applied to Bookstore3-split.avi maintains four images throughout the first two-thirds of the clip. At that point it changes from four images to nine images.

15 Save the project.

Changing effects using transitions

Some effects do not include keyframes, so to change the effect over time, you can use a transition to accomplish the same thing. Simply position the transition (usually a cross dissolve) between two versions of the same clip that are identical except for the effect settings.

This method of changing an effect over time works best with certain effects such as those that control image quality, such as hue, saturation, and contrast.

Here, you'll use a cross-dissolve transition to fade changes in the Bookstore3-split.avi clip over time, returning the very first instance of Bookstore.avi to its original color. In this case, you need to use a transition to make the change, because the Black & White effect applied to one of the clips involved cannot be changed dynamically with keyframes.

1 Position the edit line in the Timeline at 00;00;32;05— the cut between Bookstore3-split.avi and Bookstore4.avi.

2 Bookstore3-split.avi and Bookstore4.avi are almost the exact same duration.

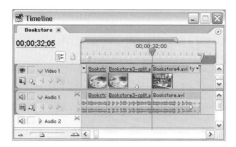

Now, you'll make a smooth lingering cross dissolve between Bookstore3-split.avi, with its four effects, and Bookstore4.avi in its original form.

3 In the Transitions palette, click the Dissolve folder and locate the Cross Dissolve transition.

4 Click the Transitions palette menu, located in the top right corner of the palette, and choose Set Default Transition if it is not currently set.

5 Next, check the Default Transition Duration by selecting that line in the menu.

The Preferences > General box appears.

6 Be certain that the Video Transition Default Duration does not exceed 190 frames. In a little while, you'll adjust it into a very long dissolve in the Effect Controls window.

Note: It's highly unlikely that yours will be set even higher than 60 frames at this point, but whatever duration you have will be changed soon.

7 Drag the Cross Dissolve transition from the Transitions palette to the Video 1 Transition track, placing it at the edit line so that it starts at the cut between the two clips at the current time indicator.

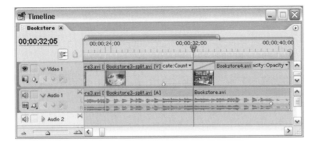

8 Click on the transition on the Timeline, then go to the Effect Controls window to adjust it.

9 Duration should be set to 00;00;06;10 (190 frames = 6 seconds x 30 frames +10 frames).

10 Alignment should be set to Start at Cut.

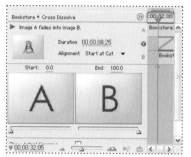
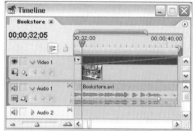

11 Preview Bookstore3-split.avi and Bookstore4.avi.

The Bookstore4.avi clip changes gradually over the duration of the clip from yellow highlights on brown shadows into full color.

12 Save the project.

Using the Scale, Rotate, and ZigZag effects

Next, you'll animate a still image by applying the Position, Scale, and Rotation effects within the Motion controls to create a pan zoom, and applying the ZigZag effect to add a swirling motion. These effects can be set to change gradually over time, in contrast to the Replicate effect you used earlier in this lesson, which can be changed only in discrete steps.

A Swirl sequence must be assembled for you to use in this lesson. You'll set up a number of actions to be initiated at the start of the sequence, which will establish several keyframes there: for Position and Scale and ZigZag. Later, you'll plot the moment in time for the scene to start spinning. Then, all effects will culminate at the same keyframe on the Out point of Always.avi.

1 In the Project window, select the Swirl sequence and double-click it to activate it in the Timeline.

2 In the timeline, select Always.avi and then go to the Effect Controls window.

3 Click on the Motion effect (⬚⬀)so that the handles appear around the image in the Program monitor. You'll reposition the image later.

4 Click on the triangle next to the Motion effect.

5 Add a keyframe at the In point of Always.avi on the Position controls by selecting the Toggle Animation button (♡) to the left of the name Position.

6 Add a keyframe at the In point of Always.avi on the Scale controls by selecting the Toggle animation button (♡) to the left of the name Scale.

When you shoot film or video, panning refers to the movement of the camera from side-to-side or up-and-down, either to follow a subject or so that the subject moves across the frame. Zooming refers to the movement of the camera (or camera lens) so that the subject progressively appears larger in the frame (closer to the camera), or smaller in the frame (farther away). You can use effects in post-production to simulate panning and zooming with the camera. In Premiere, you use the Scale and Position controls to simulate panning or to crop a clip.

Animate the image with the ZigZag effect.

7 In the Contains field of the Effects palette, type **ZigZag**. The ZigZag effect is displayed in the distort directory.

8 Select the ZigZag effect and drag it either to Always.avi on the Timeline or into the Effect Controls palette.

9 The ZigZag Settings box appears.

Now, you'll select the settings for the first keyframe, at the In point of Always.avi.

10 In the ZigZag Settings box, type **0** for Amount (represents the magnitude of distortion), type **1** for Ridges (represents the number of direction reversals of the zigzag from the center of the clip to its edge), and set Style to Around Center (which rotates pixels around the center of the clip). With these settings, the effect will have little or no effect on the clip. Click OK to close the ZigZag Settings box.

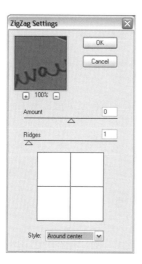

11 Add a keyframe at the In point of Always.avi on the ZigZag > Amount controls by selecting the Toggle animation button (⟳) to the left of the name Amount.

12 Add a keyframe at the In point of Always.avi on the ZigZag > Ridges controls by selecting the Toggle animation button (⏱) to the left of the name Ridges.

There are four keyframes set at the start of the Timeline.

Now, you'll select the settings for the ending keyframes in these effects. You'll work your way back up the Effect Controls window.

13 Move the timeline indicator in the Effect Controls window to the last frame of the Always.avi clip (00;00;09;00).

14 Add a keyframe at the Out point of Always.avi on the ZigZag > Ridges controls by clicking the Add/Remove Keyframe button (◈) to the right of the name Ridges.

15 Add a keyframe at the Out point of Always.avi on the ZigZag > Amount controls by clicking the Add/Remove Keyframe button (◈) to the right of the name Amount.

16 In the Effect Controls window, click the Setup icon to open the ZigZag Settings dialog box again.

17 Type **75** for Amount, type **15** for Ridges. Click OK to close the ZigZag dialog box.

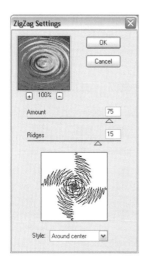

18 In the Scale control, increase the value to **290**, which will also set the end keyframe for it.

Note: the Scale slider will only go to a maximum of 100%, whereas, with the text controls, you can dial in or drag the percentage as high as 600%.

19 In the Position controls, increase the "X" (horizontal, left text field) value to **465,** and the "Y" (vertical, right text field) value to **24,** which will also set the end keyframe for it.

All is set except for an added twist to be derived from spinning the whole image along with that which will come from the ZigZag settings.

20 Click on the Toggle animation button next to the name Rotation, which will set an end keyframe for Rotation. In the number of times requested to rotate (the left text field), set the value to **1**; and in the right text field for angle of rotation, set it to one full revolution of **359.9** degrees. (You can input or use the dragging method to set it to **360**, and Premiere Pro will change it to the final value.)

21 The Rotation will commence late in the sequence, so set the current time indicator to 00;00;07;02.

22 In the Rotation controls area, add an initiating keyframe to set the final piece of the swirling puzzle by changing both the number of revolutions and angle back to **0** (zero).

23 Preview the effect you just applied or use render-scrub.

The image in Always.avi pans and zooms in while the ZigZag effect gradually intensifies, and the whole images rotates.

24 Save the project.

Applying audio effects

Audio effects and video effects are applied in about the same way. Here, you'll first remove noise from an audio clip, and then add some reverberation to the same clip.

1 Make Bookstore the active sequence on the Timeline.

2 Press Page Up or Page Down on the keyboard to set the edit line at the In point of Bookstore.avi (00;00;08;00).

3 Drag Audioeffect.wav from the Project window into the Audio 2 track so that its In point snaps to the edit line.

Note: You muted the Audio 1 track earlier in this lesson. It is best to leave it muted until the last effect is completed in the Audio 2 track.

4 Check that the box on the far left of the Audio 2 track is selected so that the speaker icon (◀ᵢ)) appears.

5 Preview Audioeffect.wav by moving the edit line to the beginning of the clip and pressing the Play button under the Program view. Notice the constant noise in the clip.

The Notch effect in Premiere can be used to remove or reduce hum (low-frequency noise) or another single-frequency noise in an audio clip. You'll use the Notch effect to remove noise from the Audioeffect.wav clip.

6 In the Contains field of the Effects palette, type **Notch**.

7 The Notch effect is displayed in three directories.

8 Select the Notch effect for Stereo tracks, and drag it to the Audioeffect.wav clip in the Timeline window. Or, if the Audioeffect.wav is selected in the Timeline window, drag the Notch effect to the Effect Controls window.

9 Open the triangle next to the name Notch, and then the Notch > Center controls after that.

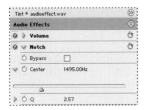

10 Click the Preview sound box (▸). Premiere plays a short loop of audio from the audio track.

The frequency of the noise in Audioeffect.wav is 800 Hz.

11 Drag the Center slider in the Notch to **9.99**, then try random settings less than 800 Hz in the effect and listen to the audio preview.

Notice that at the effect setting of 800 Hz, the noise is reduced. Set the effect just below 800 Hz.

12 Using the Center slider, set it to **770.43** Hz in the Hz field.

"Q" Specifies the range of frequencies to be affected. A low setting creates a narrow band; a high setting creates a wide band.

13 Set the Q slider to **0.12**.

14 Preview Audioeffect.wav again. The noise is now nearly inaudible. Also notice that the audio sounds flat.

Add some life to it by adding reverberation to the same audio clip. The Reverb effect simulates sound bouncing off hard surfaces in either a medium-size room or a large room.

15 In the Timeline window, select Audioeffect.wav.

16 In the Contains field of the Video Effects palette, type in **Reverb**. The Reverb effect is located and displayed.

17 Drag the Stereo Reverb effect to the Audioeffect.wav clip in the Timeline window. Or, if the Audioeffect.wav is selected in the Timeline window, drag the Reverb effect to the Effect Controls palette.

18 Click the triangle next to the name Reverb to open it, then the Custom Setup triangle as well. Graphical effect controls are displayed in the Custom Setup controls area.

19 On the far right of the Reverb name bar is a menu for selecting the size of the room being emulated in the effect. Select Medium room.

20 Set the other pods as follows, and then adjust according to taste and wow factors you want to achieve:

• Set Absorption to **10.00%**.

• Set Size to **80.00%**.

• Set Density to **100.00%**.

• Set Lo Damp to **-6.00 dB**.

• Set Hi Damp to **-6.00 dB**.

- Set Mix to **50.00%**.

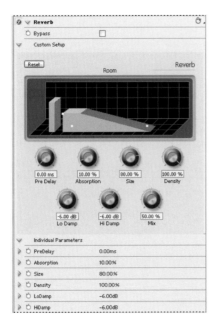

21 Preview Audioeffect.wav, which the video portion covers.

22 Turn on the audio on the Audio 1 track, and preview the entire Bookstore sequence.

You have just improved the quality of the sound in your project significantly! You have also completed the first lesson in effects. In the next lesson, you'll work with effects imported from other Adobe products.

23 Save the project.

Exporting the movie

Now that you've finished your editing, it's time to generate a movie file.

1 If you turned off audio previewing earlier in the lesson, make sure you turn it on again by clicking the icon in the track header area of each audio track so that it changes to the speaker icon (◀).

2 Choose File > Export > Movie.

3 In the Export Movie dialog box, click the Settings button. In the General settings, make sure that File Type is set to Microsoft DV AVI.

4 Select Entire Project for the Range.

5 Make sure that Export Video, Export Audio, Add to Project When Finished, and Beep When Finished are selected.

6 In the Audio section, choose 48000 Hz for Sample Rate, 16-bit for Sample Type, and Stereo for Channels.

7 Click OK to close the Export Movie Settings dialog box.

8 In the Export Movie dialog box, specify the 06Lesson folder for the location and type **06Done** for the name of the movie. Click Save.

While Premiere is making the movie, a status bar displays the time remaining to complete the process. When the movie is complete, it appears in the Project window.

9 Double-click the movie to open it into the Source view of the Monitor window.

10 Click the Play button (▶) to play the movie you've just created.

Exploring on your own

Feel free to experiment with the project you have just created and to explore various ways of working with the Audio Effects and Video Effects palettes. Here are some suggestions:

• Create and name a new folder in the Video Effects palette, using the palette menu or the New Folder button in the palette. Drag some of your favorite effects into the folder.

• Select a folder in the Audio Effects palette that you don't expect to use frequently, and use Hide Selected in the palette menu to dim the folder. Now, use the Hide Hidden command in the palette menu to hide the folder.

• Find effects to reverse an image (left-to-right), invert an image (top-to-bottom), and reverse a clip (front-to-back).

• Try this method of making an effect start changing at an exact point in a clip. Select a keyframe either by clicking it, using the keyframe navigator to move the edit line to it, or manually positioning the edit line on it. Specify where you want the change to start by making your changes using the available settings controls.

• Split a clip into a number of equal-size segments, using the razor tool, and then apply an effect to every other segment, using Paste Attributes and Paste Attributes Again.

Review questions

1 How can you tell if an effect has been applied to a clip?

2 What does a keyframe contain?

3 Why would you need to use a transition to change an effect over time?

4 What is the quickest method of applying identical effects and settings to multiple clips?

5 What does the speaker icon do in the Timeline window?

Answers

1 A blue-green bar is displayed at the top of the clip in the Timeline.

2 A keyframe contains the values for all the controls in the effect and applies those values to the clip at the specified time.

3 Effects that do not use keyframes can be changed over time only by using a transition.

4 Using the Paste Attributes command is the quickest way to apply identical effects and settings to multiple clips.

5 The speaker icon can be used to mute the audio track or unmute it.

Lesson 7

Integrating Adobe After Effects, Photoshop, and Illustrator with Premiere Pro

Interactivity and communication between video and graphics programs outside of Adobe Premiere Pro makes a complex production easier to pull together. User-friendly and Premiere Pro-compatible imports from other sources provide a range of creative possibilities for making sparkling motion pictures.

Adobe Premiere Pro can act as a server to other video and graphics programs. In this lesson you'll edit an important scene in your movie and use methods shared from other programs. You'll learn to do the following:

- Use effects found in other Adobe video programs.
- Create effects in a style consistent with Adobe After Effects.
- Apply multiple effects to the same footage.
- Use the Pen tool to make keyframes and transitions.
- Copy and adjust keyframes from one clip to another.
- Use the Radial Blur and Image Matte effects.

Getting started

For this lesson, you'll create a new project. Be sure you know the location of the files used in this lesson. Insert the DVD-ROM disk if necessary. For help, see "Copying the Classroom in a Book files" on page 4 of this *Classroom in a Book*.

1 Launch the Premiere Pro software.

2 Click New Project.

3 Click on Browse and locate the directory called C:\PrPro_CIB\07Lesson and click OK.

4 In the Name field, type **07Lesson** and click OK.

5 Create a new bin by either clicking the Bin icon (📁) at the bottom of the Project window or clicking the menu triangle button at the top right corner of the Project window and choosing New Bin.

6 In the Project window, click on the Bin 01 folder icon.

7 Choose File > Import.

8 Navigate to the 07Lesson folder and click Open.

9 Select Admire1.avi, Admire2.avi, Admire3.avi, Aged.avi, Baby.avi, Embrace.avi, Entrance.avi, Kiss.avi, Propose.avi, Tomb.avi, and Wedding.avi while holding down the Control key.

10 Click Open.

11 Choose Window > Workspace > Effects. This lesson uses the Effects Workspace.

Viewing the finished movie

To see what you'll be creating, you'll first take a look at the finished movie.

1 In the Project window, create a new bin and name it **Resources**.

2 Click the triangle next to the Resources bin to open the bin. Then choose File > Import and select the 07Final.avi file in the Finished folder within the 07Lesson folder. Click Open.

The 07Final.mov file is located in the Resources bin.

3 Double-click the 07Final.avi file so that it opens in the Source view of the Monitor window.

4 Click the Play button (▶) in the Source view in the Monitor window to watch the video program.

Using effects from other Adobe programs

Throughout the lessons in this book, you'll work with a number of video and audio effects. Some of them were first developed for Adobe After Effects, a professional editing system that is a powerful companion of Premiere Pro. Combined, the two programs provide a producer with a myriad of options for creating theatrical, broadcast, and commercial motion pictures.

Add the ability to import files from Adobe Photoshop and Illustrator and the scope broadens even more. The early 1990s unveiled the advent of 3-D animation special effects, known in the entertainment industry as computer generated imagery (CGI). Virtually every movie and television commercial requires the use of CGI. The graphics programs from Adobe are used by studios around the world to achieve convincing special effects in either subtle or spectacular ways.

You can move easily between Adobe Premiere Pro and Adobe After Effects because they work similarly. Import layered Adobe Photoshop files as flattened clips, or as Timelines with each layer on a separate track. Export projects as AVI and MPEG files for use in Adobe Encore DVD, a creative tool for authoring sophisticated multilanguage DVDs. Timeline markers from Adobe Premiere Pro become DVD chapter points.

For information on how to use Adobe Premiere Pro with Adobe Photoshop and Adobe Illustrator files, see the section on "Importing still images" in the *Adobe Premiere Pro User Guide*. For information about using chapter marks for use in Adobe Encore, see the section on "Using markers" in the *Adobe Premiere Pro User Guide* and Lesson 14, "Working with Adobe DVD Encore," in this book.

For more information on special effects, see Lesson 6 of this book and "Applying Effects" in the *Adobe Premiere Pro User Guide*.

Creating effects with Adobe Photoshop files

When *Books & Beans* was shot to digital video tape, the set was a former coffee store. The facade of the building was simply painted green. All of the signs were removed when the business closed. You may have noticed in the final movie file that there are signs on the front green wall of the store. The signs were created by applying effects and opacity attributes to a layered Photoshop file.

With this flexibility, you can create colorful and creative images outside of Premiere Pro, and then utilize all of the special aspects of the image when it is animated or embedded into a Premiere project.

Creating effects with Adobe Illustrator files

In a similar manner, you can import outlined, vector illustration art from Adobe Illustrator into Premiere Pro. In fact, the logo for *Books & Beans* was originally designed in Illustrator, rendered into Photoshop as a layer, where it was tweaked before it was implemented in the production of the set decoration of the store.

Illustrator is a superior matte generating program that has been used in Premiere for many years. It is especially suited to creating complex angles and making changes to curved objects.

For more information on using Adobe After Effects, Photoshop, and Illustrator, see the *Adobe After Effects User Guide*.

After Effects and Photoshop "inside" Premiere Pro

It is very straightforward to import a clip rendered in After Effects into Premiere Pro. That would not give you, however, much of a look at its potential. To gain insight into how After Effects differs from Premiere Pro, you'll build a scene with many clips in the "After Effects style." Using a different track for each clip in the sequence, you'll create transitions and effects using keyframes.

Adobe Photoshop is used widely by artists of all disciplines. Photoshop files are implemented into Premiere Pro as either flat or layered compositions. Depending on whether or not the Photoshop file has layers, or mattes, or is a flat bitmap file, you can use it for masking superimposed clips.

In the following scene, the girl of Hero's dreams enters the store, where Hero falls immediately into a reverie about her and himself. You've already imported the clips into Bin 01. These fantasy clips were individually rendered in After Effects using a Screen filter to "burn out" the images.

1 In the Project window, locate Sequence 01 and rename it **Entrance**.

You'll add eight video tracks to the Timeline default number of three, because you have eleven clips to affect.

2 In the track header area of the Video 3 track, right click and choose Add Tracks.

The Add Tracks dialog box appears.

3 In the Video Tracks field, type **8**.

4 For Placement, choose After Last Track.

5 Click OK.

There are now eleven video tracks in the Entrance sequence.

6 From the Project window, drag Admire1.avi to the Video 1 track at the start of the sequence.

7 In the Timeline window, press Page Down to advance the edit line to the end of Admire1.avi (at 00;00;01;04).

To manage your tracks, you may choose to rename them to correspond to the name of the clip on them. In the track header area of the Video 1 track, right-click the name and choose Rename. In the selected name field for the track, type **Admire1**, *and so forth.*

8 In the Project window, select Entrance.avi and drag it to the Video 2 track so that its In point is at the current time indicator (at 00;00;01;04).

9 Set the edit line 15 frames from the tail of Entrance.avi to 00;00;05;26 (6.11 - 15 = 5.26). This will be the first instance of overlapping clips.

10 From the Project window, insert Admire2.avi at the edit line on the Video 3 track.

This manner of trimming clips is commonly used in After Effects. The first 15 frames of Admire2.avi superimpose Entrance.avi, because Admire2.avi is on the next track or layer. Later you'll actually trim it to achieve the final effect in the sequence.

As you may recall from the final movie, several key timing issues need to be addressed as you proceed. The fourth clip begins the quick succession of cross dissolves that characterize Hero's fantasy life upon seeing Dreams for the first time.

11 Shuttle the current time indicator to the end of Admire2.avi (at 00;00;08;00).

12 Insert Embrace.avi on the Video 4 track at the edit line.

13 Excess black frames were rendered into Embrace.avi. Move the current time indicator (CTI) to the location where the black frames begin.

14 Trim the Embrace.avi clip at the edit line. If you use the razor cut to trim, be sure to clear the black frames from the project. (For more information, see Lesson 2, "Sequencing and Basic Real-Time Editing".)

15 Save the project.

Constructing the sequence for layered effects

First, you'll set your media pieces onto the Timeline.

1 In the Timeline, shuttle the edit line back to 15 frames from the end of the clip
Embrace.avi (at 00;00;10;16).

2 From the Project window, insert the Propose.avi clip at the edit line on the Video 5
track.

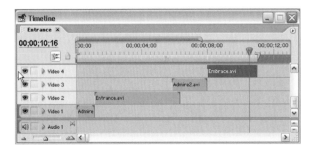

3 Shuttle to 15 frames shy of the end of Propose.avi (at 00;00;11;09).

4 From the Project window, insert the Wedding.avi clip at the edit line on the Video 6
track.

5 Continue in this manner for the next four clips until you achieve the configuration of the Entrance sequence as shown. Of these last insertions, only the Admire3.avi clip will snap to the end frame of the clip on Video 10 track (Tomb.avi). Make your edits as follows:

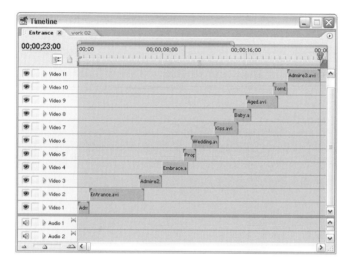

- Insert Kiss.avi on Video 7 track at 00;00;13;13.

- Insert Baby.avi on Video 8 track at 00;00;15;08.

- Insert Aged.avi on Video 9 track at 00;00;16;17.

- Insert Tomb.avi on Video 10 track at 00;00;19;01.

- Insert Admire3.avi on Video 11 track at 00;00;19;27 so that its in point is located at the end point of Tomb.avi, creating no overlap or superimposed frames.

6 Preview the project, so far without effects. In the next section, you'll change some of the straight cuts into After Effects-style cross dissolves.

7 Save the project.

Creating a Cross Dissolve with keyframes

The life cycle fantasy sequence is an accelerated series of clips. You'll create a Cross Dissolve with keyframes by working with opacity controls either in the Timeline or in the effect controls window. In this exercise, you'll learn another efficient keyframe technique using the pen tool (✏).

1 In the Tools palette, select the pen tool.

In the default state of the pen tool functions as a selection cursor and as a mover tool.

2 Set the current time indicator to the end of the Embrace.avi clip (at 00;00;11;01).

3 Select the Propose.avi clip on the Video 5 track.

4 In the track header area of the Video 5 track, click on the Collapse/Expand triangle to gain access to the keyframe and display options.

5 Click on the Show Keyframes menu button and choose Show Keyframes.

6 Click on the small menu button on top of the Propose.avi clip name and choose Opacity, if is not already selected.

7 To make a keyframe at the edit line, press and hold down the Control key. A "plus" sign will appear in the cursor (⌖+) when you can add a keyframe along the yellow line. Press the Control key while clicking on the edit line.

A keyframe appears at the edit line in Propose.avi.

8 In the track header area of the Video 4 track, click on the Collapse/Expand triangle to access the keyframe and display options.

9 Click on the Show Keyframes menu button and choose Show Keyframes.

10 Add a keyframe to the last frame of Embrace.avi at the edit line (at 00;00;11;01) by using the pen tool. (Press the Control key while clicking on the yellow line.)

11 Press the Page up key to locate the first frame of Propose.avi (at 00;00;10;16).

12 Add a keyframe to the first frame of Propose.avi by using the pen tool.

13 Add a keyframe to the Embrace.avi clip on the Video 4 track at the edit line.

Now you have four keyframes: two on the overlapping portion of the Propose.avi clip on the Video 5 track and two keyframes on Embrace.avi on the Video 4 track.

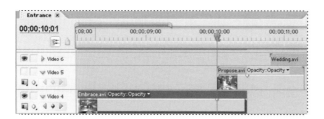

14 With the pen tool, locate, the second keyframe in the Embrace.avi clip. The cursor will display a keyframe icon (◊) when the point of the pen reaches the keyframe to be adjusted.

15 Drag the second keyframe in the Embrace.avi clip to zero opacity. (Drag toward the bottom of the track display.)

16 Drag the first keyframe in the Propose.avi clip to zero opacity. (Drag toward the bottom of the track display.)

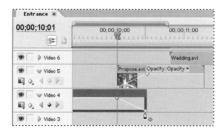

17 Preview the first cross-fade.

18 Save the project.

Duplicating effects using effect controls

In this exercise, you'll complete the cascading staircase of cross dissolves. Opacity attributes cannot be copied and pasted directly into a clip on the Timeline. Instead, you'll copy and paste keyframes, then adjust them using the Effect Controls window.

1 Shuttle the current time indicator to the first frame of Wedding.avi.

2 Select the Propose.avi clip on the Video 5 track.

3 Press the Control key and hold it down, while making a keyframe at the edit line with the pen tool.

4 Press the Page down key to locate the last frame of Propose.avi (at 00;00;11;09).

5 Set a keyframe at the last frame of Propose.avi.

6 Drag the last keyframe in the Propose.avi clip to zero opacity. (Drag toward the bottom of the track display.)

Now you'll transfer the keyframes to the clips in Video tracks 6-10.

7 Select Propose.avi in the Entrance sequence.

8 Locate the Effect Controls window. If it is not displayed, choose Window > Effect Controls. Dock the Effect Controls window with the Source view of the Monitor window.

9 In the Effect Controls window, select the name Opacity.

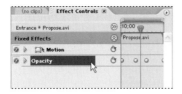

The keyframes embedded in the Propose.avi clip are indicated in the Timeline view of the Effect Controls window by shaded, raised circles. This signifies that the Opacity settings are collapsed.

10 Choose Edit > Copy.

11 In the Entrance sequence, select the Wedding.avi clip on the Video 6 track.

12 Go to the Effect Controls window and select the Opacity settings.

Notice that the Timeline area for Wedding.avi doesn't display any keyframes.

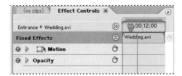

13 Choose Edit > Paste to add the opacity keyframes to Wedding.avi.

The keyframes copied to Wedding.avi match the fade at the beginning of Propose.avi, but not at the end. This is because the Copy command replicates the run length encoded in the source clip's (Propose.avi's) keyframes. Propose.avi is shorter than Wedding.avi. In the following exercise, the fade-out keyframes are moved to the tail end of Wedding.avi.

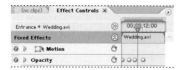

14 Save the project.

Selecting and moving multiple keyframes

To match the effect from the Video 5 track on up through the Video 10 track, you'll select the two end keyframes and reposition them at the ends of each clip.

1 To access the Opacity keyframes in the Wedding.avi clip displayed in the Effect Controls window, click on the triangle next to the name Opacity.

The circular symbols in the Timeline view become editable diamonds and half-diamonds.

2 Press down the Control key and click on the last two diamonds.

3 Drag them to the last frame in the Timeline view.

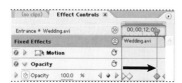

4 Repeat this procedure for the clips in Video tracks 7–10:

- Select the clip in the sequence.

- Go to the Effect Controls window and open the Opacity settings.

- Paste the Propose.avi keyframes.

- Select the last two keyframes and move them to the right to the end of the clip.

5 For the Tomb.avi clip on the Video 10 track, select the last keyframe on the right, and move it to the out point. (The Tomb.avi clip is shorter than the run length of the source clip for the keyframes. Thus, the fourth keyframe fell outside of the Tomb.avi clip.)

The clips Tomb.avi and Admire3.avi are edited as a straight cut in the final short feature that you are building.

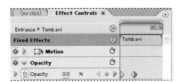

Last two keyframes in Tomb.avi are deleted.

6 Preview the effects that you've just created.

You've created a series of special effects in a manner similar to After Effects, resulting in a set of precise cross fades.

7 Save the project.

Using an effect from Adobe After Effects

After Effects can be regarded as "Photoshop in motion". Designed to work with still images, it enlivens them with an infinite array of enhancements. The motion controls in Premiere Pro are similar to those in After Effects. Documentary editors often use close ups of photographs and then zoom out and pan around the image to illustrate an episode through animation. The significant technique involved in the After Effects interface is setting, adjusting, and manipulating keyframes. The layout of the sequencing area is vertical as opposed to horizontal. While time is indicated horizontally, each piece of media is a separate vertical layer that corresponds to a Timeline track in Premiere Pro.

You can import a layered Photoshop composition and animate each layer over time, then export that motion into a movie that is then compiled with other movies in Premiere Pro. Conversely, two Premiere files can be color balanced in After Effects, then embellished before becoming part of a project in Premiere.

Adobe Premiere Pro includes over 30 effects from Adobe After Effects in the Effects palette. With practice, these effects (filters) and plug-ins can become powerful development tools for your video productions. The Channel Blur, Blend, Lightning, Ramp, and Twirl effects are discussed next:

Channel Blur

This effect blurs a clip's red, green, blue, or alpha channels individually. Use it to create a glow effect. The Edge Behavior/Repeat Edge Pixels option allows you to either prevent the edges from becoming transparent or makes the edges semitransparent.

Blend

This effect blends two clips, using different modes; the original clip fades in while the new clip fades out. The different modes include:

The Blend with Layer   This mode specifies that the track containing the clip must be blended with the original clip.

Mode   This selection allows you to choose from the following Blend options:

• Cross-fade fades between the original clip and the secondary one.

• Color Only colorizes each pixel in the original clip based on the color of each corresponding pixel in the secondary one.

• Tint Only tints pixels in the original clip only if they are already colored.

• Darken Only darkens each pixel in the original clip if it is lighter than the corresponding pixel in the secondary clip.

• Lighten Only lightens each pixel in the original clip if it is darker than the corresponding pixel in the secondary clip.

Blend with Original   This selection specifies the fading level between the blended clip and the original one. A setting of 100% shows only the first clip, while 0% shows only the secondary clip.

If Layer Sizes Differ This selection specifies how to position the clips.

To use the Blend effect:

1 Make sure the two source items to be blended have been added to the Timeline.

2 Apply the Blend to the first clip. Then in the Blend with Layer menu, choose the name of the track on which the second clip is located.

3 Hide the second clip by clicking the video switch for the track.

Lightning

The lightning effect creates lightning bolts between specified points in a clip. It uses start and end points to specify where the lighting bolt begins and ends. Stability and Pull Force settings create a "Jacob's ladder" effect, which is automatically animated across a time frame without keyframes.

Ramp

This effect creates linear or radial ramps in which the color and position may vary over time. It creates a color gradient by blending it with the original image.

Twirl

The twirl effect twirls the pixels of an image around a specified point at a specified amount. The angle specifies which direction to twirl the image. Positive angles move the image clockwise; negative angles move the image counterclockwise. The Twirl Radius tells how far the twirl extends from its center.

Note: *For more information about how to use any of these effects, see "Applying Effects" in the* Adobe Premiere Pro User Guide.

The following Adobe After Effects are compatible with Premiere Pro and can be used in your Premiere video projects if you own Adobe After Effects: Color Balance, Compound Blur, Gamma/Pedestal/Gain, Beam, Offset, Corner Pin (Production Bundle only), Displacement Map (Production Bundle only), and Scatter (Production Bundle only).

Applying the Radial Blur effect

You'll now use two Premiere Pro effects that are also found in After Effects. When *Books & Beans* was shot, the glare from outside had to be diffused with a scrim material known as Rosco. Rosco is like a screen mesh that allows light in but not glare. It is tacked up with duct tape or masking tape. The Entrance sequence, where Dreams arrives at the shop, reveals tape on the Rosco.

To cover the illusion-busting pieces of masking tape, you'll apply the Radial Blur effect to Dreams' first clip. It will remove the tape from view and give her an ethereal glow, which is how Hero perceives her at first sight.

1 In the Entrance sequence, use the selection tool to select the Entrance.avi clip on the Video 2 track.

2 Trim the tail of Entrance.avi to the head of Admire2.avi in the Video 3 track.

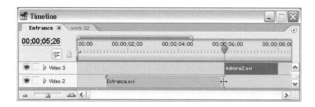

3 Select the Entrance.avi clip on the Timeline, then double-click it to store a version of this edit in the Source view of the Monitor window. You'll need it later to complete the effect.

4 In the Effects palette, type **blur** in the Contains area to locate the Radial Blur filter.

5 With Entrance.avi still selected in the Entrance sequence, drag the Radial Blur effect to the Effect Controls window.

The Radial Blur settings box appears.

6 In the Amount field type **9**, for Blur Method select Spin, and for Quality select Best. Click OK.

The Radial Blue effect is applied.

The masking tape is indistinguishable, but Dreams is blurred along with the background. To remedy this, you'll mask off the portion of the screen occupied by Dreams.

7 Save the project.

Applying the Image Matte Key

For a heightened effect, Dreams will appear in sharp contrast to the swirling background, which is what the extra copy of the Entrance.avi clip will convey.

1 From the Source view, drag Entrance.avi to the Video 3 track, placing it exactly above the first instance of it on the Video 2 track. Make sure the tail of Entrance.avi snaps to the head of the Admire2.avi.clip.

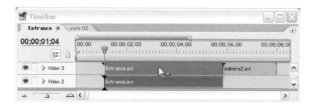

In all four of the Adobe graphics programs highlighted in this lesson—Premiere Pro, After Effects, Photoshop, and Illustrator—masking (or the use of mattes) is a vital technique to learn. You'll mask out or "key out" the background of the second instance of Entrance.avi. The foreground will remain opaque.

The Image Matte Key requires a matte. You'll be linking it to Entrancematte.psd, a Photoshop file located in the 07Lesson folder.

2 Select the second instance of Entrance.avi, which is on the Video 3 track.

3 In the Effects palette, type **matte** in the Contains area.

The matte effects are displayed, one of which is the Image Matte Key.

4 Drag the Image Matte Key from the Effects palette into the Effect Controls window.

5 Click on the Setup icon (→▣).

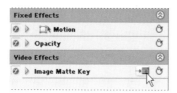

The Select Matte box appears, which allows you to find a file on one of your drives.

6 Locate and select the Entrancematte.psd file in your 07Leson folder, and click Open.

7 Click the triangle to the left of the Image Matte Key name.

8 From the Composite Using menu, choose Matte Luma, which isolates the foreground pixels by making them opaque. The background pixels become transparent in order to be masked or keyed out.

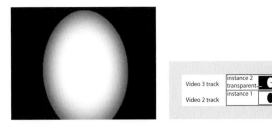

The Entrancematte.psd allows the blurred edges between the foreground and background on the clip below it to appear, but leaves the foreground opaque.

9 Preview the two effects.

10 Save the project.

You'll add the musical score to this scene in Lesson 10, "Advanced Editing Two: Nested and Multiple Sequences", and you will work with another Adobe product in Lesson 14, "Working with Adobe DVD Encore."

Exporting the movie

Now that you've finished editing, it's time to generate a movie file.

1 Choose File > Export > Movie.

2 In the Export Movie dialog box, click the Settings button. In the General settings, make sure that File Type is set to Microsoft DV AVI.

3 Select Entire Project for the Range.

4 Make sure that Export Video, Export Audio, Add to Project When Finished, and Beep When Finished are selected.

5 In the Audio section, choose 48000 Hz for Sample Rate, 16-bit for Sample Type, and Stereo for Channels.

6 Click OK to close the Export Movie Settings dialog box.

7 In the Export Movie dialog box, specify the 07Lesson folder for the location and type **07Done** for the name of the movie. Click Save.

While Premiere is making the movie, a status bar displays the time remaining to complete the process. When the movie is complete, it appears in the Project window.

8 Double-click the movie to open it into the Source view of the Monitor window.

9 Click the Play button (▶) to play the movie you've just created.

For a complete understanding of all of the export options available in Adobe Premiere Pro, see "Output" in Lesson 13.

Exploring Photoshop and Illustrator in Premiere Pro on your own

Here are some of the things you might want to try while working with Photoshop and Illustrator in Premiere Pro:

• Layers of Adobe Photoshop and Adobe Illustrator files can be animated over time. Import the separate layers, each one becoming footage. Then apply them to a sequence and add effects.

• Find out how different mattes react within the context of a movie clip.

• Import a large, high-resolution image. Use the Motion controls to pan and zoom the picture. This is a technique documentary filmmakers like to use.

Review questions

1 What are three names for keying?

2 What are some of the aspects of Premiere Pro that most resemble After Effects, Photoshop, and Illustrator?

3 How can you make an image file into a movie?

4 What are two methods for creating keyframes?

5 How can you make a transition without using one from the Video Transitions folder in the Effects palette?

Answers

1 Creating or using Alpha Mattes, Alpha Channels, and Masking are three ways to "key" out image areas of superimposed clips.

2 The Adobe video and graphics programs are similar with regard to layers (tracks) and mattes.

3 Import a layered image or illustration with each layer becoming a separate clip. Place the clips on the Timeline and animate them over time.

4 Two ways to make keyframes are in the Effect Controls window, using the keyframe navigator in conjunction with the timeline area, and in the Timeline, using the pen tool.

5 Create cross fades with overlapping clips by changing the opacity of the overlapping frames. The tail of the frame fades out under the head of the consecutive frames, which fades in.

Lesson 8

8 Fundamentals of Multipoint Editing

When fine-tuning a scene, it is often necessary to separate, remove, or resynchronize the audio and video portions. Premiere Pro provides many different ways to design your projects.

In this lesson, you'll fine-tune a segment of the movie, when Son orders a brownie. In editing this segment, you'll learn the following techniques:

- Making three-point and four-point edits.
- Making six-point edits.
- Targeting video and audio tracks.
- Linking, unlinking, and synchronizing video and audio clips.
- Creating a split edit, using the link override function.
- Closing a gap with the Ripple Delete command.

Getting started

In this lesson, you'll open an existing project with the clips already assembled in the Timeline. Make sure you know the location of the files used in this lesson. Insert the *Classroom in a Book* DVD-ROM disk if necessary. For help, see "Copying the Classroom in a Book files" on page 4.

1 Launch the Premiere Pro software.

2 In the Premiere Pro Welcome window, click Open Project.

3 In the Open Project dialog box, browse to the 08Lesson folder that you copied into your hard drive from the DVD-ROM.

4 Locate the 08Lesson.prproj file in the 08Lesson folder and click Open. (You can also double-click on the 08Lesson.prproj file to open it.)

5 If necessary, rearrange windows and palettes so that they don't overlap, by choosing Window > Workspace > Editing.

Viewing the finished movie

To see what you'll be creating, take a look at the completed movie for this lesson.

1 In the Project window, choose File > New > Bin.

A new bin appears in the Project window.

2 Select the new bin and double-click in the name field to edit it.

3 Type **Resources** and then press Enter.

4 Click on the triangle next to the directory icon in the Resources bin.

5 Select the Resources bin by clicking on it.

6 Choose File > Import and double-click the 08Final.wmv file in the Finished folder, inside the 08Lesson folder.

The movie is imported into the Resources bin in the Project window.

7 Double-click 08Final.wmv to make it active in the Source view of the Monitor window.

8 Click the Play button (▶) under the Source view in the Monitor window to view the movie.

9 You may choose to keep the Resources bin for further reference during the lesson. To delete it, click on the bin and then click the Clear icon (🗑) at the bottom of the Project window.

Viewing the assembled project

Take a look at the project as it has been assembled so far. There are no transitions, filters, or other effects used in this project.

1 Make sure the edit line is at the beginning of the Timeline.

2 To view the project, click the Play button (▶) under the Program view in the Monitor window.

Although the assembled project looks much like the finished movie you viewed earlier, you may notice some small problems that could be solved by further editing. In this lesson, you'll use some editing tools that are especially useful in dealing with the matching of video and audio clips from different sources.

Multipoint editing techniques, which are discussed in this lesson, preserve the duration of a project or the range of frames.

Understanding three-point and four-point editing

In some situations, you may want to replace a range of frames in the program with a range of frames from a source clip. In Premiere Pro, you can do this using a three-point edit or a four-point edit. Both are standard techniques in video editing.

In previous lessons, you worked with *source In and Out points*—the first and last frames of a clip that were added to the video program. In addition, it's important to understand *program In and Out points*—the location in your video program where you will apply an editing technique. Being able to specify In and Out points for both the source and the program gives you more control, making your edits as precise as possible. You'll need to set source and program In and Out points for the three- and four-point editing exercises in this lesson.

Three-point editing   Use three-point editing when at least one end point (In or Out) of the source material or the program material it replaces is not critical. The three-point edit is more common than the four-point edit because you set only three points, and the ranges do not have to be the same duration. Premiere Pro automatically trims the point you don't set so that the source and program material are the same length. This is called a three-point edit because you specify three points: any combination of In and Out points in the program material being replaced and in the source material being added.

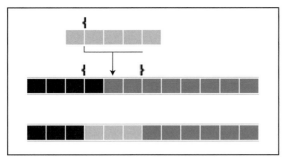

In a three-point edit, you set three points and Premiere Pro sets the fourth point.

Four-point editing   Use four-point editing when you want to replace a range of frames in the program with a range of frames of equal duration in the source. This is called a four-point edit because you specify all four points: the In and Out points both for the source material being added and for the program material being replaced.

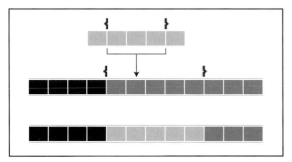

In a four-point edit, you set all four points. If source and target material have different lengths, you can tell Premiere Pro to make the source material fit the target area.

If the source material you've selected is not exactly the same duration as the material you're replacing, Premiere Pro gives you one of two options for completing the replacement, depending on the situation: *fit to fill* or *trim source*. If you select Fit to Fill, the duration and speed of the source frames change to fit into the duration of the frames being replaced. If you select Trim Source, Premiere changes the Out point of the source frames, effectively making this a three-point edit instead of a four-point edit.

In the next exercise, you'll make a three-point edit.

Making a three-point edit

You'll use a three-point edit to overlay a sound with another sound, Dooropen.avi, replacing parts of Byebye.avi in the program. As part of this edit, you'll also eliminate an unwanted dialogue fragment at the end of Byebye.avi. First, you'll open the source clip in the Source view and preview it.

1 In the Timeline window, use the Time Zoom controls so that you can view the sequence clearly. (Type a "\" reverse slash to fit the entire contents of the sequence in the Timeline view.)

2 In the Project window, double-click Dooropen.avi, which is in the Bin 01 folder. The movie opens in the Source view of the Monitor window.

3 Preview the clip by clicking the Play button (▶). The critical frames are the sounds of Father opening the door as he exits. The sound occurs off-screen, so you'll be concerned with capturing the audio only.

Now you'll set the In point of Dooropen.avi to the moment just before Father opens the door.

4 In the Source view of the Monitor window, use the shuttle control to locate the frame just before the door opens. You'll hear the door opening and view a sliver of light between the door, when they open.

💡 *Alternatively, you can click the location timecode and type* **220** *(00;00;02;20), then press Enter. In projects that you create on your own, you will have to figure out the in and out points. For more information about using the shuttle and jog controls and precision editing, see the* Adobe Premiere Pro User Guide.

5 In the Source view of the Monitor window, click the Set In Point button (ᵻ) to set the In point in Dooropen.avi.

6 Step forward 22 frames in the Source view monitor.

7 Click the Set Out Point button (ᵼ) to set the second point of the 3-point edit.

8 In the Timeline window, adjust the Time Zoom level controls so that the audio waveforms in the Byebye.avi clip can be easily seen in the Timeline.

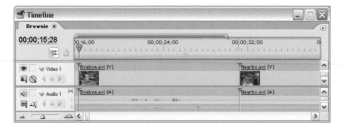

Next, locate the corresponding frame in the Byebye.avi clip on the Timeline, which will be the third point.

9 Use the shuttle control to locate the frame where Father opens the door (at approximately 00;00;30;08). Position the CTI at this point.

The three points are set.

At this point, the duration timecode (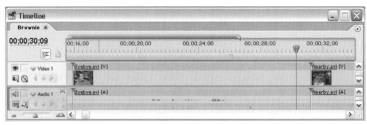) in the Source view reads 00;00;00;23, which is the duration from the source In point to source Out point.

Whenever you add clips to the Timeline using the keyboard or Monitor window controls (as you're about to do), you need to tell Premiere Pro which tracks you want to use. You'll designate the track for the destination of the edit, and specify what portion of the source clip to use with the Toggle Take Audio and Video button located in the Source view.

10 In the Timeline, click the track header area on the Audio 1 track to identify the Audio 1 track as the target track for the edit.

Audio 1 track is selected as the target for the three-point edit.

Because a video file already exists in the Video 1 track, you'll take only the audio portion of Dooropen.avi, so as not to disturb the Video 1 track.

11 In the bottom right area of the Source view of the Monitor window, click the Toggle Take Audio and Video button and select Audio only (🔊).

Now that you have specified source In and Out points and a program In point, totaling three points, and set the target track for your edit, you are ready to replace the program material with the source material.

12 In the Source view of the Monitor window, click the Overlay button (🔳).

The range of frames marked in the audio track of Byebye.avi is replaced with an equal amount from Dooropen.avi.

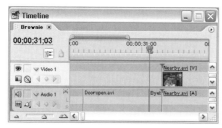

The audio portion of Dooropen.avi is targeted to the Audio 1 track.

13 Preview the three-point edit.

14 Save the project.

For more information about how to specify source and target tracks, see "Specifying source and target tracks" in the *Adobe Premiere Pro User Guide.*

Linking and unlinking clips

In Premiere Pro, you can link a video clip to an audio clip to move the two clips together. When you drag the video portion into the Timeline, the linked audio portion moves with it, and vice versa. Linked video and audio clips are identified regardless of which clip was selected. The name of each clip in the set is underscored.

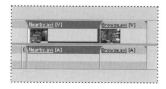

You can override a link temporarily to edit linked clips. When you want to work with linked clips individually, you temporarily turn off synchronized behavior by choosing Clip > Unlink Audio and Video or right-click in the context menu.

When linked mode is on, both clips of a linked pair behave as a single unit. In this mode, all Timeline tools affect both clips in a linked pair; both clips are affected when you select, trim, split, delete, move, or change the duration or speed of either clip. When linked mode is off, linked clips can be edited independently, as if they were not linked.

Sound recorded on a video camera can be captured and imported into a Premiere Pro project already linked to its video clip. Breaking a link is useful when you want to replace linked audio. Or you may want to break a link to edit In or Out points independently. You'll use this technique later in this lesson to create an L-cut. (See "Making an L-Cut" on page 304.)

In this exercise, you'll perform three separate tasks. First, you'll link a video clip with an audio clip. Then you'll resynchronize a pair of linked clips. Finally, you'll use the link override command to create a *split edit*. A split edit (also known as an L-cut or a 6-point edit) extends the audio only, from one clip into an adjacent clip. In this case, the audio will begin to play before the corresponding video appears.

Linking clips

First, you'll unlink a linked pair of clips and delete the audio, then you'll align a different audio clip to the video clip and link them. Although Pay.wav is longer than Pay.avi, they'll begin at the same point.

1 In the Timeline window, use the Time Zoom controls so that you can view the sequence clearly. (Or type a "\" reverse slash to fit the entire contents of the sequence in the Timeline view.)

2 In the Program view, click the Go to Previous Edit Point button (⊩) until the edit line moves to the beginning of the Brownie sequence. (Or press the Home key if no clips are selected, otherwise the Home key returns the edit line to the beginning of the selected clip.)

The Pay.avi clip is in the wrong position in the Brownie sequence. You'll unlink its video and audio, delete its audio, then relink the video to a different audio clip before moving the hybrid clip to its proper spot in the program.

3 In the Timeline, select the Pay.avi clip.

4 Choose Clip > Unlink Audio and Video.

5 Deselect both parts of the clip by clicking elsewhere in the Timeline. The names are no longer underscored, indicating that they are unlinked.

6 Select the audio portion only of Pay.avi, and choose Edit > Clear.

7 In the timecode field of the sequence, type **4329** to set the current time indicator.

8 Drag Pay.wav from Bin 01 in the Project window to the Audio 2 track so that it snaps to the edit line, which is at the beginning of Pay.avi (at 00;00;43;29).

9 Select both clips, Pay.avi and Pay.wav, by holding down the Shift key.

10 Choose Clip > Link Audio and Video.

Pay.avi and Pay.wav are linked. Try moving one of them and you'll notice that they both move in tandem. In the next exercise, you'll learn more about linked clips.

Making an L-Cut

In this exercise, you'll reposition the Pay.avi/Pay.wav clip in the Timeline without losing any of its audio or video footage.

1 In the Tools palette, select the selection tool (➤).

To prevent unintentional edits, always deselect a tool when you are finished using it, unless it is the selection tool. The easiest way to deselect a tool is to select the selection tool.

The action in the clips you just linked is supposed to take place when Father pays for Son's brownie, so let's reposition them earlier in the Timeline.

You'll move the Pay.avi scene and its linked audio, Pay.wav, to the moment Son finishes saying "I want a brownie." Right then, Father begins to reach into his pocket to pay (at 00;00;12;16).

2 Set the current time indicator to 00;00;12;16, either by typing **1216** into the timecode field, or scrubbing the edit line.

3 In the Timeline, select Pay.avi.

4 Be sure to click on the Audio portion as you drag to the left and down keeping the Pay.wav clip upon the Audio 2 track. Watch the head and tail frames of each clip as they are displayed in the Program view.

This allows you to create an L-cut without disturbing the audio on the Audio 1 track.

Pay.avi and Pay.wav are now overlaid at 00;00;12;16, with Pay.wav forming an L-cut.

Notice that none of the video clips shifted to the left, so a gap the size of Pay.avi remains. The default application of a clip in Premiere Pro is Overlay, thus the video portion overlaid the Order2.avi clip. Don't worry about the gap created by moving Pay.avi. You'll fix that later.

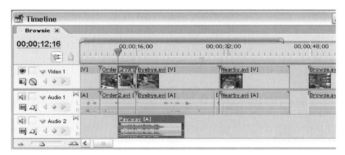

The results of shifting Pay.avi linked to Pay.wav are gaps the size of Pay.avi;
Pay.wav has shifted as a linked clip with it along the Audio 2 track.

5 Preview the Brownie sequence.

6 Save the project.

Handling unsynchronized linked clips

For video clips that have audio linked to them when they are imported into a project, Premiere Pro stores sync information, and attempts to keep these clips synchronized.

In the Project window, for instance, observe that Dooropen.avi has its own audio track. When they are moved out of sync, both clips display a white tag on a red background at the In point with a red number to indicate the extent of the out of sync condition. This tag displays the amount of time the clip is out of sync with its accompanying video or audio clip.

In some situations, clips may be accidentally shifted out of sync during an edit. When this happens, it is an easy matter to resynchronize them.

In order to produce an out of sync condition, you'll unsync the video and audio portions of Nearby.avi.

1 In the Timeline, select either the Nearby.avi audio or video clip. Both clips will be selected, because they are linked.

2 Choose Clip > Unlink Audio and Video.

To make sure the clips have been unlinked, select the Nearby.avi audio clip. Only the audio should be selected, not the video portion, because the audio has been unlinked from its video track.

3 Drag the Nearby.avi audio clip to the right, about halfway through the empty space next to it.

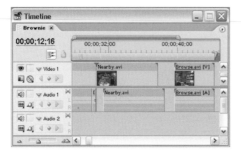

4 Select the audio and video portions of Nearby.avi by holding down the Shift key.

5 Choose Clip > Link Audio and Video.

6 Tags appear at the In point of each clip, indicating that Nearby.avi audio and video are out of sync by 00;00;01;11. (Your number may differ.)

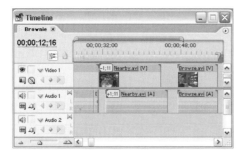

7 To relink out of sync clips, right-click on the tag at the In point of the Nearby.avi video or audio clip and choose Move into Sync.

The audio portion of Nearby.avi is in sync with the video portion, and the red markers disappear. To ensure that video and audio are now in sync, you'll preview Nearby.avi.

To set the start of the work area bar, press and hold Control + Shift and then double-click on the textured portion of the title bar at its center. The work area bar conforms to the length of the visible area of the Timeline. To set the left end of the work area bar, drag the work area markers (at either end of the work area bar) to specify the beginning and end of the work area. Be sure to drag the marker; otherwise, you'll grab the edit line instead.

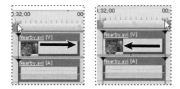

8 After you resize the work area bar to cover Nearby.avi, press Enter to preview it.

You can tell if the clips are in sync. Turn up the audio volume and enlarge the view of the Program monitor.

9 Restore the clip to its original position, with its In Point snapped to the Out Point of Byebye.avi (at 00;00;31;08). Leave the gap that was created earlier by repositioning Pay.avi and Pay.wav.

10 Save the project.

Creating a split edit

Earlier, you created a type of split edit, also known as an L-cut or a 6-point edit, by breaking the link between the video and audio clips. Here, you'll use a new technique to create a split edit, temporarily overriding a link. In this split edit, you'll extend the audio both before and after a video clip to which the sound is synchronized.

1 Use the Time Zoom controls to view the entire Brownie sequence in the Timeline.

You'll edit an audio clip independently of its linked video.

2 Select the Pay.avi/Pay.wav clip.

You'll reposition the Pay.wav clip so that it extends on both sides of the Pay.avi video clip.

3 Press the Alt key as you drag the Pay.wav audio clip to the left.

You've just moved a linked and synced clip without unlinking its audio from its video. The clip names are underscored, indicating that the clips are still linked.

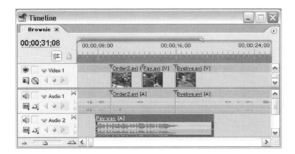

Now you'll restore them back into sync.

4 Choose Edit > Undo.

5 Save the project.

Closing a gap with the Ripple Delete command

Earlier in this lesson, you moved Pay.avi, which left a gap between Nearby.avi and Browse.avi. You'll use the Ripple Delete command to remove this gap. The Ripple Delete command eliminates the selected gap by moving all clips that are on the right of the gap. Unlike the ripple edit tool, you must select either a gap or one or more clips in the Timeline before choosing the Ripple Delete command.

It's important to understand that you can use the Ripple Delete command only on one or more clips or a gap—you cannot use it to delete a range of frames marked by In and Out points as you can with the Extract button (discussed later in the next lesson). Also, the Ripple Delete command has no effect on clips in locked tracks.

Locking tracks

To prevent parts of the program from being affected by the Ripple Delete command, lock the corresponding track. Locking a track prevents any further changes until the track is unlocked.

1 Click the empty box to the right of the speaker icon in the Audio 1 track header area. The lock icon (🔒) indicates that the track is now locked. Cross hatches appear along the track itself.

Audio 1 track is locked.

2 In the Video 1 track, select the gap between Nearby.avi and Browse.avi.

3 Choose Edit > Ripple Delete.

After the gap is deleted, all of the clips on the track shift to the left to close the gap. Because the Audio 1 track is locked, the Browse.avi clip got out of sync.

Now, you'll close the gap on the Audio 1 track.

4 Click the Lock icon in the Audio 1 track header area to unlock the track.

5 Lock the Video 1 track by clicking the empty box in the track header area, and the lock icon appears.

6 In the Timeline window, select the gap between the Nearby.avi and Browse.avi audio clips in the Audio 1 track.

7 Choose Edit > Ripple Delete. The gap is deleted between the two audio clips.

8 Unlock the Video 1 track.

Note: You may need to resynchronize Browse.avi. If so, use the steps you learned earlier in this lesson.

9 Preview your work.

10 Save the project.

Exporting the movie

Now that you've finished your editing, it's time to generate a movie file.

1 If you turned off audio previewing earlier in the lesson, make sure that you turn it on again by clicking the icon in the track header area of each audio track so that it changes to the speaker icon ( ).

2 Choose File > Export > Movie.

3 In the Export Movie dialog box, click the Settings button. In the General settings, make sure that File Type is set to Microsoft DV AVI.

4 Select Entire Sequence for the Range.

5 Make sure that Export Video, Export Audio, Add to Project When Finished, and Beep When Finished are selected.

6 In the Audio section, choose 48000 Hz for Sample Rate, 16-bit for Sample Type, and Stereo for Channels.

7 Click OK to close the Export Movie Settings dialog box.

8 In the Export Movie dialog box, specify the 08Lesson folder for the location and type **Brownie.avi** for the name of the movie. Click Save.

While Premiere Pro is making the movie, a status bar displays the time remaining to complete the process. When the movie is complete, it appears in the Project window.

9 Double-click the movie file to open it in the Source view of the Monitor window.

10 Click the Play button (▶) to play the movie you've just created.

Exploring on your own

Feel free to experiment with the project that you have just created. Here are some suggestions:

• Perform a four-point edit, but make the source material shorter than the program material. Experiment with the options that Premiere Pro gives you to complete the edit.

• Experiment with the History palette by applying a change to some part of the project, and then observing that the new state of that project is added to the History palette. For example, if you add a clip to the Timeline window, apply an effect to it, copy it, and paste it in another track; each of those states is listed separately in the palette. You can select any of these states, and the project will revert to how it looked when the change was applied. You can then modify the project from that state.

• Try changing the name of a clip in the Project window without using Clip > Rename. Here's a hint: You don't need to use any menu items, icons, or buttons, but the Project window must be in List View. Once you've changed the name, observe what effect it has on instances in the Timeline.

Review questions

1 In addition to the Timeline window, which two Premiere windows let you move the edit line?

2 What is one advantage of using a three-point edit?

3 To edit linked video and audio clips separately without permanently destroying the link, what would you need to do before you begin editing?

4 What is one easy step that helps prevent accidental edits?

5 Which tool would you use to change the In and Out points of a clip while preserving the clip's duration?

Answers

1 You can move the edit line from the Monitor window by using the Program view controls, and from the Effect Controls window by scrubbing the edit line in the time view.

2 In a three-point edit, Premiere Pro trims the unspecified point for you.

3 Press the Alt key while editing the clip.

4 Deselecting a tool prevents using it accidentally. Locking a track is another way to prevent accidental edits.

5 You can change a clip's frame rate using either the Clip/Speed Duration box (choose Clip > Speed) or the rate stretch tool (⟷).

Lesson 9

9 Advanced Editing One: Single-Frame Techniques

Finishing a project can mean fine-tuning edits while preserving the duration of individual clips and the overall program. The techniques covered in this lesson will help prepare you for the detailed editing needed to polish a project.

Now, you'll complete the segment of the movie when the main character meets his ex-girlfriend's new boyfriend at the bookstore cafe. In editing this segment, you'll learn the following techniques:

- Removing frames, using the Extract and Lift buttons.
- Pasting a clip, using the Paste Insert command.
- Using the slip and slide tools to adjust edits.
- Editing in the Trim window.
- Adding sound effects.

Getting started

For this lesson, you'll open an existing project with the clips roughly assembled in the Timeline. Make sure you know the location of the files used in this lesson. Insert the *Classroom in a Book* DVD-ROM disk if necessary. For help, see "Copying the Classroom in a Book files" on page 4.

1 Launch the Premiere Pro software.

2 In the Premiere Welcome window, click Open Project.

3 In the Open Project dialog box, locate the 09Lesson folder that you copied into your hard drive from the DVD-ROM.

4 Locate the 09Lesson.prproj file in the 09Lesson folder and click Open. (You can also double-click on the 09Lesson.prproj file to open it.)

5 If necessary, rearrange windows and palettes so that they don't overlap, by choosing Window > Workspace > Editing.

Viewing the finished movie

To see what you'll be creating, take a look at the completed movie for this lesson.

1 Create a new bin by either clicking the Bin icon ( ) at the bottom of the project window or clicking the Clip Information menu triangle at the top right corner of the Project window and choosing New Bin.

2 Type **Resources** to name the new bin.

3 Choose File > Import and select the 09Final.wmv file in the Finished folder, inside the 09Lesson folder. Choose Open.

The 09Final.wmv file is now located in the Resources bin.

4 Double-click the 09Final.wmv file so that it opens in the Source view of the Monitor window.

5 Click the Play button (▶) in the Source view of the Monitor window to watch the video program.

6 You can either delete the Resources bin and the 09Final.wmv movie by clicking the Clear button (🗑) at the bottom of the Project window, or, you may decide to keep it as a reference.

Viewing the assembled project

Take a look at the existing project. You'll notice that there are no transitions, filters, or any other effects.

1 Make sure that the edit line is at the beginning of the Timeline. To move it to the beginning, click the Timeline window title bar and then press the Home key on your keyboard.

2 To view the project, click the Play button (▶) under the Program view in the Monitor window.

The project plays in the Program view. Although the assembled project looks somewhat like the finished movie you viewed earlier, you'll solve some problems. In this lesson, you'll use some editing tools that are especially useful in fine-tuning a project.

Much of this lesson introduces editing techniques for preserving the duration of a project or range of frames.

Understanding the extract and lift functions

Premiere Pro provides two methods for removing a range of frames or a gap from the Timeline: *extracting* and *lifting*.

Extracting Removes frames from the Timeline, closing the gap like a ripple deletion. These frames can be within a single clip or can span multiple clips, but it is important to understand that extracting removes the selected range of frames *from all unlocked tracks.* You can also extract a gap from the Timeline. This feature works only with a range of frames that have been marked with In and Out points in the Program view.

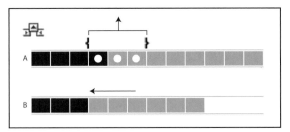

*Frames are marked in the Program view with In and Out points (**A**). The marked portion of the program is deleted and the gap is closed up (**B**).*

Lifting Removes a range of frames from the Timeline, leaving a gap. The frames removed can be within a single clip or can span multiple clips and are removed *only from the target track.* As in extracting, you select the frames you want to remove by setting In and Out points in the Program view in the Monitor window. The Lift button does not affect the duration of the other clips in the Timeline.

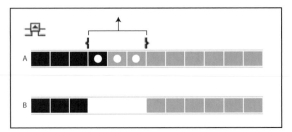

*Frames are marked in the Program view with In and Out points (**A**). The marked portion of the program is deleted, leaving a gap (**B**).*

Removing frames with the Extract button

Here, you'll use the extract feature to remove some repetitive movement in the Greet2.avi clip. Extracting the frames will split the clip into two separate clips.

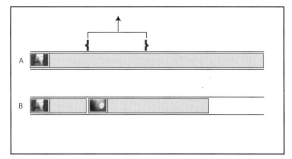

*Clip before (**A**) and after (**B**) extracting frames*

To begin, you'll set In and Out points in the Program view to define the portion of Greet2.avi to be extracted from the Timeline.

1 In the Project window, double-click the Seeya sequence to make it the active Timeline.

2 Playback in Real-Time Preview or scrub in the Timeline ruler to preview Greet1.avi and Greet2.avi. Note the repetition between the two clips.

3 Locate the point in Greet2.avi after New Boy says, "Hey, dude," and before Hero sticks out his hand to shake New Boy's, while saying, "Hey," (at 00;00;10;26). (Use the jog and shuttle controls in the Monitor window, or type **1026** in the timecode and then press Enter.)

The edit line should be at the point where Hero begins to move his hand.

4 In the Program view, click the Set Out Point button ( ) to set the Out point for the frames you will extract.

5 Find the first frame of the Greet2.avi clip by pressing the Page Up key (at 00;00;06;12).

6 In the Program view, click the Set In Point button ( ) to set the In point.

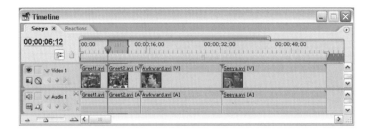

Now you'll extract the range of frames you've just defined from the Timeline. You'll specify whether to lift the sequence selection from both the video and audio tracks or just one of them. In this case, you'll remove both, because some dialogue is repeated.

7 In the Timeline window, click the Video 1 and Audio 1 track header areas to designate both tracks as target tracks for the extract command. Notice that the target tracks turn grey.

Timeline track header areas.
(l) Default;
(r) selected as target tracks.

8 In the Program view of the Monitor window, click the Extract button (⊞).

Extracting removes the range of frames in Greet2.avi marked by In and Out points. The gap is closed, which shortens the program.

9 Preview the video you just edited.

10 Save the project.

💡 *To temporarily make a track shy or to turn off the audio preview, click the speaker icon (◀) next to any audio track that contains audio clips.*

Removing frames with the Lift button

You'll use the Lift button in the Program view of the Monitor window to remove the end portion of Greet1.avi, where Hero is heard off screen to say, "Hey."

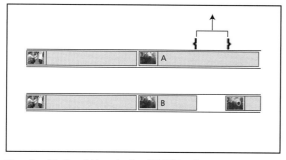

Greet1.avi before (A) and after (B) lifting frames

First, you'll define the range of frames you want to remove.

1 Use the Time Zoom controls in the Timeline window to zoom in on the waveforms displayed in the Audio 1 track.

You'll locate the point in Greet1.avi just before Hero says, "Hey."

2 Playback in Real-Time Preview or scrub in the Timeline ruler to preview Greet1.avi.

3 Use the controls in the Timeline or Monitor window to locate the point in Greet1.avi right after New Boy says, "Hey dude," and right before Hero says, "Hey." It is also where Ex's hand moves off the screen (at 00;00;04;26).

4 In the Program view, click the Set In Point button (✦) to set the In point in Greet1.avi.

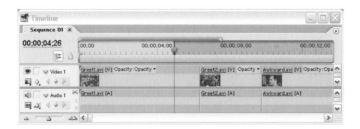

5 Move the edit line to the end of the Greet1.avi clip (at 00;00;06;12) by pressing once on the Page Down key. Click the Set Out Point button (✦).

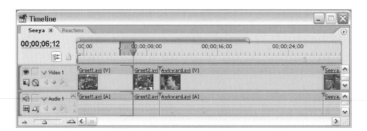

Now that you've defined the range of frames you want to remove, you'll lift this range of frames from the Timeline. You'll specify whether you will lift the sequence selection from both the video and audio tracks or just one of them. In this case, you'll remove from both tracks, because Hero says, "Hey" in each clip.

6 In the Timeline window, click the Video 1 and Audio 1 track header areas to designate both tracks as target tracks for the extract command.

7 In the Program view, click the Lift button ( ).

The portion of Greet1.avi that you marked is removed—leaving the other clips in the track undisturbed and preserving the program's duration. Next you'll remove the gap.

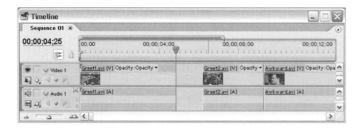

8 Save the project.

Closing a gap

Editors use the Lift button when they want to keep the program at the same duration. You can also rearrange existing clips in the Timeline by cutting and pasting. If you simply paste a clip, Premiere Pro overlays it at a selected area in the Timeline, leaving the duration of the project the same. Depending upon the length of the clip, overlaying may remove underlying footage. If you choose Edit > Paste Insert, Premiere Pro inserts the pasted clip in the Timeline, increasing the duration of the project by the length of the pasted footage.

There are a number of ways to insert material into a gap in a project, including using 3-point and 4-point edits.

1 In the Timeline window, select the gap on the Video 1 or Audio 1 track.

2 Choose Edit > Ripple Delete and the gap is removed.

3 Play back the project by using Real-Time Preview or by scrubbing in the Timeline ruler.

All the clips in the project are now in the proper order and trimmed to about the right length. In the next exercise, you'll fine-tune some critical edits.

4 Save the project.

Fine-tuning your edits

The remaining exercises in this lesson involve adjusting edits to match the action between scenes. When fine-tuning a project, it's necessary to either preserve the duration of a clip or of the entire project. In this project, we want to preserve the duration of Awkward.avi and Seeya.avi, because we'll be cutting between scenes shot from two angles, and we'll be matching action between those scenes. In the exercises that follow, you'll use the slide tool, the slip tool, and the Trim window to put some finishing touches on your project.

In the exercises that follow, you'll adjust several edits, working from left to right.

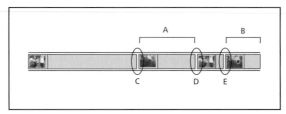

*To preserve the In and Out points and durations of Greet1.avi (**A**) and Awkward.avi (**B**), you'll refine several edits, using the slide tool on the first (**C**), the slip tool on the second (**D**), and the Trim window on the third (**E**), working from left to right.*

Understanding the slide and slip tools

Premiere provides two tools for adjusting a clip in the Timeline while preserving its duration: the slide tool and the slip tool.

Slide tool Adjusts the duration of the two clips adjacent to the target clip, while preserving the In and Out points of the selected clip. This tool also preserves the duration of the project. You can think of this as a rolling edit with a clip between the two clips being trimmed. The slide tool also preserves the duration of the selected clip. As you drag the selected clip, the location of the clip moves left or right in the Timeline.

Note: Similar to transitions, the slide tool can be used only when (and to the extent that) the adjacent clips have been trimmed so that "extra" frames are available in those clips.

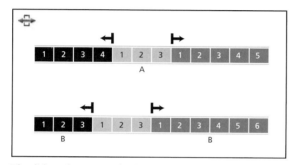

*The slide tool preserves the duration of the sliding clip (**A**) while changing the In or Out points of the adjacent clips (**B**), but only if those two clips have trimmed frames available.*

Slip tool Adjusts a clip's In and Out points while preserving its duration. As you drag in the clip with the slip tool, the clip's In point and Out point shift simultaneously in the same direction, while the duration of the clip remains unchanged. You can think of this as slipping the clip one way or the other behind a fixed window in the track. The location of the clip in the Timeline does not change.

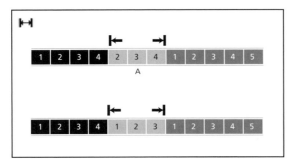

*The slip tool changes the In and Out points of a clip (**A**) while preserving its duration, provided the clip has trimmed frames available.*

Note: You can use the slip tool only on trimmed clips so that additional frames are available beyond the current In and Out points.

When you hold down the mouse button and barely instigate the dragging motion with either the slide tool or the slip tool selected, the Monitor window changes to show four critical frames: the last frame of the adjacent clip on the left, the first and last frames of the selected clip, and the first frame of the adjacent clip to the right.

Note: You can't use the slip and slide tools directly on audio clips, but when you use the slip and slide tools on video clips, any audio clips linked to those video clips will be adjusted to match the video clips.

Preparing to use the slip and slide tools

You'll use the slide tool to build tension in a close-up shot of a greeting card of Ex used as a bookmark and the awkwardness between Hero and Ex. You'll preserve the In point and Out points of Awkward.avi after it is split into two parts, and of Seeya.avi. Performing this edit shortens one adjacent clip while extending the other.

Just as ripple and rolling edits allow you to adjust a cut between two clips, the slip and slide edit tools are useful when you want to adjust two cuts in a sequence of three clips. Drag the center clip with either the slip or slide tool to the left or right. When you use the slip or slide tools, the Program view displays the four frames involved in the edit side-by-side, except when editing audio only.

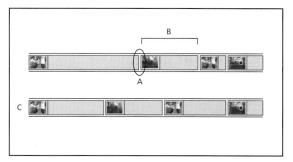

The slide tool will be used to match action at the edit point (A) between Awkward.avi and Seeya.avi, while preserving the In and Out points and duration of Seeya.avi (B). The result can be seen in (C).

1 In the Timeline window, zoom in on the Awkward.avi clip to get a close-up view.

2 Move the current time indicator to the frame where the scene cuts away from the close-up of the book (at 00;00;15;12).

You'll split Awkward.avi into two parts.

3 Choose Sequence > Razor Cut at Current Time Indicator, and Awkward.avi is split into two parts.

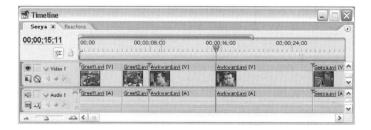

Now you'll insert a sequence of clips shot from different angles.

4 In the Project window, double-click the Reactions sequence to make it the active sequence in the Timeline window.

5 Choose Edit > Select All.

6 Hold down the Shift key while you click on the last clip in the sequence, Awkward2.avi, to deselect it. All the others will remain selected. (You'll insert Awkward2.avi later.)

7 Choose Edit > Copy.

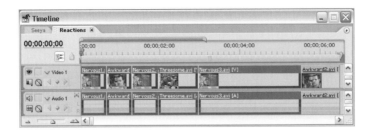

8 Click on the Seeya sequence to make it the active Timeline.

9 Select the second part of Awkward.avi, the segment after the close-up of the book, and choose Edit > Clear.

10 In the Seeya sequence, make sure that the current time indicator is set to the gap created by clearing the right portion of Awkward.avi (at 00;00;15;12). (Use the Page Down and Page Up keys.)

11 Choose Edit > Paste. The contents of the Reactions sequence are added to the Timeline.

12 Close the gap by selecting Seeya.avi and dragging it to the Out point of the pasted clips from the Reactions sequence.

Note: You can also select the gap and choose Edit > Ripple Delete.

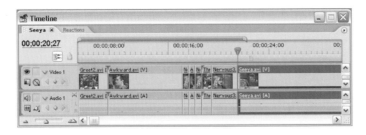

13 Save the project.

Using the slide tool

The Seeya sequence, which is composed of contiguous clips, is now ready for the frame accurate edits that you'll apply to finish this lesson.

1 Zoom into the Seeya sequence so you can see Nervous1.avi, Awkward1.avi, and Nervous2.avi.

2 Make sure the Selection tool is active and select the Nervous1.avi, Awkward1.avi, and Nervous2.avi clips.

3 Choose Marker > Set Sequence Marker > In and Out Around Selection.

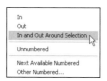

The three clips can be reviewed easily in the Program view.

4 In the Program view, click the Play In to Out button ( ) to review the footage.

Notice that the timing is off on the In point of Nervous2.avi. You want her eyes and head to move up on the cut, so the clips will read more dynamically. From the bookmark being seen, you'll have Ex look down, followed by Hero looking up, followed by Ex looking up.

5 In the Seeya sequence, set the current time indicator to the frame in Nervous2.avi where Ex's eyelids open and she gazes at Hero (at 00;00;17;02).

6 In the Timeline, click on the Snap button so that it toggles to the off position. (The white background and outline around the Snap button turn to gray.)

7 Hold the Shift key while clicking on Nervous1.avi and Nervous2.avi to deselect them. Awkward1.avi is still selected.

8 In the Tools palette, select the slide tool (⊕).

Note: If the Tools palette is not displayed, go to the title bar and choose Window > Tools.

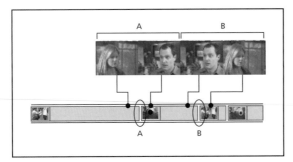

*You can view the edit between Nervous1.avi and Awkward1.avi (**A**) and the edit between Awkward1.avi and Nervous2.avi (**B**). Here, you'll move (A) toward (B) to a specific frame.*

💡 *You may want to change the Monitor to Single View by clicking the menu button at the top of the Monitor window and choosing Single View. Make the Monitor window display as large as possible so that you can spot subtle changes in motion in small areas of the frame.*

9 Position the cursor on Awkward1.avi, and then press and hold down the mouse button.

The Program view displays the critical frames of the three clips.

Notice that the Monitor window displays four frames: the Out point of the adjacent clip on the lower left (Nervous1.avi); the In point and Out points of the clip in which the tool is being used (Awkward1.avi, displayed in the upper row); and the In point of the adjacent clip on the lower right (Nervous2.avi).

10 In the Timeline, drag right to the current time indicator (at 00:00;17;02) where she begins to look up from the bookmark). This moves the Out point of Nervous1.avi and the In point of Awkward1.avi later in time.

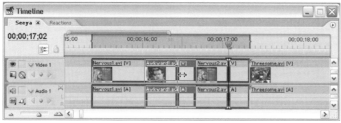

Note: If your Program view is too small to notice the subtle eye movements, use the Timeline window to view the edit. Look for the place where the edit line bisects the Out point of Awkward1.avi and the In point of Nervous2.avi. With snap turned off, you'll be able to adjust the edit to this moment in time.

Note: Use the zoom controls for more precise results.

11 Select the selection tool ( ) to deselect the slide tool.

When you release the mouse button, Premiere Pro updates the In and Out points for the adjacent clips, displaying the result in the Monitor window. The duration of the program and the Awkward1.avi clip are not changed. You have slid the right clip's position in the Timeline back toward the start of the project without changing its duration. It's as if you slid a film strip to the "left" and "behind" the Awkward1.avi clip, but kept the run length of the footage the same. Nervous2.avi now begins and ends later.

You've just matched the action between the Out point of Awkward1.avi (C) and Nervous2.avi (D), ignoring the other two frames.

12 Preview the change.

13 Save the project.

Using the slip tool

You'll use the slip tool to match the action between Nervous3.avi and Seeya.avi. To do this, you'll move the In point of Nervous3.avi while preserving the clip's duration. The In and Out points of Nervous3.avi will appear in the two middle frames of the Monitor window as you use the slip tool. The edited clips remain in the same position on the Timeline. The range of visible frames slips into position.

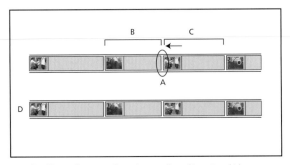

*Use the slip tool to match action at the edit point (**A**) between Nervous3.avi (**B**) and Seeya.avi (**C**). The tool changes the In and Out points of Nervous3.avi while preserving its duration. Adjacent clips, such as Threesome.avi, are unaffected. The result can be seen in (**D**).*

The slip edit motion involves dragging nine frames to the right.

Because there is no movement in the clip, there is no visual reference other than the four frames displayed in the Program view. You can watch the position of the cursor during the edit in the Info palette as a quantitative reference.

1 Scroll through the Nervous3.avi clip and the first part of the Seeya.avi clip.

Notice that Ex lays her head on New Boy's shoulder at the end of Nervous3.avi and also in Seeya.avi. You'll use the slip tool to create a lead into the Seeya.avi clip by eliminating the first instance of Ex resting her head on New Boy.

2 Position the current time indicator to the frame in Nervous3.avi where Ex moves to cuddle against New Boy's shoulder (at 00;00;20;19).

3 In the Tools palette, select the slip tool ().

4 Position the pointer on the Nervous3.avi clip in the Timeline, and then press and hold down the mouse button.

As you move the slip tool, the Monitor window displays the Out point of Threesome.avi, the In and Out points of Nervous3.avi, and the In point of Seeya.avi.

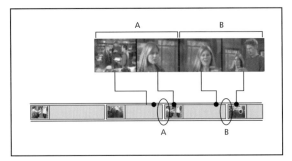

*You can see the edit from Threesome.avi and Nervous3.avi (**A**) and the edit between Nervous3.avi and Seeya.avi (**B**). Here, you'll fix the second edit.*

5 Drag right until the action in the third frame (the Out point of Nervous3.avi) matches the action in the frame displayed at the current time indicator. This results in new Timeline In and Out points that reflect footage appearing earlier in the source clip. The Timecode indicator will change into a plus or minus frame count. You want to move plus seven frames (move to the upper right +00;00;00;07).

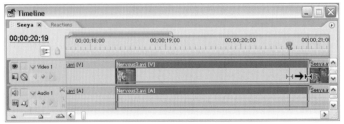

Top shows new frame 3 Out point, once the mouse is released (bottom). The frame at 00;00;20;19 will slip to the Out point of Nervous3.avi at 00;00;20;26, after the edit is completed.

6 Release the mouse button. The Monitor window now displays one frame.

7 Select the selection tool (↖) to deselect the slip tool.

8 Preview the change.

The action in the third and fourth frames should match. Premiere Pro updates the source In and Out points for the clip, displaying the result in the Monitor window. The clip and program duration are maintained. Adjacent clips are unaffected. Before moving on to the next exercise, you'll revert to the status before the slip edit.

9 Chose Edit > Undo Slip to return the Timeline to its previous state.

10 Save the project.

Understanding the Trim window

The Trim window is a separate window with specific controls for fine-tuning the cut points between clips. It is similar to the dual view in the Monitor window, except both views represent clips in the program. The left monitor view is the clip to the left of the edit point, and the right monitor is the clip to the right of the edit point. You can perform ripple edits or rolling edits at any point in a sequence, and the sequence updates as the edits are made.

Being able to see frames on either side of the edit line enables you to precisely trim each clip. This view is useful for fine-tuning the edit between two clips in which the action must match or for which the timing is critical. The Timeline updates as you perform the edit.

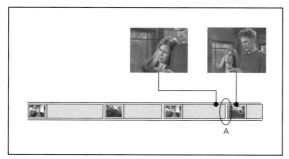

The Trim window provides a frame-by-frame ripple edit function and a view of each clip at the edit point (A).

Ripple editing in the Trim window

Now you'll use the Trim window to produce the same result as with the slip tool. You'll trim Nervous3.avi to make the action consistent with the action at the beginning of Seeya.avi. Then, you'll use a rolling edit to move the edit point between the clips. The rolling edit preserves the combined duration of the two clips.

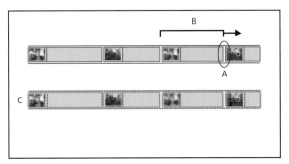

*The Trim window will be used to make the action at the edit point (**A**) between Nervous3.avi and Seeya.avi while preserving the In and Out points and duration of Nervous3.avi (**B**). The result can be seen in (**C**).*

1 In the Program view, press the Page Up or Page Down keys to set the edit line between Nervous3.avi and Seeya.avi.

2 Click the Trim button (⊞) at the bottom right of the Program view to display the Trim window.

In the Trim window, Premiere displays two frames: the Out point of Nervous3.avi on the left; and the In point of Seeya.avi on the right. You'll notice some buttons unique to the Trim window.

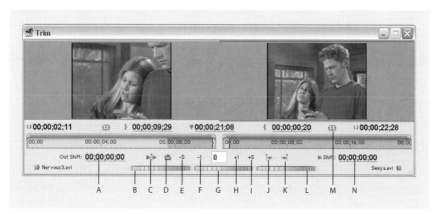

A. Out Shift B. Jog Out Point C. Play Edit D. Trim: Loop E. Trim Backward by Large Trim offset F. Trim Backward by One Frame G. Jog Roll In and Out Points H. Trim Forward by One Frame I. Trim Forward by Large Trim offset J. Go to Previous Edit Point K. Go to Next Edit Point L. Jog In Point M. Safe Margins N. In Shift

Now you'll adjust the action in Nervous3.avi to be consistent with the action in Seeya.avi.

Earlier in this Lesson (in step 2 on page 335), you located the keyframe in the clip where Ex turns to face the camera as she is moving toward New Boy. This keyframe was identified at 00;00;20;19.

3 With 00;00;20;19 as the target Out point in the Trim edit, position the cursor over the left view, which displays the current last frame of Nervous3.avi.

The cursor changes into the Ripple Edit tool when it is over the image area of the frame.

4 Click and drag the mouse to the left until the frame at 00;00;20;19 appears in the center timecode field and the target keyframe image appears above and to the left of that timecode (the left image viewed in the Trim window).

 If you go too far, use the -5 and -1 buttons to reverse the trim. Click the left frame (Nervous3.avi) and then use the +5 and +1 buttons to adjust Nervous3.avi so that the action in the Nervous3.avi Out point matches the action in the Seeya.avi In point.

Note: *The -5 and -1 buttons trim clips left, and the +5 and +1 buttons trim clips right.*

The action from one clip to the other is now consistent.

5 Preview the edit to see its effects.

The cut is tighter from Ex's close up in Nervous3.avi to where she leans her head against New Boy's shoulder in the medium shot at the beginning of Seeya.avi.

6 Save the project.

Using a rolling edit in the Trim window

Next, you'll perform an edit between clips using the rolling edit in the Trim window.

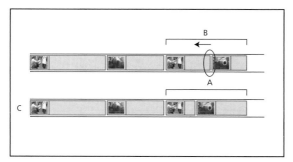

*You'll use a rolling edit in the Trim window to move the edit (**A**) between Nervous3.avi and Seeya.avi while preserving the combined duration of both clips (**B**). The result is seen in (**C**).*

Now, you'll tighten the edit at the start of Nervous3.avi, removing the blinking of Ex's eyes so that her reaction flows more continuously from her nonverbal exchange with Hero over the sensitive greeting card.

There are two keys to the Trim window. First, place the edit line inside the selected clip and second make sure to select the clip on the Timeline before you make the rolling edit.

1 With the selection tool, select Nervous3.avi. Click on the Trim button to display the Trim window if it is no longer displayed. Position the pointer in the space between the left and right views. The cursor becomes the rolling edit tool (⊞).

2 Drag the rolling edit tool to the right until the target frame at 00;00;18;20 becomes the In point on the right image. Use the following illustration as a guide.

Note: Perform a rolling edit numerically by typing a negative number to move left or by typing a positive number to move right in the text field between the -1 and +1 buttons, and then pressing Enter. The move is a total of nine frames (+00;00;00;09).

3 Choose Window > Monitor to bring the Monitor window to the front of your display.

4 Scrub in the Timeline ruler to preview the change.

5 Preview the last three clips.

6 Save the project.

For more information about performing a rolling edit in the Trim window, see "Using the Trim window" in the *Adobe Premiere Pro User Guide*.

Adding three polishing edits

To polish the end of this project, you'll add one more clip and two sound effects.

Adding a final clip to enhance pacing

You'll insert footage that is one second in length to break up the action between the Nervous3.avi and Seeya.avi clips to improve the pacing and make it more cinematic.

1 Close the Trim window.

2 In the Timeline, adjust the zoom controls to see Nervous3.avi and Seeya.avi.

3 Set the edit line at the cut between the two clips.

4 In the Timeline window, click on the Reactions sequence tab to make it the active sequence.

5 Locate the last clip in the sequence, Awkward2.avi, and select it.

6 Choose Edit > Copy.

7 Return to the Seeya sequence by clicking on its tab in the Timeline window.

8 With the current time indicator still set at the cut between the Nervous3.avi and Seeya.avi clips, choose Edit > Paste Insert.

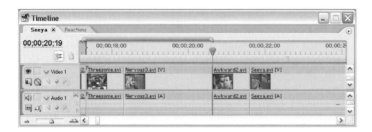

9 Preview the newly added clip and the surrounding footage to see its effect on the timing of the scene.

Adding one more cut improves the flow between the action of Nervous3.avi and Seeya.avi.

10 Save the project.

Adding two sound effects

Now you'll add two sound effects to this sequence. Throughout the scene, New Boy plays with a hand-held game. You'll add the sound of the game to the sequence for a touch of realism. Then you'll add the sound of the door slamming as Ex and New Boy exit.

1 In the Project window, open Bin 01. Double-click Game.wav so that it opens in the Source view of the Monitor window.

2 Locate 00;00;29;04 in the clip's display in the Source view.

3 Click the Set Out Point button (⌐) in the Source view.

4 In the Seeya sequence, use the zoom out controls to see the entire sequence in the Timeline.

5 In the Timeline, set the current time indicator to the beginning of the project by typing the Home key, with nothing selected, or Page Up until it is at 00;00;00;00. (Also, make sure you eliminate any Sequence Markers by right-clicking on the time ruler and selecting Clear Sequence Marker > In and Out Points.

6 Make sure no clips are selected. Click in the header area next to the Audio 2 track to make it the target track.

7 In the Source view of the Monitor window, click on the Overlay button (![icon]).

8 The Game.wav clip is placed at the beginning of the sequence on the Audio 2 track.

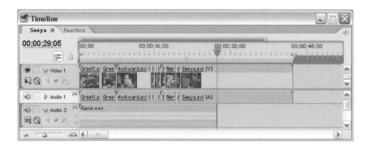

9 Preview the sound effect.

10 Save the project.

Last, add the sound of the door slamming in Hero's face, the final insult to his injured pride.

11 Locate the final frame where the door slams (at 00;00;38;27). (Scrub, drag the shuttle control, or press the arrow keys in either the Timeline or Program Monitor.)

12 Go back five frames to 00;00;38;22.

Note: Once you place the sound effect, you may need to tweak its position to match the action in the video.

13 In Bin 01 of the Project window, select the Doorslam.wav clip.

14 Choose Clip > Overlay.

15 Preview the project.

16 Save the project.

You've now completed advanced frame-by-frame editing techniques. In the next two lessons you'll assemble the entire movie, using nested sequences and some of the dynamic sound features of Adobe Premiere Pro. Then you'll learn how to make titles and credits. In the final two lessons, you'll find out about the many forms of video and audio output available to you in Premiere Pro.

Exporting the movie

Now that you've finished your editing, it's time to generate a movie file.

1 If you turned off audio previewing earlier in the lesson, make sure you turn it on again by clicking the icon in the track header area of each audio track so that it changes to the speaker icon (◀)).

2 Choose File > Export > Movie.

3 In the Export Movie dialog box, click the Settings button. In the General settings, make sure Microsoft DV AVI is selected for the File Type.

4 Select Entire Sequence for the Range.

5 Make sure that Export Video, Export Audio, Add to Project When Finished, and Beep When Finished are selected.

6 In the Audio section, choose 48000 Hz for Sample Rate, 16-bit for Sample Type, and Stereo for Channels.

7 Click OK to close the Export Movie Settings dialog box.

8 In the Export Movie dialog box, specify the 09Lesson folder for the location and type **Seeya.avi** for the name of the movie. Click Save.

While Premiere Pro is making the movie, a status bar displays the time remaining to complete the process. When the movie is complete, it appears in the Project window.

9 Double-click the movie to open it into the Source view of the Monitor window.

10 Click the Play button (▶) to view the movie you've just created.

Review questions

1 The Ripple Delete command and the Extract button provide similar functions. What is the main difference between them?

2 Which tool would you use to change the In and Out points of a clip while preserving the clip's duration?

3 How does the slide tool differ from the slip tool?

4 What features does the Trim window offer that make it well-suited for fine-tuning edits?

5 Name two techniques for matching action between the end of one clip and the beginning of the next.

Answers

1 Ripple Delete works on one or more whole clips or on a gap; the Extract button works on a range of frames in one or more clips.

2 The slip tool changes the In and Out points of a clip while preserving its duration.

3 The slide tool preserves the duration of the target clip but changes the duration of the two clips adjacent to the target clip.

4 The Trim window enables you to trim individual frames on either side of an edit point, while viewing those frames.

5 The slip tool and the Trim window controls provide you with two methods to adjust the action to make it realistic and seamless.

Lesson 10

10 | Advanced Editing Two: Nested and Multiple Sequences

Nested sequences and duplicate clips are powerful tools used to assemble a video program in Premiere Pro. Sequences allow you to organize vast databases of digital video information. Nested sequences clips combine one or more clips, effects, and transitions into a single clip to simplify the Timeline and increase your flexibility and workflow. Effects and transitions can be applied repeatedly on the same source material.

Manipulating clips and footage in a Premiere Pro project can be greatly enhanced by using nested sequences and duplicate clips. You'll learn about using nested sequences and duplicate clips by assembling all but a few pieces of the short film *Books & Beans* you have worked with throughout the lessons of this book.

In this lesson, you'll learn the following skills:

• Creating and naming duplicate clips.

• Using duplicate clips in a project.

• Creating, nesting, and editing nested sequences.

• Compiling a nested sequence into an actual clip.

• Treating sequences as clips.

• Editing multiple nested sequences.

Getting started

For this lesson, you'll open an existing project with no clips assembled in the Timeline. Make sure you know the location of the files used in this lesson. Insert the *Classroom in a Book* DVD-ROM disk if necessary. For help, see "Copying the Classroom in a Book files" on page 4.

1 Launch the Premiere Pro software.

2 In the Premiere Pro Welcome window, click Open Project.

3 In the Open Project dialog box, locate the 10Lesson folder that you copied onto your hard drive from the DVD-ROM.

4 Locate the 10Lesson.prproj file in the 10Lesson folder and click Open. (You can also double-click on the 10Lesson.prproj file to open it.)

5 If necessary, rearrange windows and palettes so that they don't overlap, by choosing Window > Workspace > Editing.

Viewing the finished movie

To see what you'll be creating, take a look at the completed movie for this lesson. Because the final result of the exercises in this lesson will be the entire movie *Books & Beans*, except for some audio and the credits, you'll reference the final movie.

1 Create a new bin by either clicking the new Bin icon (🗀) at the bottom of the project window or clicking the menu triangle at the top right corner of the Project window and choosing New Bin.

2 Type **Resources** to name the new bin.

3 Choose File > Import and navigate to the main directory you copied to your hard disk from the DVD.

4 Select the Movies directory and click Open.

5 Select Books&Beans.wmv and click Open.

The Books&Beans.wmv file is now located in the Resources bin.

6 Double-click the Books&Beans.wmv file so that it opens in the Source view of the Monitor window.

7 Click the Play button (▶) in the Source view of the Monitor window to watch the video program.

8 You can either delete the Resources bin and the Books&Beans.wmv movie by clicking the Clear button (🗑) at the bottom of the Project window, or, you may decide to keep it as a reference.

Working with multiple sequences

A single project may contain multiple sequences, which are represented by tabs in the Program view of the Monitor window and in the Timeline window. Tabs make it easy to switch between sequences. Click on a sequence tab to view the sequence in its own window.

All the sequences in a project must share the same timebase, which defines how Adobe Premiere Pro calculates time. The timebase cannot be changed after you've created a project.

Note: You can import a project into another project with a different timebase. However, the alignment of edits in the imported sequences continue to reflect the timebase of their source project. Because mismatched timebases can cause frame misalignments, you should check— and if necessary, adjust—edits in imported projects.

Nesting sequences

You can also insert, or nest, sequences into other sequences. A nested sequence appears as a single, linked video/audio clip—even though its source sequence may contain numerous video and audio tracks. You can select, move, trim, and apply effects to nested sequences as you would to any other clip. Any changes you make to the source sequence will be reflected in any of the nested instances created from the source sequence. Moreover, you can nest sequences within sequences—to any depth—to create complex groupings and hierarchies. The ability to nest sequences enables you to employ a number of time-saving techniques and to create effects that otherwise would be difficult or impossible. Nesting enables you to do the following:

• Reuse sequences. When you want to repeat a sequence—particularly a complex one—you can create it once, then simply nest it in another sequence as many times as you want.

• Apply different settings to copies of a sequence. For example, if you want a sequence to play back repeatedly but with a different effect each time, just apply a different effect to each instance of the nested sequence.

• Streamline your editing space. You can create complex, multilayered sequences separately, and then add them to the main sequence as a single clip. This prevents you from having to maintain numerous tracks in the main sequence, and reduces the chances of inadvertently moving clips during editing and losing sync.

• Create complex groupings and nested effects. Although you can apply only one transition to an edit point, you can nest sequences and apply a new transition to each nested clip—creating transitions-within-transitions. Or you can create picture-in-picture effects, in which each picture is a nested sequence, containing its own series of clips, transitions, and effects.

When nesting sequences, keep in mind the following:

• You can't nest a sequence within itself.

• Because nested sequences can contain references to many clips, actions involving a nested sequence may require additional processing time, as Adobe Premiere Pro applies the actions to all of its component clips.

• A nested sequence always represents the current state of its source sequence. Changing the content of the source sequence is reflected in the content of its nested instances. Duration is not directly affected.

ADOBE PREMIERE PRO **353**

• A nested sequence clip's initial duration is determined by its source. This includes empty space at the beginning of the source sequence, but not empty space at the end. Subsequently changing the source sequence's duration, however, does not affect the duration of existing nested instances. To lengthen the nested instances and reveal material added to the source sequence, use standard trimming methods. Conversely, a shortened source sequence causes the nested instance to contain black video and silent audio, which you may need to trim off the nested sequence.

• You can set a nested sequence's In and Out points as you would other clips.

Understanding duplicate clips

Each component of a video program has a name that describes its function in the program and its location in the Premiere Pro Workspace.

Source clip A *source clip* is a file containing video that has been digitized. All of the files currently in the Project window of this project are source clips.

Instance You can drag copies of a source clip from the Project window into the Timeline as many times as you want. Each copy you use in this manner is called an *instance*.

Duplicate clip You can also create a *duplicate clip* from a source clip in the Project window. Like a source clip, a duplicate clip appears in the Project window, and is identified by the same name with the word *copy* next to its name. You can use any number of instances of a duplicate clip in a project.

Note: Don't confuse a duplicate clip with the rename command. Applying a new name to a clip simply changes the name of the clip but doesn't create a new clip.

To create a duplicate clip that is a subset of a source clip, you must first open an *instance* of the source clip in the Source view to set new In and Out points for the duplicate clip. They will retain the new In and Out points, which you can adjust in the Source view.

Note: It's important to understand that if the source clip is deleted from the Project window, the instances and duplicate clips created from that source clip will also be deleted, both from the Project window and from the Timeline.

Understanding nested sequences

When creating duplicate clips, you make a number of clips from a single source clip. When creating nested sequences, you create a single clip from a specified area of a Timeline from another sequence, which can include any number of clips. A nested sequence can include multiple clips, tracks, effects, and transitions. It can be reused in a project any number of times. Premiere treats a nested sequence as a single clip, so you can edit it and apply settings as you would to a source clip. By using nested sequences to organize and group sequences, you can save time editing complex video programs.

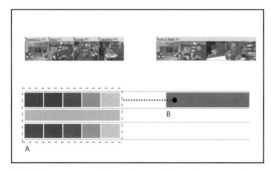

*Multiple sequences (**A**) can be combined into a nested sequence (**B**).*

For example, if you create a short sequence involving four superimposed video tracks and three mixed audio tracks, and you want to use the sequence ten times in a project, you can simply build the sequence once, create one nested sequence from it, and add ten *instances* of the nested sequence to the Timeline.

You can apply effects, transitions, or other settings to the source clips that define a nested sequence to simultaneously make global changes to all instances of the nested sequence in the Timeline. You can also apply settings more than once to the same clip. Certain effects can be achieved only by combining transitions. You cannot apply more than one transition to the same point in time. To accomplish multiple overlapping transitions you must use nested sequences.

You can also apply different settings to copies of a sequence. For example, if you want a sequence to play back repeatedly but with a different effect each time, you can create a nested sequence and just copy it for each instance in which you want it to appear with a different effect. As with duplicate clips, each clip in the source area for a nested sequence refers back to a source sequence in the Project window.

Note: *Deleting the source clip or the clip in the source area for the nested sequence will also delete the corresponding portion of each instance of the nested sequence.*

For more information on using nested sequences, see the section on "Working with multiple sequences and nested sequences" in the *Adobe Premiere Pro User Guide.*

Creating nested sequences

In this exercise, you'll create a nested sequence that will be combined with other clips to make the final project. Before you can create a nested sequence, you must assemble the source clips and sequences that will make up the nested sequence.

Assembling source sequences and clips

Now you'll assemble the source clips from which to create a master nested sequence. The resulting nested sequence will combine sequences and clips from previous lessons to create the entire feature.

Begin by observing the Project window that was set up in the 10Lesson project folder on the *Classroom in a Book* DVD-ROM.

You'll see the sequences you created in previous lessons arrayed in the Project window.

Note: The Resources bin contains all of the clips that comprise the various sequences. You'll use the sequences just exactly as if they were clips. Close the Resources bin when you're done exploring.

1 In the Project window, click on Sequence 01 and choose Clip > Rename. Type **Master** to rename Sequence 01.

2 In the Project window, select the following in order while holding down the Control key: Sequence Ex, Seeya, Brownie, and Transitions.

3 Drag them to the beginning of the Master sequence in the Timeline window so that they appear in the order selected.

The complex sequences from previous lessons are now a "flat" simple Timeline. The color scheme for sequences used as clips is different than the color scheme for ordinary clips.

Building a sequence to be nested

The first 00;03;39;06 of the movie are laid down on the Video 1 track. Now you'll build the ending sequence to import. You'll see how making changes to one affects the other without having to redo any steps.

1 In the Project window, choose File > New > Sequence.

2 In the dialog box, type **Ending** for the name and click OK.

The basic building blocks of Ending are located in the Ending bin inside the Resources bin of the Project window.

3 In the Project window, locate the Ending Bin inside the Resources bin.

4 Open the Ending bin and select the following clips in the following order while holding down the Control key: Dejection.avi, Alone.avi, Exchange.avi, and Resolve.avi.

5 Use the Automate to Sequence button to insert them onto the Timeline in Ending sequence. Be sure to place them in the Selection Order with no transitions active.

6 In the Automate to Sequence dialog box, choose Selection Order for the Ordering field, Sequentially for Placement, Overlay Edit for Method, and then set the Clip Overlap to 0 and click OK.

Now you'll prepare to place this rough draft of Ending onto the Master sequence at the end of the program. You'll create a gap in the Ending sequence.

7 Set the current time indicator to 00;00;53;11.

8 In the tools palette, select the track select tool (⊞) and click on Exchange.avi.

All of the clips to the right are selected.

9 Drag the selected clips to the right so that the head of Exchange.avi snaps to the edit line creating a gap between the Alone.avi and Exchange.avi clips.

Now you'll preview the Ending sequence from the Master sequence.

10 Make the Master sequence active by clicking on its tab in the Timeline window.

11 From the Project window, with the selection tool drag the Ending sequence icon to the Master sequence at the tail of Transitions.

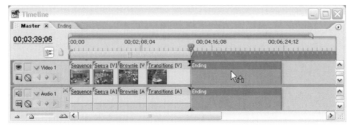

12 Play the movie.

Observe the gap you've just created, but review on an entirely different Timeline.

Viewing changes in a sequence in a nested master

Now when you edit Alone.avi in the Ending sequence, you'll learn how the two Timelines are related to each other.

1 In the Timeline window, click the Ending sequence tab to activate it.

You'll fill the gap with a duplicate of Alone.avi.

2 In the Resource bin of the Project window, locate the Ending bin and open it.

3 Select the Alone.avi clip and choose Edit > Duplicate.

The Duplicate command creates a copy of Alone.avi in the Ending bin.

4 Rename Alone.avi Copy to **Alone2.avi**.

5 Make sure that the current time indicator in the Ending sequence is at 00;00;53;11.

6 From the Project window, drag Alone2.avi to the Ending sequence so that its tail snaps to the edit line.

7 In the Tools palette, select the rate stretch tool (⟂).

The rate stretch tool changes the clip speed.

8 With the rate stretch tool, select the head of the Alone2.avi clip and drag it to the left until it fills the gap.

9 Now observe the results of the edits to the Ending sequence by previewing the Master sequence again.

Notice that the changes made to the Ending sequence are reflected in the instance of the Ending sequence on the Master sequence.

10 Click on the selection tool in the Tools palette.

11 Save the project.

Adding the first of two special effects

Now you'll make two more special effects: one of these effects will be added in the Ending sequence, and the second will be added in the Master sequence.

1 In the Timeline of the Ending sequence, set the current time indicator to the In point of Alone2.avi, which is at 00;00;41;29.

2 Select the track header area of the Video 2 track and the Audio 2 track to designate them as target tracks. (The tracks turn gray.)

3 Drag the Loveyou.avi clip so that its head snaps to the CTI.

4 With Loveyou.avi selected on the Timeline, go to the Effect Controls window and select Opacity.

5 In the Effect Controls window, click the triangle next to Opacity to expand the settings.

6 Set the opacity for the Loveyou.avi clip to **50%**.

Now you will fade the last second of the Loveyou.avi clip from 50% to 0% opacity.

7 Set the edit line to 00;00;53;18.

8 Add a keyframe by clicking on the Add/Remove Keyframe button (◈).

9 Press the Page Down key once to go to the end of the Loveyou.avi clip (at 00;00;54;18).

10 Click the Add/Remove Keyframe button to add another keyframe at the end.

11 In the Effect Controls window, change the opacity for the end keyframe from 50% to **0%**.

12 Click on the Master sequence tab to make it the active Timeline.

13 Preview the effect of the Loveyou.avi clip superimposed on the slow motion of the Alone2.avi clip created with the rate stretch tool.

Notice that the changes you've made to the Ending sequence are updated in the Master sequence.

14 Save the project.

Adding an effect to a nested sequence

In the previous exercise, you added an effect to a source sequence composed of clips. Now you'll add a series of effects to the Master sequence.

1 Click on the Master sequence tab to make it the active Timeline.

2 Make the Video 2 track the target by clicking in its track header area of the Timeline.

3 Set the edit line to the In point of the Transitions sequence clip (at 00;02;20;01).

4 In the Project window, open Bin 01 within the Transitions bin within the Resources bin and select the Vignette.psd clip.

5 Choose Clip > Overlay.

6 In the Timeline, move the edit line to the end of the first fantasy scene, after Hero runs off screen (at 00;02;29;29).

7 Using the selection tool, drag the Out point of the Vignette.psd clip to the edit line.

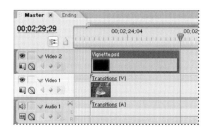

8 Press the Page Up key to place the edit line at the start of Vignette.psd.

9 With the Vignette.psd clip selected, go to the Effect Controls window.

Now you'll make the Vignette.psd clip fade in at the rate of the Cross Dissolve.

10 Add a keyframe at the edit line by clicking the triangle next to Opacity to expand the settings and then click on the Add/Remove Keyframe button (◆.)

11 In the Timeline window, locate the point in the first approach fantasy scene, where the cross dissolve ends (at 00;02;21;29).

12 In the Effect Controls window, click on the Add/Remove Keyframe button (◊) to add another keyframe (at 00;02;21;29).

13 To make the Vignette.psd clip fade in, click on the Go to Previous Keyframe button (◄), then drag the Opacity slider to zero or change the opacity value to **0**.

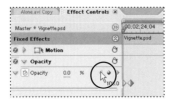

14 Preview the effect inside the Effect Controls window by scrubbing with the edit line.

Vignette.psd fades in at the pace of the cross dissolve below it, and the scene is framed in a dreamy glow.

15 Save the project.

Now you'll repeat this process for the other three fantasy segments.

16 In the Timeline window, locate the start of the dissolve to the second approach fantasy scene (00;02;34;27). If you step forward a frame at a time, you'll see that the transition begins to fade in at that point. Place the edit line at 00;02;34;27.

17 Select the Vignette.psd clip on the Video 2 track and choose Edit > Copy.

18 Deselect Vignette.psd.

19 Make sure the target track is the Video 2 track, and then choose Edit > Paste.

The second instance of Vignette.psd is overlaid at the edit line.

20 Place the edit line at the Out point of the bouquet fantasy scene (at 00;02;40;29).

21 Using the selection tool, trim the Out point of the second Vignette.psd to the edit line.

22 Repeat this pasting process for the third instance of Vignette.psd (at 00;02;44;14) and fourth instance (at 00;03;05;01).

23 Trim the Out points of the third and fourth instances of Vignette.psd to 00;02;53;05 and 00;03;15;19, respectively. (The fourth trim will increase the duration.)

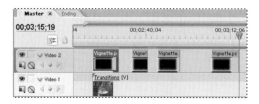

24 Preview the four fantasy scenes.

Note: To apply the same effects to the Transitions sequence, you have to copy and paste them into it. If you build them in the Transitions sequence, they will be updated in the Master sequence.

25 Save the project.

Refining and polishing the nested sequence

Now that you have assembled the source sequences, you are ready to polish the edits of your nested sequence into a movie.

In this exercise, you'll:

• Remove repetitive segments that arose from using the same clip at the end of one sequence and the beginning of the next in a separate lesson. You'll fix two of those instances.

• Add Dreams' entrance sequence, and Hero's celebratory, "Yes," when he figures it out that Dreams is not part of Father and Son's family.

• Insert a transition between two sequences.

• Apply most of the music clips to the Audio 2 track of the Master sequence.

You'll add more music in Lesson 12, "Audio".

Editing and trimming nested sequences

To this point, you've added effects to the Master sequence. Now you'll do some edits that add an establishing shot to Sequence Ex and remove the repeated sequences in the cut from Sequence Ex to Seeya, and the cut from Transitions to Ending.

1 First, in the Project window, locate Sequence Ex and double-click it to make it the active timeline.

Note: You can also click on the tab if it is visible in the Timeline window.

2 In Sequence Ex, set the current time indicator to the moment the book starts to slip from under Hero's armpit, at 00;00;09;26.

3 In the Tools palette, select the ripple edit tool (⁜).

4 Click on the Pieplease.avi clip to make it active. Drag right from the In point to Ripple edit the clip to the edit line.

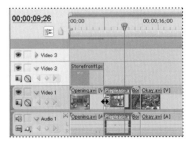

5 Use the Page Up key to move the edit line to the Out point of Opening.avi (at 00;00;06;05).

6 In the Project window, select Cup.avi in Bin 01 within the Ex bin within the Resources bin.

7 Choose Clip > Insert.

You've added a new angle for the Pieplease scene.

8 Activate the Master sequence, in the Timeline and review the new footage.

Now, you'll adjust the moments when Hero and New Boy encounter each other.

9 In the Master sequence play the last few seconds of Sequence Ex to learn the cue you'll be editing to: the words, "You two know each other" (at 00;00;42;17).

10 Now set the edit line to that cue point in Seeya (at 00;00;46;12).

11 Ripple edit the nested Seeya sequence in the Master timeline to the edit line from the In point, dragging to the right.

12 Preview the edit to be sure the cut is smooth.

13 Save the project.

A similar adjustment is needed at the end of the nested Transitions sequence and the first frame of the Ending sequence.

14 Set the edit line in the Master timeline to the place right after Hero packs up his belongings and exits (at 00;03;59;01).

15 With the ripple edit tool, trim the Ending sequence from the left to the edit line.

16 Preview the edit to be sure the cut is smooth.

17 Save the project.

Inserting a sequence into nested sequences

The first rough cut of the Master sequence omits Dreams' glowing entrance into the coffee shop.

1 Set the edit line in the Master sequence to the cut between Seeya and Brownie.

2 In the Timeline window, select the track header area of the Video 1 and Audio 1 tracks to designate them as the target tracks.

3 In the Project window, select the Entrance sequence.

4 Choose Clip > Insert.

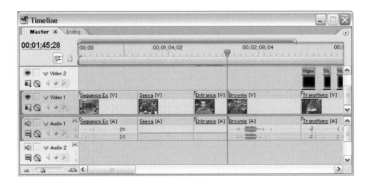

5 Preview your changes.

6 Save the project.

Now you'll add the triumphant Yes.avi clip to the Brownie sequence to update the Master sequence.

7 In the Project window, double-click the Brownie sequence to activate it in the Timeline window.

8 In the Timeline window, locate the place in the Brownie sequence after Father and Son leave the store and Dreams says, "Bye bye now" (at 00;00;28;09).

9 In the Project window, select the Yes.avi clip in the Brownie bin within the Resources bin.

10 Make sure the Video 1 and Audio 1 tracks are selected as the target tracks. Choose Clip > Overlay to preserve the duration of the sequence.

11 Return to the Master sequence to preview this adjustment.

12 Save the project.

Adding a transition to nested sequences

You can add transitions just like any other effects between two sequences nested in another one. Here you'll make a cross dissolve between the departure of Ex and New Boy and Hero seen later reading the book and sipping his drink.

1 In the Effects palette, type **Cross Dissolve** in the Contains area. (To open the Effects palette, choose Window > Effects.)

2 Make sure Cross Dissolve is the default transition. (The icon should be outlined in red.)

3 Click the menu triangle button in the upper right corner of the Effects palette and choose Default Transition Duration.

4 In the Preferences dialog box, make the Video Transition Default Duration **60** frames and click OK.

5 In the Master sequence, make the Audio 2 track the target track by clicking in the track header area.

6 Locate the cut between Seeya and Entrance by using the Page Up and Page Down keys.

7 Choose Sequence > Apply Video Transition.

The Cross Dissolve is applied between the two sequences. Because there is no trim area to the tail of Seeya, Premiere Pro places the transition at the head of Entrance.

8 Select the transition on the Timeline.

9 In the Effect Controls window, use the time zoom controls to center the dissolve between the two sequences, Seeya and Entrance.

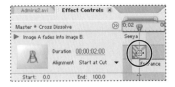

In the Timeline, after the transitions have been applied, you can set the current time indicator to one second before the cut, then drag the transition until it snaps to the edit line. This will perfectly center it. The cross hatches indicate where the transition had to "borrow" frames from Seeya to make the transition work as a center to cut transition.

10 Preview the transition.

11 Save the project.

Adding audio to nested sequences

As you've seen in these exercises, you treat nested sequences just like any other clip. You'll now add music for the first half of the movie to the Audio 2 track. The balance of the music and sound effects for the entire film are added in exercises in Lesson 12, "Audio."

By inserting the music that opens the movie, you'll create a gap when you synchronize it to Hero's first word, "Hello." In the next Lesson, "Titles and Credits," you'll add the video portion of the title scene.

1 Make the Master sequence the active timeline.

2 Set the current time indicator to the beginning of the movie by using the Page Up or Home key.

3 Click on the Audio 2 track header area to make it the target track.

4 In the Project window, locate the Title.wav clip in Bin 01, which is within the Ex bin inside the Resources bin and select it.

5 Choose Clip > Insert.

The result is a video gap so that most of the Title.wav clip will play over black.

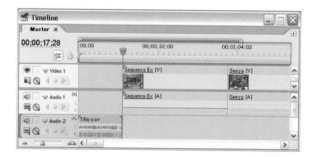

6 Navigate to the first few seconds of Sequence Ex until you find the moment Hero begins to speak to the clerk (at 00;00;26;05), and place the edit line there.

7 Select Title.wav and drag it to the right until its Out point snaps to the edit line.

8 Select the gap to the left of Title.wav at the start of the Audio 2 track.

9 Choose Edit > Ripple Delete.

10 Preview the opening music and first speech.

11 Save the project.

You'll add three more music clips to complete this lesson on nested sequences.

12 Navigate the edit line to where Hero is about to say, "Not much," and the scene cuts away to a lonely mountain top (at 00;00;40;08).

13 In the Project window, locate the Gothic.wav clip in Bin 01, which is inside the Ex bin within the Resources bin.

14 Making sure that Audio 2 track is still the target track, choose Clip > Overlay.

15 Jog, shuttle, or step back to the last frame on the mountain top and place the edit line there (00;00;43;20).

16 Trim Gothic.wav to the edit line by dragging left from the Out point until it snaps to it.

17 With the Gothic.wav clip selected, select the Volume effect in the Effect Controls window.

18 Open the Volume triangle and then the Levels triangle to locate the Volume slider.

19 Lower the volume to -10.37dB.

Note: In Lesson 12, "Audio," you'll learn how to adjust the volume interactively while the music plays.

20 Preview the effect of adding Gothic.wav to the scene.

21 Save the project.

The third piece of music covers the exit of Ex and New Boy. The cue for the melancholy passage is Ex saying, "Seeya around sometime, maybe."

22 Place the edit line to the point in time immediately after Ex says, "Maybe" (at 00;01;19;11).

23 In the Project window, select the Seeyablues.wav clip in Bin 01 within the Seeya bin, which is inside the Resources bin.

24 Choose Clip > Overlay.

25 Preview the end of the relationship underscored by the music.

26 Save the project.

Last, add the choral music that accompanies the "mystical" entrance of Dreams.

27 Jog, shuttle, or step forward and place the edit line where Hero beholds Dreams in the open doorway and the camera zooms in on her (at 00;01;42;11).

28 In the Project window, select the Chorale.wav clip in Bin 01 within the Entrance bin, which is within the Resources bin.

29 Choose Clip > Overlay.

30 Preview the emotions dramatized by the music.

31 Save the project.

Congratulations, you have completed the lesson on nested sequences.

Exporting the movie

Now that you've finished your editing, it's time to generate a movie file.

1 If you turned off audio previewing earlier in the lesson, make sure you turn it on again by clicking the icon in the track header area of each audio track so that it changes to the speaker icon (◀).

2 Choose File > Export > Movie.

3 In the Export Movie dialog box, click the Settings button. In the General settings, make sure that File Type is set to Microsoft DV AVI.

4 Select Entire Sequence for the Range.

5 Make sure that Export Video, Export Audio, Add to Project When Finished, and Beep When Finished are selected.

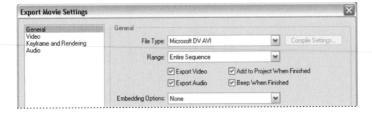

6 In the Audio section, choose 48000 Hz for Sample Rate, 16-bit for Sample Type, and Stereo for Channels.

7 Click OK to close the Export Movie Settings dialog box.

8 In the Export Movie dialog box, specify the 10Lesson folder for the location and type **Nested.avi** for the name of the movie. Click Save.

While Premiere Pro is making the movie, a status bar displays the time remaining to complete the process. When the movie is complete, it appears in the Project window.

9 Double-click the movie to open it into the Source view of the Monitor window.

10 Click the Play button (▶) to play the movie you've just created.

Exploring on your own

Feel free to experiment with the project you have just created. Here are some suggestions:

• Use the razor tool to cut one of the nested sequences into several segments and apply different effect settings to each segment.

• Add the Strobe Light effect to the last nested sequence you created. Set Visible Frames to 4, Hidden Frames to 1, and pick a bright color. Set keyframes identical to those used in the Invert effect.

Review questions

1 What are two ways to rename a clip?

2 What is the advantage of nesting sequences while creating effects and transitions?

3 To create a new clip that appears in the Project window, would you use a duplicate clip, an alias, or a nested sequence?

4 What are the advantages and disadvantages of compiling a nested sequence?

5 Can a duplicate clip contain more than one source clip?

6 Can a nested sequence contain more than one source clip?

7 What are three ways to change the duration of a still image?

Answers

1 Choose Clip > Rename or change the name in the Project window with the list view selected.

2 You can use transitions and effects more than once on the same material.

3 A duplicate clip.

4 Compiling a nested sequence protects it against being accidentally modified, eliminates the need to keep its source material in the project, and shortens the preview time. Once a nested sequence is compiled, however, you can change it by modifying the source material.

5 A duplicate clip cannot include more than one source clip.

6 A nested sequence can consist of more than one source clip. It can also consist of more than one nested sequence.

7 You can change the duration of a still image in the following ways:

• Before importing the clip into the project, change the number of frames for the Video Transition Default Duration in the Preferences General dialog box.

• Choose Clip > Speed/Duration and then enter a new duration after the clip is imported into the project.

• Position the selection tool pointer on the edge of the clip and drag to a new location in the Timeline.

Lesson 11

11 | Titles and Credits

Text and graphics play an integral role in conveying information in a video program. The Title Designer in Premiere Pro allows you to create text and graphics that you can import and superimpose over existing video. The files can also run alone as a self-contained clip. This Titler program contains many graphics tools for developing a vast variety of credits, whether they are designed to be static, rolling, or crawling.

In this lesson, you'll use the Title Designer in Premiere Pro to create the opening titles and closing credits for *Books & Beans*. You'll be using text, rolling text, and graphic tools. Then you'll import the titles and superimpose them over movie clips in the project Timeline. Specifically, you'll learn to do the following:

• Enter text and change text attributes such as kerning.

• Add shadows and color.

• Create graphics.

• Apply opacity values, texture, gradients, and sheen to graphics and text.

• Create and preview rolling type.

• Add titles to a project.

• Superimpose a title over a video clip.

• Edit titles for timing, position, and effect.

About titles and the Title Designer

You'll be able to create broadcast-quality title sequences that include text and graphic elements using the Adobe Title Designer. Whether you're crafting a highly choreographed opening sequence that integrates text and graphic elements with moving footage or producing a straightforward credit roll, you can create high-quality results using time-saving features right within the Adobe Premiere Pro program. Some of those features are:

Professional typographic controls Such as leading, kerning, baseline shift, rotation, slant, and more mean you can refine your titles with the precision of Adobe Illustrator text. You can also apply special edge treatments such as outlined text, embossing, or bevels to help a title pop off the screen.

Drawing tools, including the Adobe-standard pen tool Use the Pen tool to draw free-form vector shapes that range from simple to complex forms, or use other drawing tools to create simple, regular shapes such as circles, polygons, rectangles, and lines.

Styles for text and shapes Work with predefined text and object styles, or create your own custom Styles. Styles are easy to manage, and you can save and load Styles from other title projects.

Time-saving templates Create your own Templates, or modify the over-100 Templates included with Adobe Premiere Pro to create customized looks.

Precise animation controls Once your titles are formatted, you can add motion either by using the roll or crawl options in the Adobe Title Designer or by animating the completed title file in the Premiere Pro Timeline.

Seamless import from other programs You can create titles, using a graphics or title application, saving it in a format compatible with Premiere Pro, such as pict (.pct), TIFF (.tif), Photoshop (.psd), or Illustrator (.ai or .eps), and importing it into your Premiere Pro project.

You access the Titler when you first launch Premiere Pro—with an untitled Project window open—or with an existing or new project. You can also have up to four Title Designer windows open at the same time.

Viewing the finished movie

To see what you'll be creating, take a look at the finished movie.

1 In the Project window, choose File > Import and select the Books&Beans.wmv file in the Movies folder in the main directory of your CIB lesson files.

The movie opens in the Project window.

2 Double-click Books&Beans.wmv to make it appear in the Source view of the Monitor window.

3 Click the Play button (▶) in the Source view to watch the video program. When the movie ends, the final frame will remain visible in the viewing window.

Working from the existing project file

For this lesson, you'll resume the project from the previous lesson on nested sequences. All of the video and most of the audio is in place. You'll add closing credits and the opening titles. The final movie uses the Myriad Pro font, but if you don't have it in your system, choose another font that you feel is suitable for the genre of the film.

1 To open the existing file, double-click 11Lesson.prproj in the 11Lesson folder that you previously copied to your hard disk.

2 If necessary, rearrange windows and palettes so that they don't overlap, by choosing Window > Workspace > Editing.

You're ready to add titles.

3 Choose File > New > Title to open the Title Designer window.

The Title Designer appears.

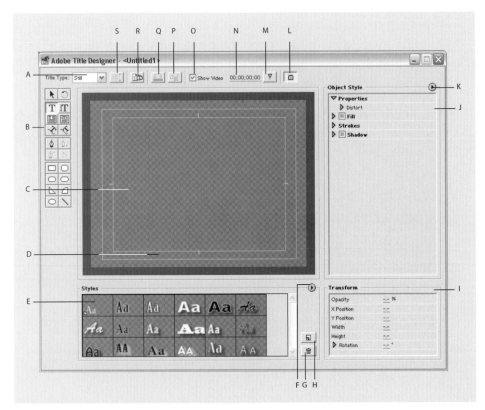

Title Designer window A. Title Type menu B. Tools C. Title area D. Title-safe zone E. Font Styles area F. Font Styles options menu G. Delete Style button H. New Style button I. Transform area J. Object Style area K. Object Style options menu L. Send Frame to External/Monitor button M. Sync to Timeline button N. Background Video O. Show/Hide video source preview P. Font Browser Q. Tab Stops R. Templates menu S. Roll/Crawl Options

Overview of the Title Designer window

Title Type menu Choose to make still, rolling, or crawling titles.

Tools A wide variety of text and vector and bitmap graphics tools are provided.

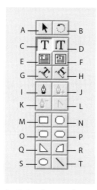

A. Selection tool
B. Rotation tool
C. Type tool
D. Vertical Type tool
E. Area Type tool
F. Vertical Area Type tool
G. Path Type tool
H. Vertical Path Type tool
I. Pen tool
J. Add anchor point tool
K. Delete anchor point tool
L. Convert anchor point tool
M. Rectangle tool
N. Clipped Corner Rectangle tool
O. Rounded Corner Rectangle tool
P. Rounded Rectangle tool
Q. Wedge tool
R. Arc tool
S. Ellipse tool
T. Line tool

Title The Title area is your canvas for creating with the Title Designer.

Title-safe zones Not all monitors, TVs, or displays have the same viewing area. Placing key elements inside the safe zones assures that they will be easily visible on virtually any kind of viewing screen. The inner rectangle is the text-safe zone. The outer rectangle is the image-safe zone. You can turn these margin lines on or off by choosing Title > View. See the section on "Overscan and safe zones" on page 19 in this book.

Note: To turn title-safe and action-safe margins on or off, Choose Title > View > Safe Title Margin or Title > View > Safe Action Margin. The margin is on if a check mark appears next to its name.

Font Styles area The Adobe Premiere Pro Title Designer displays all the system fonts available to you for use in creating titles.

Font Styles options menu Add, modify, and save Font Styles.

Transform Move, rotate, change opacity, and scale objects in the Title Designer.

Object Style Modify colors, adjust properties, and enhance the appearance of objects in the Title Designer. The properties in this area change depending on the selected object. Map textures onto text, apply multicolored gradients, emboss or bevel edges, make subtle drop shadows, and modulate transparency.

Templates button Choose from dozens of predesigned broadcast-quality, title-sequence templates, including still layouts, rolls, and crawls. Alternatively, you can create your own templates and styles, and save and share them.

Working in the Titler

1 Reposition the Titler window so that it does not obscure the Project window.

2 Resize the Titler window if you like by dragging the lower right corner of the window.

The main title work area is bounded by two concentric white-line boxes. The inner box represents the *title-safe zone*; the outer box represents the *action-safe zone*. Text placed outside the title-safe zone may appear blurry or distorted on some television monitors. Graphic images beyond the action-safe zone may not be visible on some television monitors. Various *tools* are grouped at the upper left corner in the Titler window.

Line Width and Object and Shadow colors can be specified in the Object Style area, as can the *Gradient and Transparency settings* and the *Shadow Offset. Positions and rotations* are adjusted in the Transform area.

You'll be using the style and transformation areas in the Titler window itself for most of the exercises in this lesson. When you start a new Title Designer window, however, note that Premiere Pro adds *Title* to the main menu in the title bar at the top of the Premiere window. The Title menu contains the commands for setting the font, size, style, alignment, orientation, and Roll/Crawl title options.

Click Title and review the available menu items.

💡 *You can also access the main menu items directly from the Title area if you right-click anywhere in the selected text or graphic object.*

Setting up a new title

Once you open the Adobe Title Designer window, you can either create a title from scratch or load one of the existing templates. The Adobe Title Designer drawing area is the same size as the frame size specified in the Project Settings dialog box.

Using templates

The Adobe Title Designer includes many templates that provide you with title area configurations to help you build a title. For instance, some templates include art that may be pertinent to your project's subject matter. Other templates have special designs, such as letter boxed or pillar boxed drawing areas. If you change a template, you can save it as a new title file or import it as a template for use in other projects. You can use any saved title as a template.

Templates are transferable between users and across platforms. If you share templates, make sure that each system includes all the fonts, textures, logos, and images used in the template. For information on textures, see "Loading textures" in the *Adobe Premiere Pro User Guide.*

Creating a simple title

First, you'll create a simple, text-only title. In this exercise, you will add a sample frame to the Title Designer window, add text, change the text attributes, add a shadow, and kern the text.

Importing graphics and titles

You can import graphics to use in titles from other software programs such as Adobe Photoshop and Adobe Illustrator. You can import entire title sequences created in other software such as Adobe After Effects. You can also import an individual layer from a multilayer Photoshop file.

For more information on importing graphics and animations for titles, see the section on "Capturing and Importing Source Clips" in the *Adobe Premiere Pro User Guide.*

An alpha channel is a fourth channel in an RGB image that defines which parts of the image are transparent or semitransparent. Many programs, such as Adobe Illustrator and Photoshop, use alpha channels. Premiere Pro preserves alpha channels when you import graphics that include them.

For more information on using alpha channels in titles, see "Adding a title to a project" in the *Adobe Premiere Pro User Guide.*

You can use the Edit Original command in Premiere Pro to open a clip in its original application, such as Adobe After Effects. Then you can edit it. The changes are automatically incorporated into the current project without exiting Premiere Pro or replacing files.

For more information, see "Editing a clip in its original application" in the *Adobe Premiere Pro User Guide*.

Displaying a sample frame for reference

Before you enter text, by default you'll find the sample background frame to be displayed in the Title area. This sample frame will help you determine the best colors to use for the title text. Sample frames are only for reference and do not become part of the title. When you save and close the title, the reference frame is not saved with the file.

When you open 11Lesson.prproj, by default the Premiere Pro Titler makes the frame at the Timeline marker visible in the Title area. The Show Video box at the top of the Titler window is selected. The first frame is black and is therefore displayed in the Title area background. You'll be starting this lesson by creating the closing credits, because they are composed entirely of text.

1 To construct the first line of the credits with a background frame for reference purposes, locate the Show Video box at the top of the Title Designer window.

2 Make sure that its default state is on, indicated by a check mark in the box.

3 To the right are the Hot Text Controls and above them the timecode field. Set the timecode to 00;05;57;00.

The frame at 00;05;57;00 becomes the background for designing the credits.

Creating text and changing text attributes

Premiere Pro lets you change the text attributes of words, and of individual characters within a word, using any font available in your operating system.

1 In the Tools area, select the type tool (T) and click in the center of the Title area.

2 In the Title Designer, choose Object Style > Properties > Font to specify the font family. Click on the Browse option at the top of the menu.

The Font Browser appears.

3 For Font and Style, select Myriad Pro Bold, and then click OK.

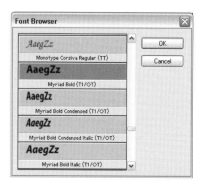

Adjusting values by using hot text controls

Hot text controls give you a dynamic interface without having to type.

You can specify the font size you want either by selecting and typing it into the entry box, or by holding the cursor on the number you wish to adjust until it changes into a pointing finger with arrow heads pointing left and right.

1 Click on the font size entry box, and drag along it until the number **42** appears for the font size.

Note: *As a general rule for video, use a font size of 16 points or larger. Anything smaller may not be legible on a TV monitor.*

2 At the text cursor in the Title area, type **Books & Beans**. If the text is not centered, you will learn how to center it later in this lesson.

3 Choose File > Save As. If necessary, open the 11Lesson folder, and then type **Credits.prtl** for the name. Click Save.

Changing the text color

The default color for text is white. An Object Color swatch button () and Color Picker Eye Dropper (✐) are displayed in the Fill section of the Object Styles area, making it easy to see and change the color of an object.

▽ ☑ Fill		
Fill Type	Solid	▾
Color		⇨
Opacity	100 %	
▷ ☐ Sheen		
▷ ☐ Texture		

Clicking on the Object Color swatch button opens the Color Picker.

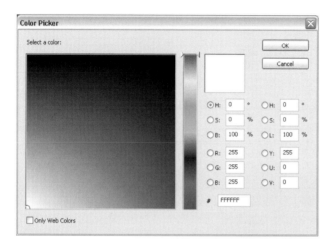

You can choose colors in the Color Picker by selecting a color in the color box or by entering values in the Red, Green, and Blue text boxes. The black, white, and gray values are located along the left side of the color box.

The Eye Dropper may also be used to select a color visible in the Titler interface. Experiment with the Eye Dropper by selecting it and rolling it over different colors. You'll see the results on the Color Swatch button. To deactivate the Eye Dropper, click on it again.

Now you'll change the color of the words "Books & Beans."

1 Use the selection tool ( ) to select "Books & Beans" if it is not already selected. When selected, a small box or handle appears on each of the four corners and at the midpoint on each line of the object's bounding box.

2 In the Object Style area go to the FIll area and click on the Object Color swatch button.

The Color Picker appears with the original (default) color of white displayed as the current color in the upper right corner of the Color Picker dialog box.

3 In the Select a color box, click on deep blue to select it. Now the color box in the upper right corner displays the deep blue color you selected.

4 To specify a color that could be used in your final movie, type **51** for Red, **0** for Green, and **176** for Blue. (White was used in the sample film on the DVD-ROM.)

Note: Adobe Premiere Pro Title Designer displays RGB, HSB, HSL, and YUV colors in the Color Picker. Some fully saturated colors can trigger a color gamut warning, which is indicated by a triangle in the Color Picker (⚠). This warning signifies colors that are not NTSC-safe. Clicking on the small color gamut square beneath the warning triangle changes your selection to the next closest NTSC-safe color in the range you have chosen.

Colors that are not NTSC-safe may bleed or blur when displayed on an NTSC monitor. Because the movie you are creating now will only be played on a computer monitor, you don't need to be concerned with RGB values. However, if you are creating a movie that will ultimately be played from an NTSC monitor, you will need to use NTSC-safe colors to ensure optimal playback.

5 Click OK to accept the color change or cancel to leave the color white.

6 Save the title by choosing File > Save.

Adding a shadow

You can add a default shadow to any image or text object in the Titler window. Select the object and then click on the Shadow box in the Object Style area of the Titler window. (You may need to scroll down to locate the Shadow box.)

1 With "Books & Beans" selected, click on the Shadow box and a checkmark appears.

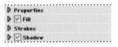

Now, you'll change the shadow from black, which is the default color, to yellow.

2 With the word "Books & Beans" still selected, open the Shadow section of the Object Style area by clicking on the triangle to the left of the Shadow check box.

3 Click on the Shadow Color Swatch.

4 To use a color compatible with the background, type **211** for Red, **163** for Green, and **60** for Blue. Click OK.

5 The default shadow angle is 155 degrees, but an angle of 120 degrees is less severe. Change the angle to 120 degrees in one of three ways: dialing it with the Hot Text controls, typing **120** in the Angle field of the Shadow section, or clicking on the triangle to the left of the word Angle and setting the wheel to 120.

6 Now make the Distance **5**.

7 Click anywhere in the Title area to deselect the text.

8 Save the title.

Changing opacity

The *opacity* controls in the Title Designer let you set different levels of transparency for graphics, text, and shadows. To change the opacity of text and graphic objects, click on the triangle to the left of the Fill box in the Object Style area. In the Opacity settings area, specify the amount of transparency in the Opacity entry field or adjust the slider to the desired amount along the dotted line.

Shadows have a default opacity value of 54%. Here you'll increase the overall opacity of the shadow, making it more opaque.

1 Use the selection tool to select the words "Books & Beans."

2 In the Shadow section of the Object Style area, change the shadow opacity to **75%**.

3 Save the title.

For more information on varying the opacity in the Title window, see "Using the Adobe Title Designer" in the *Adobe Premiere Pro User Guide*.

Kerning text

Kerning means changing the distance between two characters in a word. To kern selected text in the Title area, you use the text tool to select the text and then you adjust the amount in the Kerning entry box of the Properties section in the Object Style area. You can either select the text tool and then highlight the two adjacent letters you want to kern, or you can select the text tool and then place the text tool cursor between the two letters you want to kern. In either case, you adjust the kerning as often as needed to increase or decrease the space between the letters.

Dragging left in the Kerning entry field decreases the distance between letters; dragging to the right increases the distance.

The text tool and the selection tool affect text in different ways:

Selection tool Lets you select everything within the bounding box. If you change the font, color, opacity, shadow, or gradient with the bounding box selected, all the text is affected.

Text tool Lets you kern or edit individual characters to change only the font or font attributes of the highlighted characters.

1 Select the type tool (T), and then click after the "s" of "Books", and drag to select the ampersand sign (&) and the spaces on both sides of it.

2 In the Object Style area go to the Properties area. Drag the cursor to the right on the Kerning entry field to widen the space between the letters to a setting of **3.**

3 Kerning caused the spaces to widen without changing the rest of the text.

Aligning text

Two types of text alignment are possible in the Titler window. You can align the text inside its own bounding box and you can align the text's bounding box inside the Title area. Here you'll align the words using both alignment techniques.

First, you'll align the text within the bounding box. This will not be especially noticeable.

1 Make sure the whole title is selected and choose Title > Type Alignment > Center.

The words shift to the center of the bounding box.

Now you'll move the bounding box to the top of the title-safe area before centering it.

2 Using the selection tool, drag the title to the top of the window so that the letters are just inside the title-safe zone. (You can also use the arrow keys to reposition the text in the Title area.)

Now you can center the bounding box in the Title area.

3 With the text still selected, choose Title > Position > Horizontal Center. The entire bounding box shifts to the center at the top of the title-safe region.

4 Save the title.

Adding more text

Now, you'll add more text to the title.

1 Use the selection tool to select the bounding box.

2 Press and hold the Alt key, then drag the text box straight down. As you drag, press and hold down the Shift key to constrain the transformation to zero degrees. This creates a new text object.

3 In the Titler, choose Object Style > Properties > Font Size. Change the font size of the duplicate text box to **24**.

4 Change the Type to read **from Adobe Press**, then click the selection tool.

The text still has a shadow but doesn't require one, so you'll remove it.

5 With the smaller type box selected, deselect the Shadow box in the Object Style area.

6 Using the selection tool, move the new text into the top one-third of the Title window, directly under the words "Books & Beans."

💡 *You can also move selected objects by pressing the arrow keys.*

7 Save the title and close it. Credits.prtl appears in the Project bin area.

8 Make a new bin in the Project window called **Titles**, and move Credits.prtl into it.

For more information, see "Using the Adobe Title Designer" in the *Adobe Premiere Pro User Guide.*

The Title area lets you create simple graphics. You can use the drawing tools to create rectangles, squares, rounded squares, circles, ovals, lines, and polygons. You can also use the drawing tools to create outlined shapes or filled shapes.

Using a title as a background frame for a new title

First, you'll use a graphic as a sample frame.

1 From the Project window, create a new sequence and name it **Titles**.

2 Double-click the Titles sequence to activate it in the Timeline.

3 With the Titles bin of the Project window still active, choose File > Import.

4 In the 11Lesson folder locate Ampersand.psd, and click Open.

5 When the Import Layered File box appears, choose Choose Layer > Layer 1 and Footage Dimensions > Layer Size, then click OK.

6 From the Titles bin of the Project window, select and drag Layer1/Ampersand.psd onto the Video 1 track of the Timeline, snapping its In point to the first frame of the project (at 0;00;00;00).

7 Choose File > New > Title.

Ampersand.psd appears as the background frame for your new title. The background footage does not become part of your new title, because it is only a reference, not a saved component of the title file.

8 Choose File > Save As. Make sure the 11Lesson folder is open. Type **Ampersand.prtl** for the name of the new title file and click Save.

Now you'll add some graphics to Ampersand.prtl using Ampersand.psd as a template.

Drawing a polygon using the pen tool

The *pen tool* ( ) lets you create random shapes and curves. Select the pen tool. Then, click in the Title area to set a start point. Move the tool in any direction and then click to create connected end points for each line in your intended shape. To close the polygon, click the first point you created when you see the little completion circle appear next to the cursor.

Now, you'll draw a coffee mug using the pen tool.

1 Select the pen tool ( ) in the Title Designer window.

2 Position the cursor in the lower left corner of the mug in the background image, and click to make the first point.

3 Move the cursor up the left side of the cup to the upper left corner and click to make the second point.

4 Continue to click across and down to create the basic mug shape, ignoring for now the handle. You can use the following image as a guide.

Note: If you make a mistake, rather than start over, you can continue adding points. Click to enclose the shape, then use the selection tool to adjust individual points. To remove excess points, click once on them with the delete anchor point tool ( ). To add more points, use the add anchor point tool ( ).

5 To close the shape, place the cursor over your first point, looking for the little indicator circle before clicking the final point.

Premiere Pro draws a line from the last point to the first point, closing the object.

Now you'll remove the white outline and fill the polygon with a solid color.

6 With the image selected, find Properties in the Object Style area.

7 In the Graphic Type menu, choose Filled Bezier. By default, the Line Width for a Filled Bezier will change to **0**.

8 Click the triangle next to the Fill section of the Object Style area to see its settings.

9 Click on the Object Color Swatch button.

10 In the Color Picker, change the color values to Red **52**, Green **0**, and Blue **226**. Then click OK.

11 With the coffee mug selected, drag to the left on the Opacity entry field to change it to **50%**. (Alternatively, type **50%** in the entry box.)

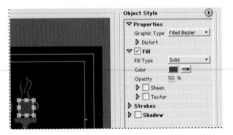

12 Using the selection tool, click anywhere outside the cup in the Title area to deselect everything.

13 Save the title file.

Repositioning objects

You can reposition text and images in the Title window by bringing them to the front or sending them to the back. Here, you'll draw another group of shapes with a different opacity setting, and then send it to the back.

1 In the Title Designer window, select the pen tool ( ).

2 To create the first point of your new shape, click and drag up on the bottom of the left curve of steam rising above the mug, creating angle handles that are used for tracing complicated curved structures.

3 Click and drag up again to make the second point while following the curved shape.

4 Complete the first steam curl with two more points.

5 To set and start a new object, you'll need to click on the Pen tool again.

6 Trace the last two steam curls, being sure to click on the Pen tool before starting the third curl. If you have difficulty with the second one, try starting from the top and from the bottom of the one on the right.

7 With the three steam objects selected, go to the Opacity level under the Fill setting in the Object Style area and change it to **25%**. (Click on the entry field and drag left, or type **25%** in the entry box**.**)

To draw the cup handle, you'll need to temporarily move the cup portion first; otherwise it will interfere with the Pen tool.

8 With the Selection tool select the cup object and move it to the left about half its own width.

9 Use the Pen tool to trace the cup handle.

10 When completed, change the color. Type **51** for Red, **0** for Green, and **176** for Blue. Do not convert the line to a closed object.

11 Change the opacity of the cup handle to **50%**.

12 In the main menu, choose Title > Arrange > Send to Back.

13 Select the main cup object and restore it to its position on the template.

The handle is positioned behind the coffee mug and shows through slightly.

14 Turn off the background image template, so that you can see your work. (Deselect the Show Video box).

Since you don't have to match the illustration perfectly, you can give it your own whimsical flair.

15 Save the title.

Creating a smooth polygon

Now, you'll use the pen tool to draw the main body of the ampersand. This time, you'll smooth the lines, because the character is smooth and round, not pointy.

1 Begin by selecting the Show Video status box.

2 Using the selection tool, click anywhere inside the Title area (but outside of the drawn objects) to deselect everything.

3 Select the pen tool ( ).

4 Make your first point in the inverted "V" shape underneath the eyeglasses and the circular stroke around them at about the center of the title area. Click and drag toward the lower left of that curve.

5 Click and drag the anchor point down and to the left. Draw your own ampersand using the following images as a guide. (It may take several tries if you are not experienced at vector art.)

6 Close the shape by clicking your first point. Remember to look for the "o" before clicking the final point to ensure that the cursor is directly above the first point.

To adjust the object, select the individual anchor points and drag to reposition them. Rotate the extended anchor points (handles) to change the smoothness or the direction of the curves. Take your time to make it as crisp as you can.

7 In Object Styles > Properties > Graphic Type, choose Filled Bezier.

8 Select the shape you just created and click the Object Color swatch button.

9 Pick a rich gold color from the color box, or you can type **186** for Red, **136** for Green, and **56** for Blue. Then click OK.

10 Set the opacity to 100%, which is completely opaque.

11 Save the title.

Adding a shadow to the ampersand

Now you'll add a light green shadow to the ampersand.

1 Use the selection tool to select the ampersand image if it is not already selected.

2 With the ampersand image selected, click the Shadow box.

Now, you'll change the shadow from black, which is the default color to green.

3 With the ampersand image still selected, open the Shadow section of the Object Style area by clicking on the triangle to the left of the Shadow check box.

4 Click on the Shadow Color Swatch button.

5 Click a light green color in the color box. Or type **72** for Red, **156** for Green, and **56** for Blue. Then click OK.

6 The default shadow angle is 155 degrees. You can change the angle by clicking and dragging in the entry field with the cursor, or typing 155 into the Angle field of the Shadow section. You can also click on the triangle to the left of the word Angle and then use the wheel to adjust the angle settings.

7 Make the Distance **10**.

8 Click anywhere in the Title area to deselect the graphic.

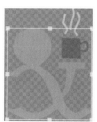

Displayed with Show Video turned off.

9 Save the title.

Using the ellipse tool

You can use the ellipse tool to draw ovals and circles of any size. To make a circle using the ellipse tool, constrain the tool by pressing the Shift key while drawing. You can also make squares, rounded squares, and 45-degree lines by pressing the Shift key while using the rectangle, rounded rectangle, or line tools.

Now you'll add a nose rest and a frame to the eyeglasses in the logo. Then you'll copy and paste to create a second one.

1 Click on the Show Video box and select the ampersand and move it right so that you can see the eyeglasses on the background image.

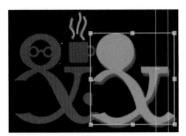

2 Select the pen tool, and make a small curve with two points that trace the nose rest of the eyeglasses.

3 Select the ellipse tool.

4 Hold down the Shift key to constrain the oval to be a circle, and draw a small circle on the left frame of the eyeglasses.

5 From the main menu, choose Edit > Copy. Then choose Edit > Paste. Premiere Pro pastes a copy of the circle directly on top of the original.

6 Position the selection tool over the circles, and then drag the center of the new circle to the right, next to the first circle.

7 Press and hold down the Shift key while clicking both of the circles at the same time.

8 In the Object Style area go to Graphic Type under Properties and change the style to Closed Bezier.

9 Set the Opacity to 100%, if it is not already.

💡 *If you accidently stretch the circle instead of moving it, choose Edit > Undo. Deselect the circle and then reselect it. Use the arrow keys to move it.*

10 Click any empty space in the Title area to deselect everything.

11 Use the ellipse tool to draw the inner ellipse of the ampersand. Start at the top center and pull down and slightly toward one side to create the oval shape. (It may take several tries.)

The default fill color of the ellipse is white.

Note: *You may wish to view without the background image to get a better idea of what you're creating in front of it.*

12 In the Object Style area go to the Fill area and then go to the Color area. Make the oval color the same as the shadow color, but at 100% opacity. Type **72** for Red, **156** for Green, and **56** for Blue.

13 From the main Premiere Pro menu, choose Title > Arrange > Send to Back.

14 With the selection tool, select the ampersand and move it into place. Then send it to the back by choosing Title > Arrange > Send to Back.

15 Save the title file.

Leave the Ampersand.prtl file open, as you'll apply effects to it in the next sections.

Mapping a textured fill

The Object Style area of the Title Designer allows you to develop text and graphics with deeper and deeper levels of realism. In the special effects industry, this process is known as mapping material values, or materials editing.

Now, you'll add a texture to the ampersand, then make it appear more spherically rounded with a radial gradient effect. Finally, you'll put a sheen on it to reflect bright light filtering down from above.

1 With the selection tool, select the image of the ampersand.

2 In the Object Style area, click on the triangle next to the word Fill.

3 Click on the triangle next to the word Texture.

4 Click the Texture box to select it.

The taller section called Texture on the next line is the Texture Thumbnail button.

The two Texture sections:
Upper: Texture check box
Lower: Texture Thumbnail

5 Click on the Texture Thumbnail button.

6 Browse to your 11Lesson folder and locate the Beans.psd file. Click Open to load it into the Titler.

Note: *The Load Texture box appears with a default list of several dozen preset textures that you can use in your projects.*

The ampersand now appears to have a coffee bean texture, but the texture is too overpowering, so you'll blend it with the original golden Bezier fill.

7 Click on the triangle next to the word Blending in the Texture area of the Object Style area.

8 Change the Mix value to **13**.

Making a gradient fill

To make the ampersand more spherical, you'll add a radial gradient over the blended texture and Bezier Fill.

1 In the Object Style area go to the Fill area and click on the Fill Type menu. Select Radial Gradient.

2 Move the left color bucket ( ) all the way to the left end at 100% opacity. Because of the base color of the ampersand, the color values should be: **186** for Red, **136** for Green, and **56** for Blue.

3 The color bucket on the right, which represents the center color of a radial gradient, should be changed to white if it isn't already.

Note: Feel free to make your own mixes and experiment with gradients, both radial and linear.

4 Gradually adjust the right color bucket and the repeat value until a glowing, rounded light appears in the ampersand's mid-section. (Repeat value of **1.0**.)

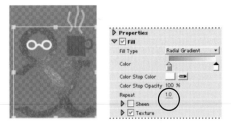

Adding sheen to the object

Now, to put a finishing bit of charm onto the object, you'll add sheen to its top to represent a light source from above.

1 In Object Style area, go to the Fill area and click the Sheen box to add a default sheen.

2 Change the Opacity to **75%**.

3 Change the Size to **22**.

4 The angle in this sample is **90**.

5 Make the Offset **77**.

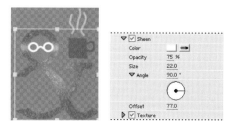

The texture mapping and materials editing is now completed.

6 Save Ampersand.prtl and close the file. Ampersand.prtl appears in the Project window, ready to be inserted into your production.

Rolling titles and crawling titles

Adobe Premiere Pro allows you to add motion to titles in rolling titles and crawling titles. *Rolling titles* move across the screen vertically, usually rolling up. *Crawling titles* move across the screen horizontally, usually crawling left-to-right.

Creating a rolling title

To create a rolling title, use the *text tool* and enter text in a rolling title scroll box. In this lesson, you'll create a rolling title that rolls up.

1 Make Titles the active sequence in the Timeline window.

2 Start a new title window.

3 At the top left of the Title area, choose Roll from the Title Type menu.

4 Select the type tool (T).

5 With the type tool selected, click and drag inside the title-safe area to define a *rolling title scroll box*. Start from the upper left corner and drag down to the right about one-third of the way. Be sure that the box stays within the title-safe area. Use the following image as a guide.

A title text box appears with a blinking text cursor at the top.

6 Verify that the font is Myriad Pro Regular. (If you chose a different font, then verify that the font information is correct.)

7 Change the font size to **24**.

8 Now, you'll left-justify the text. In the main menu, choose Title > Type Alignment > Left.

9 For legibility, use the default Object Color, which is white.

10 There is no shadow in this exercise, so be sure the Shadow check box is deselected.

A common style in the industry is to use facing tabbed text for title and names on the same line of type. Facing tabs have the left portion set to a right justified mark; while the right portion is set to a left justified mark. The tiles and names "face" each other across a small gap at the center.

Now you'll enter the first credit of three using the facing tab style.

11 Begin by pressing the Tab key.

12 Type **Edited by,** and then press Tab.

13 Type **Your Name** (or whatever name you would like to use for this exercise) on the same line, and then press Enter.

14 Select the words "Your Name," and change the font and style to Myriad Pro Bold.

Left: Original input.   Right: "Your Name" converted to Myriad Pro Bold.

Note: *As the text input box grows, the vertical scroll bar on the right side of the Title area adjusts. Click and drag on any word to highlight it and make any corrections.*

15 Make sure the cursor is active anywhere in the text.

16 In the main menu, choose Title > Tab Stops.

The Tab Stops box appears.

17 Position the Tab Stops box so that its "0" (zero) tick mark is in line with the left edge of the text box.

18 Select the right tab justification arrow and then click just to the left of what lies below the center mark in the Titler window, or at about "**250**" on the tab stop ruler. Notice that as you are in the act of setting the tab, a vertical line will appear to guide the final placement.

19 Click on the tab stop ruler about an inch to the right of the first tab stop arrow. A second right justification position will be established.

20 With the second tab stop mark still selected, click on the left justification arrow to convert the second stop to a left justification stop.

21 Position the second tab stop with the words "Your Name" just to the right of the center tick mark indicated on the title safe zone in the Title Designer window.

The words are adjusted to the new tab stops in facing center positions.

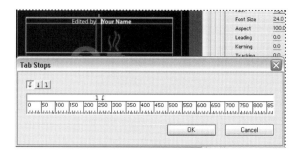

22 Click OK to accept the positioning.

23 Save the title file in your 11Lesson folder and name it **Creditslist.prtl.**

Add two more lines of type, and conform them to the same specs as the first line: plain type in the title and bold type in the name.

24 Place the cursor at the end of the line of type and press Enter.

25 On the second line of type, enter **Produced by** in plain type and **Adobe Systems** in bold type.

26 Format the second line like the first by pressing the Tab key to align the segments.

27 Place the cursor at the end of the second line of type and press Enter.

28 The text for the third line is: **Directed by** in plain type and **Classroom in a Book** in bold type.

29 Save the project.

Timing the motion of titles

When you add a moving title to a video program, the speed at which it rolls or crawls is determined by the duration specified in the Timeline. For example, if you specify a duration of 20 seconds for a rolling title, and then change the duration to 10 seconds, the title must roll twice as fast to move the same number of lines across the screen in half the time.

To have more control over the rolling or crawling motion in your program, you'll specify values in the Roll/Crawl Options box. With a title text and graphics selected in the Titler, you can choose Title > Roll/Crawl Options and select various timings.

Start Off Screen specifies that the scroll begins out-of-view and scrolls into view.

End Off Screen specifies that the scroll continues until the objects are out of view.

Pre-Roll specifies how long, in frames, the title should hold before starting to move.

Ease-In specifies how many frames are used to accelerate the title clip up to normal speed. Type 0 (zero) to start moving the title at normal speed. To accelerate more gradually, specify more frames.

Ease-Out specifies how many frames are used to decelerate the title clip to a halt. For faster deceleration, specify fewer frames. Type 0 (zero) to stop the title immediately. To decelerate more gradually, specify more frames.

Post-Roll specifies how many frames you want the title to appear motionless, starting with the frame in which the title stops and ending with the Out point of the title clip.

1 In the main menu, choose Title > Roll/Crawl Options to access the Roll/Crawl Options box.

2 Leave Start Off Screen selected and deselect End Off Screen. Then, click OK.

3 Choose File > Save.

Creating a crawling title

To create a crawling title, with the text moving horizontally across the screen, you use the same tools but choose Crawl as the Title Type.

1 Choose File > New > Title to open a new Title Designer window.

2 In the Title Type menu choose Crawl.

3 Select the type tool.

4 Drag inside the title-safe area to specify the size of the rolling title scroll box that will contain the crawling title.

5 Verify or reset the Object Color swatch, the font (Myriad Pro), style (Bold), size (24), and left alignment settings.

6 Type the text as follows:

Books & Beans was Written for the Screen, Produced, and Directed by special arrangement with Adobe Press.

This time, don't press Enter after each word or segment; just type the paragraph continuously until the box overfills.

Note: As the text input box grows, the horizontal scroll bar at the bottom of the Title area adjusts, allowing you to continue to input as well as review the text. Click and drag on any word to highlight it if it needs to be corrected.

7 In the main menu, choose Title > Roll/Crawl Options to access the Roll/Crawl Options dialog box.

8 Verify that Start Off Screen and End Off Screen are still selected from the earlier exercise. Then, click OK.

9 For crawl direction, choose left to right.

10 Choose File > Save As, open the 11Lesson folder if necessary, and then type **Crawl.prtl** for the name. Click Save.

11 Save and Close all Title files. They have automatically been imported into the Project window as clips to be used in your production.

Using titles in a Premiere Pro project

You'll have titles to place in the Timeline of your project when they are saved in the Title Designer workspace. When added to the Timeline on Track two or higher, they become superimposed over a video clip. *Superimpose* means positioning a clip, such as a title, still, or video clip, on top of another clip, so that they play at the same time. Clips in these superimpose tracks play over the clips in the corresponding lower tracks.

When using titles, Premiere Pro automatically assigns opacity and masking values, so clips on the lower tracks display through the title's background.

How you add a title clip to a Premiere Pro project depends on whether you are creating a new clip or adding an existing clip to a project.

Adding a new clip A new title clip can be added to a new or existing project.

• Open a new or existing project for which you want to create a new title clip. Use the Titler to create the title. Name and save the new title file. When you save the new title, Premiere Pro automatically adds it to the project and lists it in the Project window. Remember to save the project to keep the title with the Project.

• Open a new (untitled) project and use the Titler to create a new title. When you save the new title clip, Premiere Pro automatically adds it to the new (untitled) project. Close the untitled project without saving it; the new title clip will be available for use in any project because you named and saved the title file.

Adding an existing clip An existing title clip can be added to a new or existing project.

• Open an existing or new project, then choose File > Import > File, specify the name of the title file, and click Open. As with any imported clip, this method adds the title clip to the project without opening the title clip.

Adding titles to the Timeline

So far in this lesson, you have created some title clips and Premiere Pro has added them to the project automatically. You will superimpose two of the titles over the Master video sequence. To do this, you'll use another superimpose track on the Timeline.

You preview a rolling or crawling title by placing it on a sequence Timeline. Once it is saved, the title appears and behaves like any other clip in the Project window. Premiere Pro plays back the rolling or crawling text object in the Monitor window.

1 From the 11Lesson.prproj Project window, use the selection tool to click and select Creditslist.prtl. Drag it onto the Video 2 Track of the Master sequence, so its In point is at the point where Hero catches up to Dreams after their scene at the car (at 00;05;58;23).

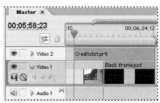

2 Preview either by pressing Enter/Return, or by holding Alt/Option as you scrub/drag the Edit line across the Timeline.

Duration and timing of credits

You can change the speed of a rolling title by changing its duration. The shorter the duration, the faster the title plays; the longer the duration, the slower the title plays.

When you started the preview, the text was off the screen at the beginning of the roll. When the roll ends, the last line has exited at the top of the screen.

Titles are clips and images with a default duration of five seconds. You can change the duration of a title clip. Select the title, then choose Clip > Duration and specify a new duration. You can also change the duration by trimming it once it is on the Timeline.

Note: *If you want to use the actual credits for the Books & Beans film, you'll need about a minute for them to roll. Experiment with making the end credits roll the way they do on the sample film. Use End credits.prtl, which contains the actual credits.*

For information on changing the still image duration preference, see Lesson 10, "Advanced Editing Two: Nested and Multiple Sequences" in this Classroom in a Book.

1 Select Creditslist.prtl on the timeline and choose Clip > Speed/Duration.

2 Change the Duration to **1000** (00;00;10;00).

3 Preview to see how changing the duration slows down the rolling titles.

4 Now extend the duration of Creditslist.prtl to the end of the project.

5 Place Ampersand.prtl on the Video 2 track so that its In point snaps to the Out point of Creditslist.prtl.

6 Make the duration of Ampersand.prtl 10 seconds (00;00;10;00).

7 Add Credits.prtl to the Video 3 track so that its In point snaps to the In point of Ampersand.prtl.

8 Extend Credits.prtl to be the same duration as Ampersand.prtl.

9 Preview the closing credits segment of the sequence.

Layering rolling credits

You can further alter credits by rolling them in front of the ampersand and behind the two lines of title text.

1 With the Selection tool, select Credits.prtl on the Video 3 track of the Timeline, and move it up to the Video 4 track.

2 Now move Creditslist.prtl into the space where Credits.prtl was on the Video 3 track.

3 Adjust the In points and durations of Ampersand.prtl, Creditslist.prtl, and Credits.prtl so that they are all the same.

Because titles created in Premiere Pro automatically have transparent backgrounds, you don't need to apply opacity values.

4 Preview the credits segment. The rolling credits move in front of Ampersand.prtl and behind Credits.prtl.

5 Save the project.

Placing a crawling title

Now you'll exchange Crawl.prtl for Creditslist.prtl.

1 In the Project window, select Crawl.prtl.

2 Drag it onto the Timeline so that it overlays Creditslist.prtl.

3 Select and clear Creditslist.prtl.

4 Drag Crawl.prtl so that its duration is the same as Creditslist.prtl.

5 Preview the crawling title segment. Adjust its vertical position as necessary in the Title Designer.

6 Review again to your satisfaction.

7 Save the project.

Updating a title in the Titler window

You can open the Titler window and update a title by double-clicking the title in either the Timeline or Project window. As soon as you save your changes to the title file, Premiere Pro updates all the references to it in your project.

Using other programs to create titles

The logo portion of the opening title sequence for *Books & Beans* was created with Photoshop. In the previous lesson, you left a video gap at the start of the Master sequence for the opening titles.

1 Into the Titles bin of the Project window, import Adobe.prtl, Presents.prtl, and Logo.psd from your 11Lesson folder. The Import Layered File dialog box appears for Logo.psd. Import as Footage. Choose Layer 2 and select Document Size.

2 In the Titles bin of the Project window, select Adobe.prtl. Choose
Clip > Speed/Duration.

3 Change the Duration to **600** (00;00;06;00). Click OK.

4 In the Titles bin of the Project window, select Presents.prtl, and then choose
Clip > Speed/Duration.

5 Change the Duration to **300** (00;00;03;00). Click OK.

6 In the Titles bin of the Project window, select Logo.psd, then choose Clip > Speed/Duration.

7 Change the Duration to **611** (00;00;06;11). Click OK.

8 Set the current time indicator to the beginning of the Master sequence (at 00;00;00;00).

9 Drag Adobe.prtl to the Video 1 track with its In point at the start of the project.

10 Move the edit line to 00;00;03;00.

11 In the Titles bin of the Project window, select Presents.prtl and drag it to the Video 2 track so that its In point snaps to the edit line.

12 In the Titles bin of the Project window, select and drag Logo.psd to the Video 2 track so that its In point snaps to the Out point of Presents.prtl.

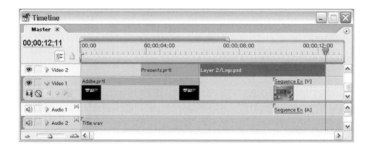

13 Play the rough cut of the opening titles.

14 To make the changes less abrupt for Adobe.prtl, try a 45-frame (00;00;01;15) fade in from **0%** opacity at the In point to **100%** opacity at 00;00;01;15. Create keyframes at the two timecodes.

15 For Presents.prtl, add a 15-frame (00;00;00;15) fade in from **0%** opacity at its In point (00;00;03;00) to **100%** opacity at 00;00;03;15, by creating keyframes at the two timecodes.

16 For Logo.psd, add a 41-frame (00;00;01;11) fade out from **100%** opacity at the In point of Sequence Ex to where the fade begins (00;00;09;22) to **0%** opacity at its Out point (00;00;12;11), by creating keyframes at the two timecodes.

17 Preview your titles and credits clips.

18 Save the project.

Exporting the movie

It's time to generate a movie file.

1 Choose File > Export > Movie.

2 In the Export Movie dialog box, click the Settings button. In the General settings, make sure that File Type is set to Microsoft DV AVI.

3 Select Entire Project for the Range.

4 Make sure that Export Video, Export Audio, Add to Project When Finished, and Beep When Finished are selected.

5 In the Audio section, choose 48000 Hz for Sample Rate, 16-bit for Sample Type, and Stereo for Channels.

6 Click OK to close the Export Movie Settings dialog box.

7 In the Export Movie dialog box, specify the11Lesson folder for the location and type the name of the movie. (Premiere Pro will add the AVI extension.) Click Save.

While Premiere is making the movie, a status bar displays the time remaining to complete the process. When the movie is complete, it appears in the Project window.

8 Double-click the movie to open it in the Source view of the Monitor window.

9 Click the Play button (▶) to play the movie you've just created.

Exploring on your own

Experiment with the Title window and the 11Lesson.prproj project. Here are some suggestions:

• Experiment with the many templates provided with Adobe Premiere Pro.

• Apply a gradient fill to the ampersand in the Ampersand.prtl title file. Adjust the left and right color buckets to achieve a glow around the color.

• Use the Rolling Title Options to apply special timing options to the crawling text so that it slows down as it exits the screen.

• Create a graphic in Adobe Illustrator or Photoshop, import it into a Premiere Pro project, then use the Edit Original command to modify the graphic. See how it affects a title sequence.

Review questions

1 How do you create a new title?

2 How do you change the color of title text?

3 How do you add a shadow?

4 How do you change the opacity of text or a graphic?

5 How do you adjust the speed of a rolling title?

6 What is a reference frame?

7 What is the difference between rolling and crawling text titles?

8 How do you add a title to a video program?

Answers

1 Choose File > New > Title.

2 Select the text, click the Object Color swatch, and pick a new color in the Color Picker.

3 Check the Shadow button.

4 Select the text or graphic, then drag the right opacity slider to a new setting.

5 The duration of a title clip can be changed once it has been placed onto the Timeline of a project.

6 A reference frame is a frame from another title, still image, or video clip that you can copy to your title and use as a reference to help determine colors, precise positions for text over an image, or to provide a guideline for drawing an image.

7 Rolling text moves across the screen vertically, either top-to-bottom or bottom-to-top. Crawling text moves horizontally, either left-to-right or right-to-left.

8 Premiere Pro automatically adds a new title to the project that is open when you name and save the new title file. To import an existing title, with the project file open, choose File > Import and specify a previously saved title to import into the project.

Lesson 12

12 | Audio

The right music or sound effects add impact to your video program. Adobe Premiere Pro makes it easy to add additional audio, mix the sound, and carefully control the volume for maximum effect.

The movie is almost complete, except for some music, audio, and sound effects, which you'll add in this lesson. Specifically, you'll learn how to do the following:

• Navigate the Premiere Pro Audio workspace.

• Adjust audio manually and automate the mixing process.

• Add music and sound effects.

• Create 5.1 surround audio.

• Adjust audio levels, panning and balancing, cross fading, using markers to synchronize clips, and performing other related activities.

Getting started

Before you begin, you'll need to open the project file. Make sure you know the location of the files used in this lesson. Insert the *Classroom in a Book* DVD-ROM disk if necessary. For help, see "Copying the Classroom in a Book files" on page 4.

1 Launch the Premiere Pro software.

2 In the Premiere Pro Welcome window, click Open Project.

3 In the Open Project dialog box, locate the 12Lesson folder that you copied onto your hard drive from the DVD-ROM.

4 Locate the 12Lesson.prproj file in the 12Lesson folder and click Open. (You can also double-click on the 12Lesson.prproj file to open it.)

5 If necessary, rearrange windows and palettes so that they don't overlap, by choosing Window > Workspace > Audio.

Note: 12Lesson.prproj is similar to the project you finished in Lesson 11. You'll use the 12Lesson.prproj project, so that In and Out points will match the instructions in the following exercises.

To keep things organized, create a separate bin for sound files, and then move the audio files into the Audio bin.

6 Create a new bin by either clicking the Bin icon (⬛) at the bottom of the Project window or clicking the menu triangle button at the top right corner of the Project window and choosing New Bin.

7 Change the name of the bin to **Audio.**

8 With the Audio bin active, choose File > Import.

9 Hold down the Control key and click on Credits.wav, Dooropen.wav, Doorslam.wav, Earlymusic.wav, Excuseme.wav, Footsteps.wav, Gazeapproach.wav and Sigh.wav. Click Open.

Now, the audio files needed for this lesson are in the Audio bin.

Note: When you import an audio file, Premiere Pro automatically converts the file to the project's current audio sample at 32-bit quality. This process provides audio that is consistent with other audio in the project and that you can play back at high quality without further manipulation. However, the conforming process may take a few minutes. (Premiere Pro displays its progress.) Your system's performance may decrease while audio is conforming. In addition, conforming can result in very large audio files that are stored on your system.

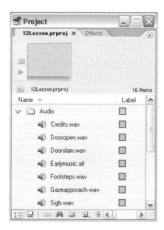

Finally, you'll save the project.

10 Choose File > Save.

Getting to know the Audio workspace

In Premiere Pro, you can edit, add effects, and mix up to 99 tracks of audio. There are several ways to process an audio clip. You can control volume and pan/balance settings of audio tracks directly within the Timeline, or use the Audio Mixer window to make changes in real time.

You can also use the Audio Mixer to create a submix, which combines audio signals from specific audio tracks or track sends in the same sequence. Use a submix when you want to work with more than one track in the same way. For more information about submixes, see the section on "Working with submixes," in the *Adobe Premiere Pro User Guide.*

You can select the Audio workspace at almost any time while working on a project. The Audio workspace uses your current workspace with the following adjustments: the Audio Mixer is open, and no palettes are displayed. You customize the audio workspace by rearranging the windows and changing their settings. Saving a workspace preserves the locations of the Project, Monitor, Timeline, and Audio Mixer windows.

1 Begin by opening the Audio workspace. Choose Window > Workspace > Audio.

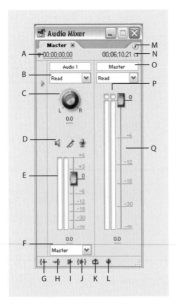

A. Timecode B. Automation options
C. Pan/balance control
D. Mute/Solo Track/Record Enable buttons
E. VU meters and faders F. Output
G. Go to In Point H. Go to Out Point
I. Play J. Play In to Out K. Loop Enable
L. Sequence Record Enable
M. Window menu N. In/out program
duration O.Track names
P. Clipping indicator
Q. Master VU meter and fader

Note: If the Audio Mixer window is ever closed or hidden, you can choose Window > Audio Mixer to display it again.

The Audio Mixer window, like a professional sound studio-style audio mixing console, contains a set of controls for each audio track. The controls are numbered according to the corresponding audio track in the Timeline. This window also contains a volume fader labeled Master, which controls the overall volume for the entire project.

In addition, in the Audio Mixer window, you can adjust the volume level and pan/balance of multiple audio tracks while listening to them and viewing the video tracks. Premiere Pro uses automation to record these adjustments and then to apply them as the clip plays back. You'll learn more about automating the mixing process later in this lesson.

Now, you'll adjust the volume level with the Volume Fader in the Audio Mixer window.

2 In the Timeline window, click the Collapse/Expand triangle next to the Audio 3 track to expand it.

3 Click the menu button in the upper right corner of the Audio Mixer window and choose Show/Hide Tracks.

The Show/Hide Tracks box appears.

4 In the Show/Hide Tracks box, make sure that all three tracks are selected. If they are not, click Show All. Click OK.

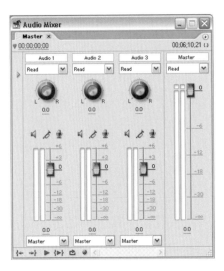

Note: You can also display audio tracks by clicking and holding the expand/contract area in the lower right corner of the Audio Mixer window and dragging to the right.

5 In the Master sequence, locate the point after the Hero's fantasies just beyond the end of the Transitions clip, where he sighs (at approximately00;03;53;03; your time code may vary a little.)

6 From the Audio bin of the Project window, locate and select Sigh.wav.

7 Drag Sigh.wav to the edit line on the Audio 2 track with its In point snapping to the edit line.

8 In the Timeline window, select Sigh.wav.

9 Choose Marker > Set Sequence Marker > In and Out Around Selection.

This option sets the In and Out points for Sigh.wav.

10 In the Audio Mixer window, click the Loop button (⊜) at the bottom of the window.

11 In the Audio Mixer window, click the Play In to Out Point button (⇅) at the bottom of the window.

Because you also clicked the Loop button, the selection will play repeatedly until you click the Stop button.

12 While Sigh.wav is playing, set the volume level of the Audio 2 mixer by doing one of the following:

• Drag the volume fader up or down to increase or decrease volume level.

• Click the editable decibels (dB) value that appears in blue directly below the volume fader and type a new dB value from +6 to −100.

• Use the hot text control that is represented by a dotted line directly below the editable dB value.

***Note:** Audio level is represented graphically by a segmented VU meter to the left of the volume fader. The small indicator at the top of the VU meter turns red when the level is high enough to cause clipping, or distortion. To avoid clipping, adjust the volume so that the VU meter does not display red.*

13 In the Audio Mixer window, click the Stop button at the bottom of the window.

Now you'll adjust the gain uniformly throughout a clip. Setting the gain is useful to balance the gain levels of several clips or to adjust a clip's audio signal when it is too high or too low.

14 In the Timeline window, select the Sigh.wav audio clip in the Audio 2 track.

15 Choose Clip > Audio Options > Audio Gain.

16 Do one of the following:

• Click the editable decibels (dB) value that appears in blue and type a gain value. A value above 100% amplifies the clip. A value below 100% *attenuates* the clip, making it quieter.

• Click Normalize to have Premiere Pro optimize gain automatically. This gain value represents the percentage of amplification necessary to boost the loudest part of the clip to full strength (the loudest sound your system can reproduce) without clipping.

17 Click OK.

Automating the mixing process

In the Audio Mixer window, you can adjust the volume level and pan/balance of multiple audio tracks while listening to them and viewing the video tracks. Premiere Pro uses automation to record these adjustments and then to apply them as the clip plays back. You can start and stop recording automation changes at any point in the audio track by using the transport controls at the bottom of the Audio Mixer window.

For each audio track, the following options on the Automation menu determine the automation state during the mixing process:

Off (⊘) Ignores the stored volume and pan/balance data during playback. Off allows you to use the mixer controls in real time without interference from the paths in the Timeline.

Read (🖢) Reads the stored volume and pan/balance data and uses it to control the audio level of the track during playback. Read is the default mode.

Write (🖉) Reads the stored level and pan/balance data for an audio track and records any adjustments you make to these settings, using the volume and pan/balance controls in the Audio Mixer window. These adjustments are stored as new handles on the Volume and Pan/balance paths when you choose Show Track Volume from the Timeline track header area. The default setting for Write is Switch to Touch after Write. You can toggle this option from the Audio Mixer menu.

Latch (🖢) Identical to Write, except that the automation doesn't start until you begin to adjust a value, and the value will remain where it was when you stopped adjusting it.

Touch (🖢) Identical to Write, except that the automation doesn't start until you begin to adjust a value. When you stop adjusting a property, its value will return to where it was before the current automated changes were recorded. The rate of return is determined by the Automatch Time.

Adjusting audio levels using the Audio Mixer controls

Now, you'll adjust audio levels in the Audio Mixer window using automation. In this exercise, you will adjust audio levels for the Approach fantasy scenes.

1 Drag the edit line in the Master sequence on the Timeline to the point where Father and Son have exited and Hero is happily stuffing his face with pie (at 00;02;34;11).

2 From the Audio bin in the Project window, select Gazeapproach.wav and drag it to the Audio 3 track. Make sure that the beginning of Gazeapproach.wav snaps to the edit line.

3 On the Timeline, select Gazeapproach.wav and choose Marker > Set Sequence Marker > In and Out Around Selection.

This option sets the In point and the Out point for Gazeapproach.wav.

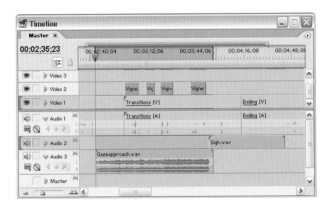

4 In the Audio 3 track header area, click the Show Key Frames button and select Show Track Volume.

5 If the Audio Mixer window is not open, choose Window > Audio Mixer.

6 In the Audio Mixer window, locate the Audio 3 mixer track, which corresponds to the Audio 3 track in the Timeline window.

7 If it is not already selected, select Write from the Audio 3 mixer track Automate menu.

Use your visual sense to work the timing in these next steps. The timecodes are approximate. This is the way live television audio, theatrical, and concert sound are controlled. Some of your time codes will be different from those indicated.

8 In the Audio 3 track of the Audio Mixer window, drag the volume fader to 0.

9 Click the Play In to Out button (▶ǀ) to play the program from the In point to the Out point. As the program is playing, drag the Audio 3 volume fader down to **–18** at the point where Hero approaches Dreams for the first time (at approximately 00;02;55;09).

10 As Hero says, "Sorry to bother you" (at approximately 00;03;05;09), slowly and smoothly drag the Audio 3 volume fader back to **0**.

11 Before Hero presents the flowers and says, "Duh-duh!"(at approximately 00;03;10;07), slowly and smoothly drag the Audio 3 volume fader down to **–18**.

12 After Hero says, "Duh-duh!" (at approximately 00;03;11;07), slowly and smoothly drag the Audio 3 volume fader back to **0**.

13 After the flower sequence, when Hero approaches Dreams for the third time and says, "Hey" (at approximately 00;03;19;24), slowly and smoothly drag the Audio 3 volume fader down to -**18**.

14 When Hero and Dreams start to kiss (at approximately 00;03;28;15), slowly and smoothly drag the Audio 3 volume fader back to **0**.

15 After Hero approaches Dreams for the fourth time, when Hero's hand reaches the back of the chair (at approximately 00;03;40;09), drag the Audio 3 volume fader down as far as it will go to fade out the music.

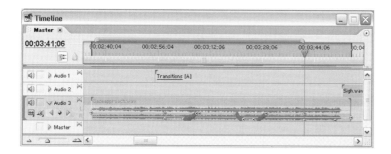

Recording stops automatically when the edit line reaches the Out point. By default, Write reverts to Touch in the Audio 3 Automation menu.

16 To Prevent accidently overwriting automation that has already been applied, select Read in the Audio 3 Automation menu.

17 Preview your volume changes.

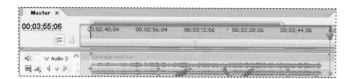

18 Once the adjustments have been recorded, fine-tune your changes directly in the Timeline by dragging the handles on the volume paths in the Gazeapproach.wav clip. To see the volume paths, click the Collapse/Expand triangle next to the Audio 3 track to expand it.

19 Save the project.

Understanding the Pan/Balance control

You can pan a monophonic audio track to set its position in a multichannel track. You can balance a multichannel (stereo or 5.1) audio track to redistribute its channels among the channels of another multichannel track.

In this exercise, you'll experiment with panning. You won't record your panning adjustments now, but Premiere Pro does allow you to do so.

1 In the Timeline window, click the triangle to the left of the Audio 2 track to expand it.

2 In the Audio 2 track, drag the edit line to the point where Hero is attracted to Dreams as she enters the scene (at 00;01;42;11).

3 Choose Marker > Set Sequence Marker > In.

4 In the Audio 2 track, press the Page Down key once to move the Edit line to the end of the Chorale.wav audio clip.

5 Choose Marker > Set Sequence Marker > Out.

6 If the Audio Mixer window is not open, choose Window > Audio Mixer.

7 In the Audio Mixer window, locate the Audio 2 mixer track, which corresponds to the Audio 2 track in the Timeline window.

8 In the Audio Mixer window, click the Play In to Out button (▮◂) to play the program from the In point to the Out point.

9 While the clip is playing, click and hold the pan control in the Audio 2 mixer track and drag inside the circle. Drag clockwise to pan or balance right; drag counterclockwise to pan or balance left.

You can also pan a track in either of these two ways:

• Click the editable pan value that appears in blue directly below the pan control knob and type a new value from –100 to 100.

• Use the hot text control that is represented by a dotted line directly below the editable pan value.

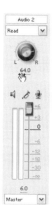

Working with Mute, Solo, and Record Enable

Now you'll use the Mute and Solo buttons in the Audio Mixer window to specify the track or tracks that you want to hear. You'll also see how the Record Enable button lets you record, or capture, an audio source.

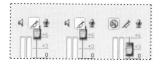

Mute (⊘) Allows you to temporarily silence selected tracks.

Solo (👂) Allows you to monitor selected tracks. When you click the Solo button for a track, other tracks that you haven't soloed will be muted.

Record Enable (👂) Allows you to use audio that is not yet in digital form, such as an analog cassette or a live voiceover.

Creating and adjusting audio effects

Premiere Pro contains enhanced audio capabilities for creating surround-sound and other multichannel audio effects. You can apply up to five effects to an audio track through the Audio Mixer window.

Unlinking the video and audio

Typically, when you shoot a scene with your camera, you capture both video and audio at the same time. When you digitize the footage, the video and audio are linked together in one file, known as a hard link. You can break these links to replace or edit audio and video independently.

When you add a clip containing video and audio to the program, and you've specified adding both the video and audio portions, the video portion appears in a video track and the audio portion appears in an audio track. The video and audio portions of the clip are linked so that when you drag the video portion in the Timeline window, the linked audio moves with it. If you split the clip, the video and audio are still linked within the two resulting clips. Video can only be linked to audio—a video clip cannot be linked to another video clip.

In many situations, it is useful to link or unlink clips manually. For example, you may want to move previously unlinked audio or video clips together, or edit the In or Out point of the video or audio portion of a clip independently. You don't have to unlink clips if you only want to delete one clip or the other.

You'll start by adding a video clip to the project.

1 In the Master sequence Timeline, select the nested Seeya sequence.

2 Choose Clip > Unlink Audio and Video.

The underline is removed from the name Seeya.avi in the Video 1 and Audio 1 tracks, indicating that the audio and video portions are unlinked. Now you can select the audio and video clips independently.

3 Undo or Relink the Seeya Audio and Video.

4 Save the project.

For more information about linking and unlinking clips, see Lesson 8, page 301.

Using markers to synchronize clips

When working with audio clips that are not linked to video, you'll occasionally encounter situations where you need to synchronize the audio to the video clip. The most straight-forward method of synchronizing these clips is to insert markers at matching events in both clips.

> ### Using markers
>
> *Markers indicate important points in time and help you position and arrange clips. Each sequence and each clip can individually contain up to 100 numbered markers (labeled from 0 to 99) and as many unnumbered markers as you want. In the Monitor window, markers appear in each view's time ruler as small icons. Clip markers also become icons within the clip as it appears in the timeline, and sequence markers appear in the sequence's time ruler. In general, use clip markers to signify important points within an individual clip. (For example, use a clip marker to identify a particular action or sound.) Use sequence markers to specify significant time points in terms of a sequence.*

For more information about using markers to synchronize clips, see the "Using markers" section of the *Adobe Premiere Pro User Guide*.

Adjusting audio levels in the Timeline

When you expand the Audio track in the Timeline, you'll notice that an audio clip is represented by a waveform. Running through the center of the waveform is a white line, called the volume rubberband, which allows you to adjust the volume level of a clip at any point. Adjustments are make with keyframe editing techniques in the Timeline or in coordination with the Effect Controls window. The volume for a segment can be adjusted separately.

Wherever a keyframe is established, you can drag its handle up or down to change the audio level. You can also cross-fade two audio clips automatically so that one fades out as another fades in. The path that has been formed out of the rubberband in the Timeline corresponds to the volume fader in the Audio Mixer window, and serves the same purpose. To create fades in the Timeline, you visually adjust levels. For each track in the Timeline, there is one volume rubberband per clip.

First, you'll fade out the end of the audio track linked to the Sigh.avi video clip.

1 Choose Marker > Clear Sequence Marker > In and Out.

2 In the Timeline window, click the Collapse/Expand triangle to the left of the Audio 2 track to expand it and locate the Sigh.avi audio clip.

3 Adjust the Time Zoom controls so that you can clearly see the waveforms.

4 Click the Show Keyframes button (◦) in the Audio 3 track header area and choose Show Clip Volume.

5 Select the Sigh.wav clip.

6 Move the edit line to the point where Hero stops and looks back at Dreams through the shop window.

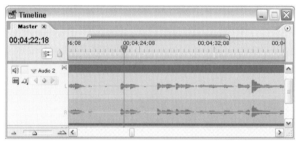

Using the Audio Units display in the sequence

You can display the scales on Timeline rulers in audio units, which are sample-based, instead of in video frames, which is the default display. The audio unit display allows you to edit audio clips in precise detail. See the *Adobe Premiere Pro User Guide* for more information about display options.

1 Click the Menu button in the upper right corner of the Timeline window and choose Audio Units.

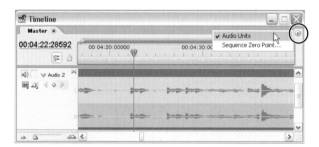

The following changes occur in the Timeline window:

• The timecode display is in audio units.

• The Timeline ruler now displays units in audio units. There are 100,000 audio units per frame.

2 Click the Menu button in the upper right corner of the Timeline window and choose Audio Units again to deselect it.

Increasing the volume of a selection

Now you'll increase the volume of the music as Hero walks away from the shop.

1 Make sure that the edit line is still where Hero looks back in through the shop.

2 Choose Marker > Set Sequence Marker > In.

3 Click the Add/Remove Keyframe button (◦) in the Audio 2 track.

Premiere Pro inserts a keyframe at the edit line.

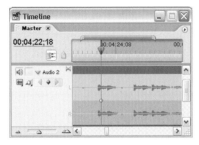

4 Step back in time three frames.

5 Click the Add/Remove Keyframe button (◦) to add a second keyframe just three frames to the left of the In point keyframe.

6 Set the edit line eight seconds forward in time.

7 Choose Marker > Set Sequence Marker > Out.

8 Click the Add/Remove Keyframe button (∘) in the Audio 2 track to insert a keyframe at the edit line.

9 Step the edit line forward in time three frames.

10 Click the Add/Remove Keyframe button (∘) in the Audio 2 track to insert a keyframe at the edit line, just three frames past the Out point.

11 In the Timeline window, adjust the view so that you can see the clip from the first keyframe to the last keyframe.

12 Move the edit line backward approximately three seconds.

13 Click the Add/Remove Keyframe button (∘) in the Audio 2 track to insert a fifth keyframe at the edit line.

14 While holding down the Shift key, click the two inner keyframes in turn so that you will have two keyframes selected, which will show goldenrod. The unselected ones will remain white.

15 While still holding the shift key, click and drag the middle keyframe you just inserted between the In and Out points up to 2.41 decibels. The three inner keyframes will move in unison.

Note that the keyframes at the In and Out points also rise to that level.

16 Play back the changes you've made to the Sigh.wav clip.

17 Save the project.

Fading audio on the Timeline

Now you'll fade out the music of Sigh.wav as Dreams and Hero finally meet.

1 In the Timeline window, move the edit line to approximately 00;04;36;14.

2 Click the Add/Remove Keyframe button (◦) in the Audio 2 track to insert a keyframe at the edit line.

3 Advance the edit line to the end of Sigh.wav.

4 Click the Add/Remove Keyframe button (◦) in the Audio 2 track to insert a keyframe at the edit line.

5 Click the keyframe that you just added and drag it down to the lower right corner of the Sigh.wav clip. A numeric display appears next to the pointing finger, indicating the current volume level.

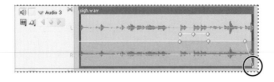

You've just created a downward slope at the end of the Sigh.wav audio clip. A downward slope fades out the audio. Because you dragged the handle as far down as possible, the audio fades out to no sound at all.

Note: If you activate the Info palette before you drag, you can watch the volume level update in the Info palette.

6 Choose Marker > Clear Sequence Marker > In and Out.

7 Play back the changes you've made to the Sigh.wav clip.

8 Save the project.

Finishing the movie with audio effects and music

Now you'll put the finishing touches on your movie. In these exercises, you'll concentrate on the final scenes from Hero's despondent exit from Books & Beans to his jubilant breakthrough when he scurries off to introduce himself properly to Dreams.

You know from the previous lessons on advanced editing that there are many layers of video operating in these scenes. Now you'll work with three levels of audio: music, sound effects, and dialog.

You'll perform the following exercises in stereo. Then, in the next section, you'll see how to work the same effects into 5.1 surround audio.

Adding a sound effect

1 In the Master sequence, place the edit line at the point where Hero stops on his way out and shoves his hands into his pockets. Notice that the door slams shut in sync with his hands.

2 Locate the Audio bin in the Project window and select Doorslam.wav.

3 Drag Doorslam.wav to the Video 3 track in the Master sequence so that it snaps to the edit line.

4 Zoom in on the Timeline to see the audio wave forms so that you can time the doorslam.

5 Adjust the placement of the sound effect with its video action.

6 Play the effect in the Timeline or in the Program view of the Monitor window.

7 Save the project.

Increasing the volume of a brief moment

In this exercise, you'll locate the point where Hero gives up on his fantasizing and lets out a sigh of acceptance. The volume of the sigh is too low for it to be heard clearly, so you'll enhance it.

First, you'll isolate the sigh by creating In and Out points for it, then increase its volume.

1 In the Master sequence, move the edit line to the point at which Hero gives up on his fantasies (at approximately 00;03;50;27).

2 In the Program view of the Monitor window, click the In point button to mark the In point.

3 In the Audio 1 track header area, choose Show Keyframes > Show Track Volume.

4 On the Audio 1 track, click the Add/Remove Keyframe button (◦) of the Keyframe Navigator to establish a keyframe at the In point.

5 Step backward one frame and add a keyframe there.

6 In the Program view, use the Jog tool to move the edit line to the end of Hero's sigh (at 00;03;52;26).

7 In the Program view of the Monitor window, click the Out point button to mark the Out point.

8 Click the Add/Remove Keyframe button (◦) of the Keyframe Navigator to establish a keyframe at the Out point.

9 In the Program view, click the Play In to Out button to hear the sigh.

10 In the track header area of the Audio 1 track, click the Show Keyframe menu button and select Show Clip Volume.

11 Move the edit line to one frame after the Out point.

12 Click the Add/Remove Keyframe button (◦) of the Keyframe Navigator to establish a keyframe at the edit line.

13 In the Tools palette, select the pen tool ( ).

14 In the Audio 1 track, raise the volume of the sigh by dragging upward to 6.02 dB.

You can also use the volume control in the Effects Control window or the Audio Mixer to make this volume change.

15 In the Audio Mixer, click the Play In to Out button (⏮) to play the program from the In point to the Out point.

16 Save the project.

Multiple audio effects in a clip

There are five audio elements that occur simultaneously during the transition from Hero's sigh to the meeting with Dreams at the car:

Dialog You added Dreams saying, "I love you," in Hero's mind in Lesson 10.

Overlapping dialog You'll add Dreams saying, "Excuse me," to Hero.

Audio effects You'll add reverberation and echo to Dreams saying, "I love you."

Music You added and adjusted the volume of the music that supports this episode in the movie (Sigh.wav).

Sound effect You'll add Dreams' footsteps as she runs to catch up with Hero.

Giving dimension to audio

Hero is walking dejectedly to his car, daydreaming about Dreams. He hears, "I love you," echoing in his head.

1 In the Project window, locate the Ending sequence, and double-click it to activate it in the Timeline window.

2 Select Loveyou.avi on the Video 2 track.

3 In the Effects window, choose Audio Effects > Stereo.

4 Select the Delay effect and drag it to the Effect Controls window.

5 Select the Reverb effect and drag it to the Effect Controls window.

6 In the Effect Controls window, activate Delay by clicking the triangle next to the name.

7 Open the Delay field to reveal the Delay slider.

8 Move the slider to **.33** seconds.

9 Across from the name Reverb, on the right edge of the name field, click on the menu triangle and choose church.

The default church settings are displayed in 3-D in the Custom Setup panel. You can have some fun tweaking the values of both effects or accept the defaults.

10 Return to the Master sequence to preview the Delay and Reverb effects applied to Loveyou.avi in the nested Ending sequence. (You may have to remove the In and Out sequence markers.)

11 Save the project.

Overlapping voice-overs

In reality, Dreams is trying to catch up to Hero. She's not saying, "I love you." She's saying, "Excuse me." You'll add this to the Ending clip nested in the Master sequence.

1 Make the Ending sequence the active Timeline again.

2 From the Audio bin in the Project window, locate Excuseme.wav and drag it to the Audio 3 track so that its In point snaps to the In point of Loveyou.avi.

3 Set the Effect Controls to the point after she says the first, "I love you."

4 With the selection tool, trim the Excuseme.wav clip from the left at the In point until it snaps to the edit line.

5 Preview in the Master sequence.

Note: You may have to use the audio mixer to independently adjust the volumes of Loveyou.avi and Excuseme.wav so that they are more in line with your editing sensibilities. If you do so, use the Write command but restore it to Read when you're done.

Layering in a sound effect

Now, the fifth piece of the puzzle, the sound of Dreams' footsteps as she follows after Hero.

1 In the Timeline, move the edit line to the start of Excuseme.wav.

2 From the Audio bin in the Project window, drag the Footsteps.wav below the Audio 3 track to automatically add the Audio 4 track. Make sure that the head of Footsteps.wav is placed on the Audio 4 track and snaps to the edit line.

3 Trim the end of Footsteps.wav to make it the same duration as Excuseme.wav.

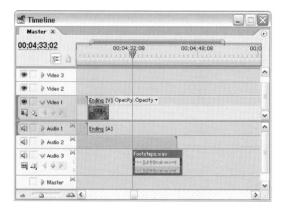

4 In the Master sequence, click Play to hear and see the multiple sound elements that are occurring at once.

5 Save the project.

Adding the final music

Now you'll add music to the final scene and the credits.

1 In the Master sequence Timeline, move the edit line to the point right after Hero crumples the note (at approximately 00;05;42;00).

2 From the Audio bin in the Project window, drag Credits.wav to the Audio 2 track. Make sure that the head of Credits.wav snaps to the edit line.

3 Save the project.

Congratulations! You have finished editing your own version of *Books & Beans.*

4 Make the Master Timeline active.

5 Type "\" (backslash) to reveal the entire movie.

6 Double-click the center ridges of the work area bar and adjust the work area to cover the entire movie.

7 Move the edit line to 00;00;00;00.

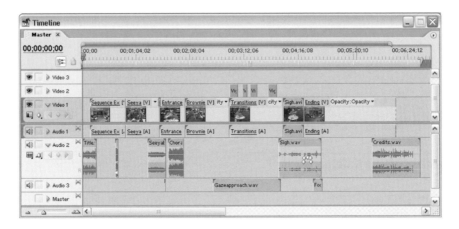

8 Press Enter to play the movie. Enjoy the show!

Working with 5.1 audio files

With 5.1 surround audio, you can set your movie's audio to play through five discrete speakers: front left, front center, front right, rear left, rear right, and subwoofer. As illustrated in the following exercises, Premiere Pro gives you complete control over your 5.1 audio mix.

Premiere Pro is compatible with some 5.1 files, including .wav files that have been compiled with 6 tracks. If you import a 5.1 file, the surround speakers will be allocated automatically. This way, you can simply import a 5.1 file, place it on the Timeline, sync it with the video action, and play it through your 5.1 speakers.

Note: If you want to monitor 5.1 surround audio, your system must have surround speakers, an appropriate audio card, and a device driver that complies with the ASIO (Audio Stream Input Output) specification.

Creating a 5.1 style edit

In this exercise, you'll learn how to create a 5.1 effect when you don't have an existing 5.1 file or the ability to create a 5.1 file. You'll begin by creating a Surround sequence.

1 Choose File > New > Sequence.

2 In the Sequence Name field, type **Surround**.

3 In the Master field of the Audio section, choose 5.1.

4 In the Mono field of the Audio section, type **5**.

5 In the Stereo field of the Audio section, type **1**.

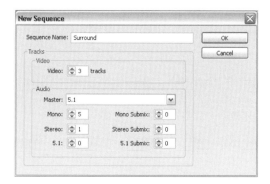

6 Click OK to close the New Sequence dialog box.

Assembling the 5.1 mix

Now you'll prepare to import the five audio files that will make up your 5.1 mix.

1 In the Project window, select the Ending sequence icon and choose Edit > Duplicate.

2 Rename Ending Copy to **5.1 Source**.

The Surround sequence becomes the active sequence.

3 Make 5.1 Source the active sequence.

4 Locate the instance of Doorslam.wav that you inserted earlier in this lesson.

This clip cannot be accessed until you change its status from Show Track Volume to Show Clip Volume.

5 In the Audio 2 track header area, choose Show Keyframes > Show Clip Volume.

6 Choose Edit > Clear. You'll be adding it back in shortly as a component of surround sound.

7 Next, select Loveyou.avi, another component of the 5.1 Sound.

8 Choose Clip > Unlink Audio and Video.

9 Shift-click on the video portions of Loveyou.avi to deselect it.

10 Choose Edit > Clear to remove the audio portion of Loveyou.avi.

11 Shift-click on Excuseme.wav and then on Footsteps.wav to select them both.

12 Choose Edit > Clear to remove them.

13 From the Project window, choose File > New > Bin. The bin appears in the Project window. Change the name of the bin to **5.1 Files**.

14 Make the 5.1 Files bin active and choose File > Import.

15 Hold down the Control key and click Doorslam-mono.wav, Excuseme-mono.wav, Footsteps-mono.wav, Loveyou-mono.wav, and Sigh-mono.wav. Now click Open.

These files include music, two overlapping dialog clips, and two sound effects.

Building a surround sound sequence

Now you'll make edits that are similar to the ones you made earlier in this lesson when you inserted Sigh.wav and Doorslam.wav.

1 From the Project window, drag the 5.1 Source sequence to the Video 1 track of the Timeline in the Surround sequence at 0.

The stereo audio linked to the video appears on the sixth audio track.

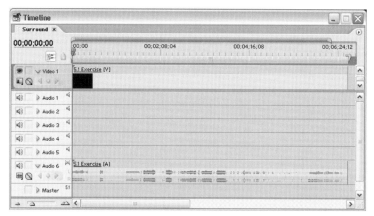

The first five tracks are mono and the Audio 6 track receives the stereo audio from the placed clip.

2 Activate the Surround sequence, then move the edit line near the start of it. This is where Hero gives up on meeting Dreams and heaves the big sigh at the dashing of his fantasies.

3 From the 5.1 Files bin in the Project window, select Sigh-mono.wav and drag it to the Audio 1 track. Make sure that the beginning of Sigh-mono.wav snaps to the edit line.

4 Move the edit line to where Hero stops to look at Dreams after he leaves the cafe–the scene where his hands are shoved in his pockets.

5 From the Audio bin in the Project window, select Doorslam-mono.wav and drag it to the Audio 2 track. Make sure that the beginning of Doorslam-mono.wav snaps to the edit line.

6 Move the edit line where Dreams begins to say, "I love you," in Hero's imagination.

7 From the Audio bin in the Project window, select Loveyou-mono.wav and drag it to the Audio 3 track. Make sure that the beginning of Loveyou-mono.wav snaps to the edit line.

8 Move the edit line to the point where Dreams is going to be following Hero after the first utterance of, "I love you."

9 From the Audio bin in the Project window, select Footsteps-mono.wav and drag it to the Audio 4 track. Make sure that the beginning of Footsteps-mono.wav snaps to the edit line.

10 Move the edit line to where Dreams would be saying, "Excuse me," over her footsteps while she is hurrying after Hero.

11 From the Audio bin in the Project window, select Excuseme-mono.wav and drag it to the Audio 5 track. Make sure that the beginning of Excuseme-mono.wav snaps to the edit line.

12 Trim Excuseme-mono.wav to end at the Out point of Loveyou-mono.wav.

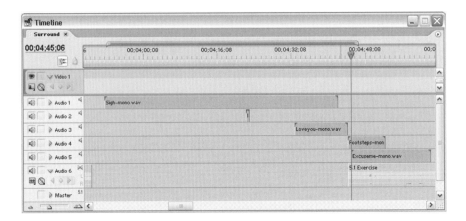

13 Preview the five edits you've just made.

Make sure that "I love you" is synced to the video. Also make sure that you can hear footsteps and "Excuse me" in the background, but that these sounds do not overpower the music. You'll make adjustments to the audio in the next exercise.

14 Save the project.

Allocating tracks to 5.1 speaker positions using the Audio Mixer

Now you'll adjust volume of the five tracks that you just inserted, and you'll put the sounds into the 5.1 fields. In this exercise, you'll be mixing a portion of your movie in true 5.1 surround audio.

1 Choose Window > Audio Mixer.

2 Click and hold the expand/contract area in the lower right corner of the Audio Mixer window and drag it to the right so that you can see all six audio tracks and the master fader.

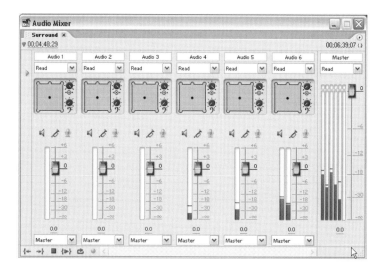

At the top of each fader, you'll see a square tray called a 5.1 surround pan/balance tray. The five pockets around the edge of the tray represent the five surround speakers. For example, the top center pocket represents the center speaker, and the top right pocket represents the front right speaker. You move the dot, or puck, within a tray to pan or balance the audio among the surround speakers.

The Center percentage knob at the top right of a tray controls the percentage of a surround audio track that is allocated to the center speaker. The LFE volume knob at the bottom right of a tray controls the volume of the subwoofer sound from the track.

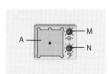

A. 5.1 surround pan/balance tray
B. Center percentage knob
C. LFE volume knob

3 In the Audio Mixer, drag the puck in the Audio 1 5.1 surround pan/balance tray to the top center pocket.

This setting pans the music to the center speaker.

4 In the Audio Mixer, drag the puck in the Audio 2 5.1 surround pan/balance tray to the bottom left pocket.

This setting pans the doorslam to the rear left speaker.

5 In the Audio Mixer, drag the puck in the Audio 3 5.1 surround pan/balance tray to the front left pocket.

This setting pans "I love you" to the front left speaker.

6 In the Audio Mixer, drag the puck in the Audio 4 5.1 surround pan/balance tray to the bottom right pocket.

This setting pans the footsteps to the rear right speaker.

7 In the Audio Mixer, drag the puck in the Audio 5 5.1 surround pan/balance tray to the top right pocket.

This setting pans "Excuse Me" to the right front speaker.

You've now set up a 5.1 audio mix so that the music comes from the center channel, Dream's voice comes from the front speakers, and the sound effects come from the rear speakers.

You can fine-tune your 5.1 mix by moving the pucks in the 5.1 surround pan/balance trays and by adjusting the Center percentage and LFE volume knobs.

Congratulations! You have now added 5.1 surround audio to your movie.

Exporting the movie as a 5.1 audio file

You've finished editing, but your video program is still composed of several video and audio files and a Premiere Pro project file. To distribute your program as a single file, you need to export it to a movie file. You'll learn various methods of creating output in Lesson 13.

In this exercise, you'll create a 5.1 audio file of the section of the movie that you worked on during the preceding 5.1 exercises.

1 In the Surround Timeline, press the Page Down key to move the edit line to the end of Excuseme-mono.wav.

2 Choose Marker > Set Sequence Marker Out.

3 In the Surround Timeline, press the Page Up key to move the edit line to the beginning of Sigh-mono.wav.

4 Choose Marker > Set Sequence Marker In.

5 As a first step to set the work area bar to the In and Out points, double-click the textured area at the center of the work area bar.

This action brings the brackets into the visible area of the Timeline.

6 Drag the left bracket until it snaps to the In point at the beginning of Sigh-mono.wav.

7 Drag the right bracket until it snaps to the Out point at the end of Excuseme mono.wav.

You are now set to export only the 5.1 part of the movie.

8 Choose File > Export Audio.

The Export Audio box appears.

9 In the File name field, type **Exercise.wav**.

10 In the Export Audio dialog box, click the Settings button. Make sure that Work Area Bar is selected for the Range. Also make sure that Add to Project When Finished is selected.

11 Click the Audio entry in the List column. The Export Audio Settings page appears.

12 In the Channels menu in the Audio page, choose Channels 5.1.

13 Click OK to close the Settings dialog box.

14 Click Save to close the Export Audio Settings dialog box and save your changes. Make sure to save to your 12Lesson folder.

Premiere Pro starts making the movie, displaying a status bar that provides an estimate of the time it will take. When the movie is complete, it appears in the Project window.

Reviewing your 5.1 audio file

Now you'll see how to play the 5.1 portion of the movie.

1 Click on the track header area to the left of the Audio 1 track in the Surround sequence.

2 Right-click the Audio 1 track header area and choose Add Tracks.

The Add Tracks dialog box appears.

3 In the Audio Tracks section, Add 1 Audio Track. For Placement, choose Before First Track. For Track Type, choose 5.1.

4 Click OK.

A 5.1 audio track is added to the Surround sequence. This track will become the new Audio 1 track. Its 5.1 attribute will be indicated in the upper right corner of the track header area.

5 With the current time indicator still set at the In point of the 5.1 Exercise, drag Exercise.wav from the Project window. Make sure that Exercise.wav snaps to the edit line.

6 Click on the Speaker icons in Audio tracks 2 through 6 to disable the speakers for these tracks. This way, you can hear only the 5.1 Exercise.wav file.

7 In the Audio Mixer, notice that Audio 1 is now a 5.1 track.

8 In the Audio Mixer, click the Play In to Out Point button ( ).

Watch and listen to your 5.1 exercise.

9 Save the project.

Congratulations! You have finished the audio lesson.

Exploring on your own

Feel free to experiment with the project that you have just created. See the "Mixing Audio" chapter in the *Adobe Premiere Pro User Guide* for more information about controlling the audio in your movie. In addition, Premiere Pro provides you with some powerful audio enhancement tools.

Review questions

1 How do you display the Audio workspace?

2 What is the difference between panning and balancing audio?

3 Why would you unlink a video clip from an audio clip?

4 What is the audio unit display?

5 What speakers are used for 5.1 surround audio?

Answers

1 Choose Window > Workspace > Audio.

2 Panning sets the position of a monophonic audio track in a multichannel track. Balancing redistributes a stereo or 5.1 audio track channel among the channels of another multichannel track

3 You unlink video and audio when you need to replace or edit audio and video independently.

4 The audio unit display shows the scales on time rulers in sample-based audio units rather than video frames. This display helps you edit audio clips in precise detail.

5 Front left, front center, front right, rear left, rear right, and subwoofer.

Lesson 13

13 | Output

Whether you want to export a sequence to DVD or create a file for viewing over the World Wide Web, Adobe Premiere Pro provides you with many options for generating your final video.

This lesson describes the techniques available for exporting movies with Adobe Premiere Pro. You'll learn how to do the following:

• Export to Tape.

• Use the File > Export > Movie command.

• Create a CD-ROM, using Adobe Media Encoder.

• Export to DVD.

• Export audio only and export a frame.

Output

When you have finished editing and assembling your video project, Adobe Premiere Pro offers a variety of flexible output options. These options allow you to:

• Record your production directly to DV or analog videotape by connecting your computer to a video camcorder or tape deck. If your camera or deck supports device control, you can automate the recording process, using timecode indications to selectively record portions of your program.

• Export a digital video file for playback from a computer hard drive, removable cartridge, CD-ROM, or DVD. Adobe Premiere Pro exports Advanced Windows Media, Real Media, AVI, QuickTime, and MPEG files; additional file formats may be available in Premiere Pro if provided with your video-capture card or third-party plug-in software.

• Use the Adobe Media Encoder export options to generate properly encoded video files for distribution over the Internet or your intranet. Adobe Premiere Pro exports QuickTime, Real Media, and Windows Media formats for download, progressive download, or streaming.

• Output a single frame as a still image in a wide variety of formats.

• Export the audio in QuickTime, AVI, or WAV format.

• Create an AAF (Advance Authoring Format) file so that you can perform offline editing based on a rough cut. This is useful when your output requires a level of quality that your system cannot provide.

• Output to motion-picture film or videotape if you have the proper hardware for film or video transfer or access to a vendor that offers the appropriate equipment and services.

Proceeding with the exercises in this lesson

There are many formats for output. Many of them have been gathered and described in this lesson. The exercises in this lesson can be performed with any project. Before you begin, locate a project with which to work and open it.

The Export to Tape command

1 Make sure your camcorder or tape deck is connected to your computer.

2 Click on the Timeline to activate it.

3 Choose File > Export > Export to Tape.

4 If your recording device has Device Control, make sure that the Activate Recording Device is selected.

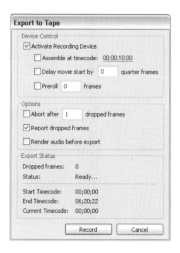

Note: If your recording device does not have Device Control, then you'll need to start the recording manually.

5 Click Record.

Premiere Pro will render any sections that need it and play it back to your tape.

Using File > Export > Movie

There are many options when exporting the movie to a file. For full details, see the section on "Producing Final Video" in the Adobe Premiere Pro User Guide.

To output the video project in this book as a full resolution DV AVI:

1 Click on the Timeline to activate it.

2 Choose File > Export > Movie.

3 Click on Settings.

4 Make sure that Microsoft DV AVI is chosen for File Type.

5 Make sure that Entire Sequence is chosen for Range. (You can also choose the area denoted by the work area bar as the range.)

6 Ensure that Export Video and Export Audio are both selected.

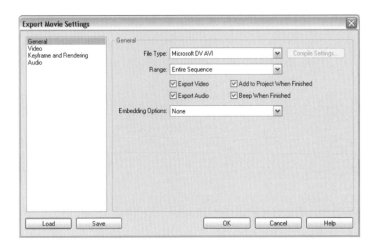

7 The default settings for Video, Keyframe and Rendering, and Audio should be fine.

Note: You can Save and Load settings files at the lower left of the dialog box.

8 Click OK to return to the Export Movie dialog box.

9 In the Export Movie dialog box, give your movie a name and location.

10 Click Save.

This AVI file can be brought into Adobe DVD Encore, After Effects, or a wide variety of other programs for further manipulation and display.

CD-ROM

Creating a file specifically for CD-ROM playback requires an intimate knowledge of the specific requirements of your project and the hardware used by your audience. You need to balance image size and quality with data rate and file size. Often, trial and error is the only way to find the optimum balance; however, a QuickTime movie reduced to 320 x 240 is often a good choice for a cross-platform file, usable on a wide variety of hardware.

To Create a CD-ROM:

1 Click on the Timeline to activate it.

2 Choose File > Export > Movie.

3 Click on Settings.

4 Choose QuickTime for File Type.

5 Make sure that Entire Sequence is selected for Range and that Export Video and Export Audio are both selected.

6 In the Video settings, for Compressor choose Motion JPEG A. Set the Frame Size to 320 h and 240 v and set the Frame Rate to 15 fps.

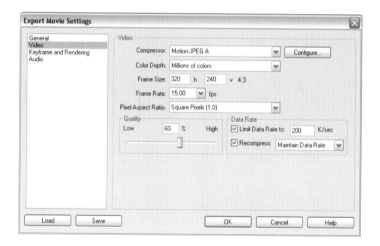

7 Set the Pixel Aspect Ratio to Square Pixels and set the Quality to 60%.

8 Click on Limit Data Rate and set it to 200 K/sec.

9 Click on Recompress and make sure it's set to Maintain Data Rate.

10 Click on Audio and for Compressor, choose IMA 4:1.

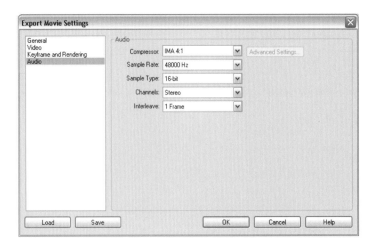

11 Click OK to return to the Export Movie dialog box.

12 In the Export Movie dialog box, give your movie a name and location.

13 Click Save.

Creating a CD-ROM using Adobe Media Encoder

In addition to manual output, Adobe Premiere Pro includes the Adobe Media Encoder, which provides many preset options for output to a wide variety of formats and data rates. It is suggested that you choose a higher bandwidth option to create a file suitable for CD-ROM.

1 Click on the Timeline to activate it.

2 Choose File > Export > Adobe Media Encoder.

3 Under Format, choose QuickTime.

Note: The preset setting depends on many factors. You may need to experiment to obtain the best setting.

4 Click OK.

5 Give your file a name and location.

6 Click Save.

Exporting a video file for viewing over the World Wide Web

Creating files for the World Wide Web is even more stringent than creating files for CD-ROM in terms of data rate and file size. Adobe Premiere Pro provides the Adobe Media Encoder to simplify the vast array of choices and possibilities available.

High-bandwidth vs. low-bandwidth With the proliferation of DSL and cable modems, many people now have access to fairly fast connections to the Internet. Nevertheless, it is a good idea to provide both a high-bandwidth and a low-bandwidth version of the movie.

Windows Media, QuickTime, and Real Media There are three major formats available for playback from the Web: Windows Media, QuickTime, and Real Media. All three require your audience to have a proprietary player on their machines. Thus, you may want to provide the movie in more than one format, rather than requiring audience members to download a specific player.

Streaming vs. progressive download There are two major ways that a Web server can send the video information to your audience's browsers: streaming, or progressive download. With streaming download, the file is sent frame by frame, like television, without ever downloading a large movie file. With progressive download, the movie file has to be downloaded; however, the movie player can usually begin playback before the entire file has been downloaded, by taking into account the file size and the connection speed. To serve streaming files, you generally have to have specific streaming software installed on your Web server. No such software is required for progressive download.

To Use the Media Encoder:

1 Click on the Timeline to activate it.

2 Choose File > Export > Adobe Media Encoder.

3 For Format, choose Windows Media.

4 For Preset, choose Windows Media Video 8 for dial-up modems (56 Kbps) for a low-bandwidth option.

5 Click OK.

6 Give your file a name and location.

Note: When exporting for the Web, it's a good idea to include some indication of the export settings in the file name, such as myMovie_56k.wmv.

7 Click Save.

8 Repeat these steps, choosing a high-bandwidth option and other media formats if you wish.

Export to DVD command

If your computer is equipped with a DVD writer, you can create a DVD directly from within Adobe Premiere Pro. These disks play automatically when inserted in consumer DVD players. Marker points can be used to create chapters on the DVD.

To create a DVD directly from Adobe Premiere Pro:

1 Click on the Timeline to activate it.

2 Choose File > Export > Export to DVD.

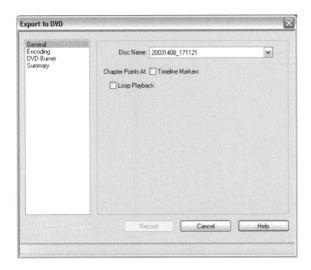

3 By default, the disk is given the date as the name. To create a different name, choose Custom from the Disc Name field.

4 Choose whether or not you want to create chapter points and looping.

5 In the Encoding settings, make sure that Entire Sequence is selected for the Export Range.

6 For this project, the defaults for the other settings should be fine.

7 Click on the DVD Burner setting and make sure that your DVD burner is recognized and that there is blank DVD media in the machine.

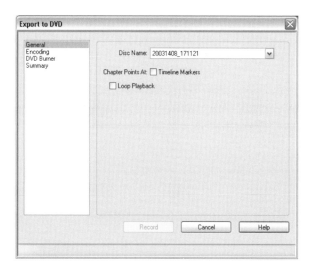

8 Click Record.

Adobe Premiere Pro renders any sections that need it and begins writing a DVD.

More and more computers are equipped with DVD writers. There are two main types: DVD-R and DVD+R. It is important to buy blank media that matches the type of writer that you have. Computers from Dell, Hewlett-Packard, and Compaq tend to ship with "+" drives, while machines from Sony and Gateway ship with "−" drives.

VCD/SVCD

The Adobe Media Encoder can also be used to create files suitable for creating Video CD (VCD) or SVCD disks. VCD and SVCD are similar to DVD, except that they are written on CD-R media rather than DVD-R or DVD+R media. Thus, a CD writer can be used. Since a CD holds about one sixth of the data of a DVD, longer programs may not fit. In addition, the quality is lower than DVD and closer to VHS or S-VHS. Finally, not all DVD players can play back VCD and SVCD disks.

1 Click on the Timeline to activate it.

2 Choose File > Export > Adobe Media Encoder.

3 For Format, choose MPEG1-VCD or MPEG2-SVCD.

4 The default preset should be fine. Click OK.

5 Give your file a name and location.

6 Click Save.

7 Premiere Pro writes out an mpeg file, which can then be burned onto a CD-ROM.

Export audio only

To export only the audio portion of your movie as a Microsoft Waveform (WAV) file:

1 Click on the Timeline to activate it.

2 Choose File > Export > Audio.

3 The default settings should be fine.

4 Give your file a name and location.

5 Click Save.

Note: You can also export audio only by choosing File > Export > Movie and deselecting Export Video in the Export Movie Settings dialog box.

Exporting a frame

1 Find the frame that you wish to export by dragging the edit line to the desired location in the Timeline.

2 Choose File > Export > Frame.

3 Click the Settings button. The default File Type is Windows Bitmap (.bmp). You can also choose from Compuserve GIF, Targa, or TIFF. Click OK.

4 You can choose a lower resolution for the output file if you wish.

5 Specify the name and location of the file.

6 Click Save.

Exporting to AAF

With Premiere Pro, you can export a project as an Advanced Authoring Format (AAF) file. AAF is an industry standard for high-end exchange of data. An AAF file allows you to preserve as much of the project's integrity as possible when transferring to another system.

To export a project to AAF:

1 Click on the Project window to activate it.

2 Choose Project > Export Project as AAF.

3 Specify the name and location of the file.

4 Click Save.

Lesson 14

14 | Working with Adobe Encore DVD

The creation of DVDs is one of the more
important aspects of multimedia
production output. Coordinating your
movie projects with DVD authoring
systems, like Adobe Encore DVD, gives
your work the opportunity to be seen in
many different environments. Learning
to master your files for maximum
viewing pleasure yet with minimum data
requirements is a desirable skill.

In this lesson you'll learn how to author DVDs using Adobe Encore DVD. Specifically, you will learn how to do the following:

• Add sequence markers in Premiere Pro.

• Export a Premiere Pro sequence as a DVD-legal MPEG2 file.

• Export a Premiere Pro sequence DVD-legal AVI file.

• Create thumbnail buttons from chapter point markers.

• Embed project information in an AVI file.

• Use the Edit Original command in Encore DVD.

Viewing the finished Encore DVD project

This lesson requires the use of both Adobe Premiere Pro and Adobe Encore DVD. You'll be instructed to move back and forth between the programs several rounds within the flow of the exercises.

To see what you'll be creating, take a look at the finished project.

1 Start Encore DVD.

2 Choose File > Open Project.

3 In the Open dialog box, select PrPro_CIB\14Lesson\14LessonDVD.ncor, and then click Open.

4 Choose File > Preview.

The Project Preview window opens, and a menu appears. The menu has two buttons.

5 Click the Chapters button. Click the different thumbnail buttons in the menu. Return to the main menu.

6 Click the Excerpt button.

7 Close the Project Preview window, and the 14Lesson end Project window.

Creating markers in Premiere Pro

1 Start Premiere Pro.

2 In Opening screen, click Open Project.

3 Select Trailer.prproj and click Open.

The Premiere Pro project opens. This simple project has one AVI file in the Timeline.

4 In the Monitor window, preview the file by pressing the Play button. Now you will add sequence markers in Premiere and export the sequence as an MPEG2 file. The sequence markers will become Chapter Point markers when the file is imported into Encore DVD.

5 Set the current time to **321** (00;00;03;21).

6 Choose Marker > Set Sequence Marker > Unnumbered.

This places a marker in the Timeline at the point in time where the current time indicator is.

Before and after adding Sequence marker

7 Set the current time to **1220** (00;00;12;20).

8 Choose Marker > Set Sequence Marker > Unnumbered.

9 Place Sequence markers at **1719** (00;00;17;19) and **2115** (00;00;21;15).

10 Save.

Exporting an MPEG2 from Premiere Pro

1 Choose File > Export > Adobe Media Encoder.

The Transcode Settings box appears.

2 For Format, choose MPEG2-DVD.

3 For the Preset, choose NTSC DV High Quality 4Mb VBR 2 Pass.

4 Click OK.

5 In the Save File box, navigate to your 14Lesson folder, name the file **14Lesson markers.m2v**, and click Save.

This may take a few minutes.

Premiere Pro exports the Timeline as an MPEG2 file that can be imported into Encore DVD. The Adobe Media Encoder is basically the same encoder as the one used by Encore DVD.

6 When the file is rendered, save and close the Premiere Pro Project

Importing an MPEG2 file with markers

Premiere Pro can export MPEG2 files that Encore DVD can import.

1 Open Encore DVD and Choose File > New Project.

2 Click OK to accept NTSC for the project settings.

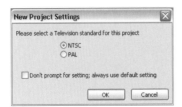

3 Choose File > Import as Asset.

When you exported the Premiere Pro Timeline, it created two files: an MPEG2 file that contains the video, and a WAV file that contains the audio.

4 Select 14Lesson markers.m2v and 14Lesson markers.wav, and click Open.

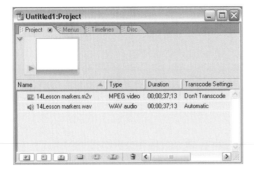

5 Select 14Lesson markers.m2v in the Project window.

6 Choose Timeline > New timeline.

A new Timeline opens with 14Lesson markers placed on the Video track. When the Timeline is created, the Monitor window opens.

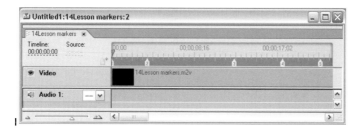

In the Timeline, notice that the markers you made in Premiere Pro have been imported. These markers have numbers, even though the markers in Premiere Pro were unnumbered.

7 You may need to click the zoom out icon in the bottom left of the Timeline so that you can see the entire Video and Audio tracks, and all of the markers.

There are five markers, even though you created four markers in Premiere Pro. This is because every Timeline in Encore DVD has a marker at the first frame.

8 Click on 14Lesson markers.wav in the Project window, and drag it to the Audio 1 track in the Timeline window.

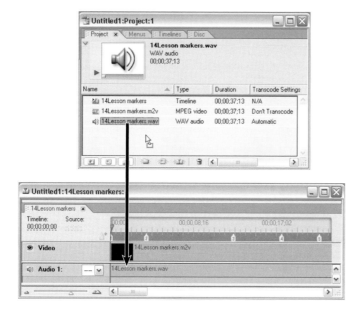

9 Click the Play button in the Monitor window to view the asset.

10 Save to your 14Lesson directory as **14LessonDVD_CIB**.

Note: To get Quicktime and Macintosh-generated assets into Encore DVD using Premiere Pro, see the Adobe Encore DVD User Guide.

Linking the chapter markers with thumbnail buttons

1 Choose File > Import as Menu. Select Chapters_menu.psd and click Open.

The file opens in the Menu window. The four cups of coffee are each buttons. There is also a Back button. Each button will link to one of the chapter points. When you play the DVD and the button is activated, the video will play from the chapter point linked to the button.

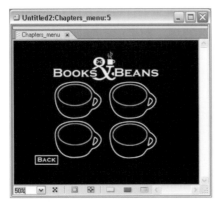

2 Make sure both the 14Lesson markers Timeline and the Menu window are visible.

3 Click on marker number 2 and drag it to the elliptical shape in the upper left coffee cup.

A thumbnail image appears in the cup. Encore DVD automatically creates a link between the button and the chapter point marker in the Timeline.

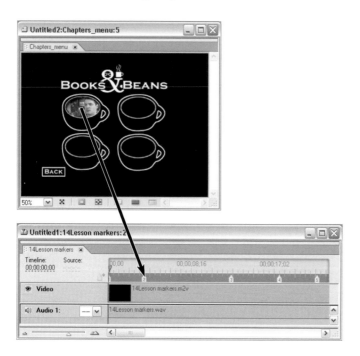

4 Drag marker number three to the upper right cup.

5 Repeat with the last two markers, dragging marker number four to the lower left cup and marker number five to the lower right cup.

When you click on a button, the video will play from the point in the timeline associated with the marker. It will play to the end of the Timeline. You want the Chapters menu to reappear when the Timeline is done playing, so you will set an End Action for the timeline.

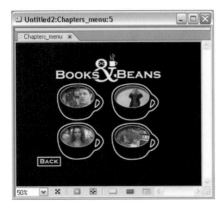

6 Make sure the 14Lesson markers Timeline is active. If necessary, click on 14Lesson markers (not 14Lesson markers.m2v) in the Project window.

7 If the Properties window is not open, choose Window > Properties.

The Properties widow displays information and settings about the 14Lesson markers Timeline.

8 Click on the menu triangle on the right edge of the End Action field, and choose Chapters_menu > 1.

When the Timeline finishes, the menu will display.

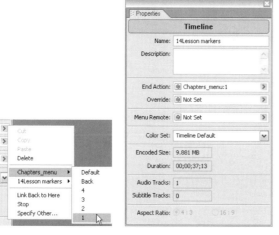

9 Save the project.

Previewing the project

1 Right click on Chapters_menu in the Project window, and choose Preview from Here.

The Project Preview window opens, and Chapters_menu displays. One of the cups is highlighted.

2 Move the cursor over the other cups. Click on one of the cups.

As you move the cursor over a cup, it is highlighted. When you click a cup, the video plays from the chapter point associated with the button. When the video is finished, the menu reappears.

3 Close the Project Preview window.

Exporting an AVI from Premiere Pro

1 Start Premiere Pro.

2 In the Welcome window, click Open Project.

3 Select 14Lesson > Scene01.prproj and click Open.

4 Click the Play button in the Monitor window.

This project has multiple clips in the Timeline. It is ready to export.

5 Make sure that the Timeline is active and choose File > Export > Movie

6 In the Export Movie dialog box, name the file **Scene01**.

7 Click the Settings button.

8 In the Export Movie Settings dialog box, Choose Microsoft DV AVI for File Type and Work Area Bar for Range.

9 Make sure that Export Video and Export Audio are checked.

10 Choose Project for embedding options.

When the AVI is rendered, information about the Premiere Pro project will be included in the file. In Encore DVD (or After Effects) the Edit Original command can launch the Premiere Pro project that created the AVI.

11 Click OK to close the Export Movie Settings dialog box.

12 Click Save.

If a warning box asks you to save the Premiere Pro project first, click Yes.

13 When the file has rendered, close the project.

Using the Edit Original command in Encore DVD

1 If necessary, open the Encore DVD project.

2 Choose File > Import as Asset and choose Scene01.avi.

3 Select Scene01.avi in the Project window and click the Create a new Timeline icon in the bottom of the Project window.

A Timeline is created with the AVI file already placed.

4 Preview in the Monitor window.

You need to trim a few seconds off of the file. Encore DVD allows you to trim the In point or Out point of the asset in the Timeline. If you need to remove a portion from the middle of the clip, you will need to use Premiere Pro.

5 In the Project window, select Scene01.avi. (Do no select Scene01, which is the Timeline.)

6 Choose Edit > Edit Original.

Because you embedded project information when you rendered the AVI in Premiere Pro, the project that created the AVI opens in Premiere Pro. If Premiere Pro is not currently running, it will launch automatically.

Using the ripple edit tool

1 In Premiere Pro, make sure that the Timeline is active.

2 In the Timeline, move the Current Time Marker to 00;00;20;19 (right before the scene of the tombstones).

This is where you want this clip to end. You will edit out the tombstones.

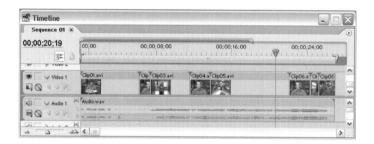

3 In the Tools palette, select the ripple edit tool (⊕) and place the cursor just to the left of the right edge of Clip05 in the Timeline. When the cursor changes to a red bracket with a double arrow (⊕), click and drag to the left. Drag the outpoint of the clip to the current time marker.

A ripple edit trims a clip and shifts subsequent clips in the track by the amount you trim.

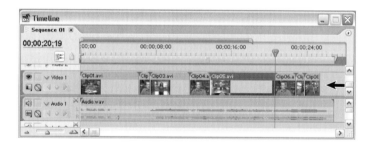

4 In the Tools palette, select the selection tool.

5 Place the cursor over the right edge of the Audio track and trim the clip until it is even with the Video track.

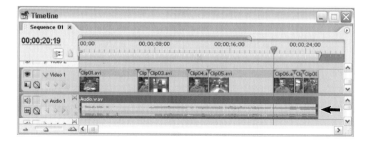

6 Save the project.

Updating the AVI file in Encore DVD

1 Make sure that the Timeline is active and choose File > Export > Movie.

2 In the Export Movie dialog box, the name of the file should be Scene01.avi. If necessary, enter the filename. It must be the same name and be in the same folder as the AVI file you imported into Encore DVD.

3 Use the previous settings.

4 Click Save.

5 A warning box asks if you want to replace the file with the same name. Click Yes.

6 When the file has rendered, close the project.

7 Make Encore DVD active.

The AVI file should update automatically.

8 Play the Timeline in the Monitor window.

The AVI file has updated in Encore DVD and the edit performed in Premiere Pro displays correctly.

Creating links and behaviors

1 Choose File > Import as menu and select Main_menu.psd. Click Open.

A new menu appears in the Menu window with two buttons.

2 With the selection tool, select the Excerpt button.

3 Open the Properties palette.

4 In the Link field, choose Scene01 > Chapter 1.

When the Excerpt button is activated, the Scene01 Timeline will play.

5 With the selection tool, select the Chapters button.

6 In the Properties palette, in the Link field, choose Chapters_menu > 1.

When the Chapters button is activated, the Chapters_menu will display.

7 Make sure that the Scene01 Timeline is active. If necessary, click on Scene01 in the Project window.

8 In the End Action field of the Properties palette, choose Main_menu > Default.

When the Scene01 Timeline finishes playing, Main_menu will display with the Chapters button highlighted.

9 In the Menu Remote field, choose Main_menu > Default.

Note: If you press the Menu button during the Scene01 Timeline, Main_menu will display.

10 Click on the Chapters_menu tab in the Menu window to make that menu active.

11 With the selection tool, select the Back button in the Menu window.

12 In the Properties palette, choose Main_menu > Default.

13 Save.

Previewing the project

1 In the Project palette, right click Main_menu and choose Set as First Play.

When the DVD plays, Main_menu will be the first item to display.

2 Choose File > Preview.

The Project Preview window opens, and Main_menu displays.

3 Click on the buttons or use the remote control icons in the bottom of the Project Preview window to navigate the project.

4 When you have checked all of the links and behaviors, close the Preview Project window.

5 Save the Project.

Burning the disc

You've come to the point in your project where it is ready for the world to see. Encore DVD provides you with a full suite of operations that you can use to make a DVD-ROM on your own system if you have a DVD Read and Write Drive (DVD RW).

In Encore DVD, choose File > Build DVD > Make DVD Disc and follow the instructions that pertain to your system and your desires for output.

Media Keep in mind that some systems use DVD-RW ("-" = a technology benchmark, not a hyphen), while others use DVD+RW ("+" = a technology benchmark, not a plus sign). Encore DVD will sense the properties of your DVD burner and direct you for the kind of media it requires.

A DVD holds over 4.5 gigabytes of information in the form of digital voice and image. Using some of the latest compression schemes like MPEG2 can allow up to two hours of high quality video and stereo or even 5.1 surround sound on a disc.

For more information, consult the operator's manual for the DVD burning equipment you have, or the *Adobe Encore DVD Users Guide,* and the FAQ area of the Adobe Web site, *www.adobe.com.*

Index

Movie Credits for Premiere Pro Classroom in a Book

<u>Books & Beans</u>

Produced & Directed by	Manuel Freedman, ASCI Advertising
Written & Edited by	Micah Freedman, Manuel Freedman
Executive Producer	Adobe Press
Assistant Producer	Judi Geringer
Director of Photography	Robert McWilliams
Sound Operator	Tony Jensen
Camera Operator	Joe La Point
Set Design	Grace Chang, Micah Freedman, Michele Rutherford
Original Music by	Rick Richards, Manuel Freedman
Make Up by	Michelle Talley

Cast

Hero	Micah Freedman
Dreams	Shanara Gabriel
Ex	Abigail Rose Solomon
New Boy	Nils Vaule
Father	Stephen Bass
Son	Michael Riskin
Clerk	Brandi Madison
Patron	Grace Chang
Patron	Mary Bartnikowski
Patron	Howard Squires
Patron	Paul Riskin
Patron	Robert Malek

Special Thanks to
The Silicon Valley WAVE Shopping Center Margie D. Francis & The Staff
Hobee's California Restaurant, Mountain View, California
Filmed on location in Sunnyvale & Mountain View, California

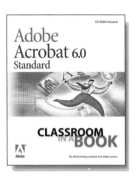
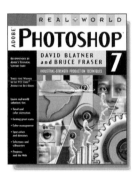

Adobe Certification Programs

 **Adobe® Certified Expert**

 **Adobe® Certified Training Provider**

What is an ACE?

An Adobe Certified Expert (ACE) is an individual who has passed an Adobe Product Proficiency Exam for a specified Adobe software product. Adobe Certified Experts are eligible to promote themselves to clients or employers as highly skilled, expert level users of Adobe Software. ACE certification is a recognized standard for excellence in Adobe software knowledge.

ACE Benefits

When you become an ACE, you enjoy these special benefits:

- Professional recognition
- An ACE program certificate
- Use of the Adobe Certified Expert program logo

What is an ACTP?

An Adobe Certified Training Provider (ACTP) is a Training professional or organization that has met the ACTP program requirements. Adobe promotes ACTPs to customers who need training on Adobe software.

ACTP Benefits

- Professional recognition
- An ACTP program certificate
- Use of the Adobe Certified Training Provider program logo
- Listing in the Partner Finder on Adobe.com
- Access to beta software releases when available
- Classroom in a Book in Adobe Acrobat PDF
- Marketing materials
- Co-marketing opportunities

For more information on the ACE and ACTP programs, go to partners.adobe.com, and look for these programs under the Join section.